OUR JOURNEY IS MY REWARD

Copyright © 2022 Gerry Lambert

All rights reserved. This book or any portion thereof may not be reproduced or used in any manner whatsoever without the express written permission of the author except for the use of brief quotations in articles or reviews.

The reader acknowledges this book is a memoir and has been produced by the author from his personal recollections, information and materials in his possession. Efforts have been made to verify and confirm details and to avoid hurting anyone and in that instance names, details and places may have been altered. In making your way through this book, if discrepancies or inconsistencies have occurred it is not through complacency but as a result of being based upon the recollections and memories of the author and others.

ISBN PRINT: 978-0-6456506-0-0
ISBN PRINT LOCAL: 978-0-6456506-1-7
ISBN EBOOK: 978-0-6456506-2-4

Book Editor, Vanessa Barrington (www.thebookdoula.com.au)
Book Cover, Typesetting and Layout Design Copyright © 2022 Maja Creative
Art Direction by Maja Wolnik of Maja Creative
Graphic Design by Monika Brzeczek of Maja Creative

OUR JOURNEY IS MY REWARD

For my children, Danita and Chantal; son-in-law, Sasha; grandchildren, Evie, Luka, Levi and Annalee; and future generations. For my extended family members Dave, Paige, Damien, and Jordan.

For the children, grandchildren, and future generations of my siblings.

This book is dedicated to the memories of my son Bradley, brother Hans, mother Martha, father Adrian, and the relatives and friends who have predeceased me.

Sketch of the Kaylaur Crescent family home by Evie Maksimovic

CONTENTS

PROLOGUE 8

INTRODUCTION 10

CHAPTER 1
THE LAMBERTS ARRIVE DOWN UNDER 11

CHAPTER 2
LIFE IN PARKES 19

CHAPTER 3
SHORT STOP IN UNANDERRA 27

CHAPTER 4
MOVE TO ALBION PARK RAIL 33

CHAPTER 5
THE FAMILY IS COMPLETED 47

CHAPTER 6
THE BLUE BIKE 65

CHAPTER 7
MY FIRST PAIR OF LONG PANTS 73

CHAPTER 8
TAKING MY OPPORTUNITY 91

CHAPTER 9
RUGBY LEAGUE AND THE MAGIC OF OUTSET 119

CHAPTER 10
WORK AND UNIVERSITY LIFE 135

CHAPTER 11
AN EYE-OPENING TRIP 157

CHAPTER 12
THE BIG MOVE 177

CHAPTER 13
THE CITY RESOURCES YEARS 191

CHAPTER 14
SINGLE PARENTHOOD AND FAMILY MARATHONS 215

CHAPTER 15
NEW BEGINNINGS AND THE VILLA WORLD FAMILY 243

CHAPTER 16
REACHING THE PINNACLE 271

CHAPTER 17
BRADLEY LAMBERT 291

CHAPTER 18
HANS LAMBERT 305

EPILOGUE 329

AUTHOR'S NOTE 349

PROLOGUE

There are a few reasons why I decided to write this book. I am probably typical of many people around my age who wish they knew more about their parents' and grandparents' lives. The reality of life is that we often don't really consider finding out more about our families until it is too late to find out directly from the relevant family members. Hopefully this book will provide some of the information about my life, my Mum, Dad, and my siblings' lives should any of the grandchildren, or their descendants, want to know down the track. I did not want Mum and Dad's story to die with the siblings.

A few years ago, my daughter, Danita, asked me to answer some grandparent questions for a school assignment for her son, Luka. They were the typical questions such as, "What was your first job? What games did you play growing up?" I emailed the answers to Danita. She called me when she received the email and said, "Dad I didn't know most of this stuff, it is really interesting". That conversation made me think more about a book.

My son, Bradley, tragically passed away in 2009. I wanted my grandkids to learn about their lively, friendly, caring uncle and hopefully obtain some understanding of his journey.

My brother, Hans, sadly passed away in 2014. I had a conversation with his son, Josh, several years later and discovered that he did not know about a significant injury Hans had sustained at a school cadet camp. That conversation with Josh sealed the deal for me to write this book. Hans was a very special person and I thought he deserved to have some of his story recorded for his future generations.

There was also probably some ego on my part. I felt like I have had a great journey, starting with being one of nine siblings, through to my own wonderful family, my corporate career, and the many special people I have met along the way.

INTRODUCTION

I am the middle child and one of nine Lambert siblings. Making it the perfect middle role I have one older sister, three older brothers, one younger sister and three younger brothers. Further, the girls are each the oldest of the two groups of four children. I have only met a few other people who are a middle child with nine siblings and have never met anyone with the same perfect configuration of brothers and sisters as me. Little did I know when I was a child how this middle role would profoundly impact my entire life and greatly contribute to the very happy, fulfilling life I have had so far.

THE LAMBERT SIBLINGS

BIRTH CERTIFICATE NAME	AUSTRALIAN 'ADOPTED' NAME	EVERYDAY/ NICKNAME
Antonia Johanna Maria	Antonia Johanna Maria	Toni/Sis
Johannes Adrianus Maria	John Adrian	John/Sticks
Johannes Theodorus Maria	Hans Theo	Hans/Harry
Reinier Petrus Maria	Renee Peter	Renee/Fuji
Gerardus Adnanus Maria	Gerald Adrian	Gerry/Ged
Diana Margaret Maria	Dianne Margaret	Dianne/Diana
Terence Johannes Maria	Terry John	Terry
Adrian Michael Maria	Adrian Michael	Adrian/Ossie
Stephen Mark	Stephen Mark	Steve

CHAPTER 1

THE LAMBERTS ARRIVE DOWN UNDER

— 1951 TO 1953 —

My story begins with my first two clear memories. We lived at 26 Pearce Street in Parkes, regional New South Wales. When I was almost five I was sent off to St Joseph's Primary School with my older siblings. On my first day we all walked to school, which was around two kilometres. Dad was at work and Mum was at home with a new baby, Dianne. I walked home during the first break to go to the toilet as I didn't know where to go at school. Also I couldn't undo the button fly we had on our shorts. Mum quickly sent me back to school. I walked back on my own.

Sometime in that first week at school the teacher asked me what my name was in front of the whole class. I responded by saying I wasn't sure, which brought some laughter from my classmates. I said that everyone calls me Ger, pronounced Jer, so that must be my name. Of course, the teacher would have known the whole time. So began a life of many nicknames and oddities associated with my name, something I shared with a few of my siblings.

Now let's go back to the start when the Lambert family came to Australia and our fantastic journey began.

My parents, Adrian and Martha (nee Van Ammers), and their three eldest children, Toni, John and Hans, were post World War II migrants from the Netherlands, and arrived in Australia in September 1951. They made this journey by aeroplane, which was reasonably novel in those days as most migrants made the long journey by boat. My brother John recalls the plane trip took three weeks and included a stopover in South Africa. Mum did this trip with three children under five years of age, and whilst pregnant with another one. This was typical of Mum; she would have just gotten on with it.

Mum and Dad met towards the end of World War II. They met after Mum got a flat tyre while riding her bicycle. Dad came to her rescue and fixed the tyre. We understand that Mum and Dad knew of each other before then but perhaps needed something to bring them together. The flat tyre did the trick and they remained together for the rest of their lives, which was just over sixty years.

Mum and Dad were married on the 23rd of February 1946 and moved to the small town of Bemmel, near the large city, Nijmegen. Dad worked as a carpenter. There was plenty of post war rebuilding work to do, particularly in that area as Nijmegen is very close to the German border. The first three children came along at a steady rate with Toni born on the 12th of July 1947, John born on the 20th of September 1948 and Hans born on the 7th of August 1950. They were all home births in the house they rented in Bemmel.

We understand that, sometime after 1946, Dad's parents, and many of his siblings, also moved to Bemmel. They all moved into the house that Mum and Dad were living in. This was probably typical of many families in the Netherlands after the war. Conditions were still very harsh after five years of German occupation during the war. Dad was the eldest of nine siblings, so their house became very crowded.

We also understand that Dad was the main instigator of that momentous decision to move to Australia, which changed or affected many people's lives. A combination of factors influenced Dad's thinking, with the main one being the prospect of a brighter future in Australia which had been much less affected by the war than the Netherlands had. Post war conditions in the Netherlands were very difficult with food shortages and a poor economy. I'm sure the Australian Government of the time had produced some rosy brochures of life in Australia. Australia desperately needed skilled migrants to replace the many soldiers who had died in the war, and to assist in the regeneration of the post war economy.

Dad went to one of the migrant recruitment centres and applied to go to South Africa, Canada, or Australia. He was notified within two weeks that they had been accepted to go to Australia. Toni recalls they were only given a short time to prepare for the trip and leave, so the farewells were very rushed.

Dad was also keen to be independent of his family, particularly one of his parents who we were told he sometimes clashed with. Dad also didn't like it that Mum couldn't be the boss in her own home. He was adventurous enough to want to join the migrant rush to Australia. He wanted to get on with life with his own little family, which didn't stay little for very long. Mum played no part in the decision to come to Australia, but she totally supported Dad.

Mum was the fifth youngest of eleven children. From the eldest down these siblings comprised three boys, five girls and then another three boys. It must have been very difficult for her to leave her siblings at that time, particularly going to an unknown country across the other side of the world. Mum's parents died when she was quite young, so she was very close to her siblings. Her mother died in 1939 when Mum was 16 and her father died in 1946 when she was 23. We believe that eight of the eleven Van Ammers siblings went on to have 67 children between them.

Dad and his siblings had 30 children between them. If they were all alive, we would have around 80 first cousins in the Netherlands today.

Upon arriving in Australia, the Lambert family's first home was the migrant hostel in Nelson Bay, New South Wales. Migrant hostels had been established all over Australia to provide migrant accommodation after World War II. Migrants and their dependants were permitted to remain in the hostels for three to twelve months and were given training to assist with re-settlement.

The fourth sibling, Renee, was born in a hospital tent at the Nelson Bay hostel on the 17th of April 1952. There were only Dutch families at the hostel, so Mum and Dad had a small Dutch community around them. Meals were provided in a central dining room. There were shared bathrooms with eight showers for about sixty people. Mum and Dad had a small hut to house the family.

While the rest of the family (Mum with four children under the age of five) stayed at the hostel Dad went to Parkes, NSW, with another Dutchman, Peter Veltmeyer, to plan a life there.

They purchased adjoining blocks of land in Pearce Street. They were large blocks of land, around 800 square metres each. They built a garage on each block for the respective families to live in and planned to live in the garages while they worked to save enough money to build each family's main house.

Parkes is situated on the Newell Highway in the central west region of New South Wales. At that time it was a country town of around 8,000 people and a shopping and business hub for the local farming community. It was almost the opposite of the town Mum and Dad had left behind in the Netherlands. With the extremely hot summers, thousands of flies, snakes, rats, mice, locusts, dirt roads, and basic shops Mum and Dad surely must have wondered what they had gotten themselves into. Further they were almost completely cut off from the families they left behind in The Netherlands. The only means of communication was telegrams or aerogramme letters. Household telephones were still a few years away.

Around the middle of 1952 the family moved to Parkes where Dad worked as a builder. He went into partnership with another Dutchman, Gerald Holman. They did a lot of building in the bush. They also had a joinery shop in Close Street, Parkes.

The Lambert family moved into the garage on the block of land at 26 Pearce Street. This garage became the family's home for around two years while Dad built the main house. It was divided into two rooms, with one room as a bedroom for the children and one room as a kitchen and living room. Mum and Dad slept on a fold out bed in the living room area and the bed was folded away each morning after they got up.

There was a laundry and a separate toilet adjoining the garage which could only be accessed from the outside. Toni recalls that all the kids bathed in the laundry tub, while Mum and Dad washed themselves from the laundry tub. They could not fit in it to have a proper bath. It appears that Mum and Dad went for a period of around two years without having a proper bath or shower.

John, Hans, Adrian, and I made a very emotional journey back to this house over forty years later to discover that the garage was intact, and the dividing wall was still there.

Not long after we moved into the garage a dog, who lived with a family at the end of our street, started coming to our place to hang around with the Lambert kids. That dog's name was Muska. She just became part of our family. The family who had her were happy for her to become our family pet as they could see how happy she was with us kids. She was a beautiful Collie dog with a wonderful temperament and was perfect for us. Muska died when I was 16 years old, and she was 18. I spent my entire childhood with the constant presence of the kind of family dog that you would think only exists in the movies.

I was born on the 26th of May 1953. Mum told me later that I lived in a bassinet on the bedroom wall for the first five months of my life - there was simply no room for me anywhere else. I must have thought it was normal to live in a bassinet. Toni was five years old then so there were five children under six years of age.

My birth certificate name was Gerardus Adnanus Maria Lambert. I did not know this was my legal name until I obtained my birth certificate, when I applied for a passport, over twenty years later. I had gone through my entire school life using the name Gerald Adrian Lambert, and only included Maria if I had to. When I finally saw my birth certificate, I asked Dad about the name Adnanus and he struggled to get the story out as he was laughing that much. He did know about it and said it was meant to be Adrianus but he had written the "r" and "i" too closely together, so they became an "n". Obviously one of my many nicknames became Adnanus. I was named after Gerald Holman, and he became my godfather.

The first eight Lambert siblings had Maria as a middle name. This was a Dutch custom for Catholics as Maria was a patron saint of the Netherlands. Only the youngest sibling, Steve, avoided having Maria in his name. Mum had asked Toni to name Steve and she went with Stephen Mark, a very Australian name.

I left my legal name as it was on my birth certificate and my passport is also in that name. Everything else, including driver's licence, bank accounts and property title documents, has always been in my Australian name, Gerald Adrian Lambert. This has only become an issue for me recently with the digital world requirements. I now have a statutory declaration on hand in case I must prove the two names are the same person. Apparently, this is not an uncommon issue with migrant families. Renee legally changed his name to his Australian name a few years ago to avoid the issues that having two names can create.

Toni and John both started school in kindergarten at St Joseph's Primary School at the commencement of the 1953 year. On Toni's first day she decided to go for a walk and left the school with one of the other girls. The walk became a long one. A farmer found them and took them to the police station. A policeman took them back to school. At that time, Toni had been in Australia for only eighteen months, and would still have been speaking Dutch more than English. Toni was probably somewhat confused on her first day and would not have understood much of what the teacher was talking about.

One of the teachers then went home to talk to Mum about what had happened. Following that discussion, they agreed to send John to school the next day with Toni so she would have someone with her. At this time John was four years and four months old so he was sent to school one full year early so his sister would have company. Not surprisingly, he repeated kindergarten the next year.

It must have been a Lambert thing to take off on the first day of school. When I started school some years later I would do the same as Toni, and so would my son Bradley when he decided to stay in the playground after the rest of the school went back to the classrooms after little lunch.

The Lamberts settled into life in Parkes with Dad working, Mum doing everything at home and the kids exploring Parkes and finding other kids to play with. Dad commenced building the family home in 1953.

CHAPTER 2

LIFE IN PARKES

— 1954 TO 1960 —

Dad continued to combine his building work with building the family home. He worked long hours, seven days a week. He eventually completed a brand new four-bedroom weatherboard house which we moved into around May 1954. This was a very special house for us. It was big, we all had beds and it was very luxurious for all of us after living in the garage. By this time Mum had an orchard of fruit trees growing in the backyard and the yard was starting to take shape.

Life for Mum and Dad would have been entirely focused on their children and getting into a family home. In those first few years it was all work, kids, school, the house, and there was no time for anything else. It appears that they drank very little alcohol, possibly for financial reasons, and their social life was centred around catching up with the other Dutch families. John recalls that they played tennis once a week with their Dutch friends.

Dad told me later in life that he liked having a drink as a youth, like most young people. It sounded like he had his share of getting drunk with his friends in the Netherlands. It is a credit to Dad that he didn't slip into a drinking lifestyle. This would have been very easy to do in a town like Parkes, where having a beer at the pub in those days would have been the normal practice for most men. I say this as Dad was a heavy smoker, so he had that propensity to become addicted. With the pressure that he would have been under, and his addictive nature, it would have been understandable if Dad had turned into a drinker.

This largely alcohol-free lifestyle continued through our lives until we left school. I can't recall ever seeing Mum or Dad have more than a few drinks and I never saw either of them get drunk.

The years from 1954 to 1960 were a joyous time for the five oldest Lambert kids, with Parkes being a very safe, friendly country town. The streets were very wide and open, houses did not have front fences, and there weren't many cars on the roads. This produced an inviting environment which resulted in people casually dropping in on neighbours or getting together in the street for a chat. The Australian people who lived in Parkes (and they were true blue Aussies) readily accepted the Dutch migrants into their town. Mum and Dad never talked later in life about experiencing any discrimination because they were migrants.

We were basically free to go wherever we wanted to. Between the five of us we had lots of friends and there was always something to do, bearing in mind that there was no television at that time. I think I just tagged along with the older boys. Muska would come wherever we went. There was endless playing in the backyard, the local paddocks and on the streets. We used to catch lots of tadpoles, particularly after heavy rainfalls, although I'm not sure Mum shared our enthusiasm for keeping them in the laundry tub.

We played marbles endlessly, and you would always know what marbles you had in your little marble bag. My overriding memory is that we were always outside. I think we just came in at dinner time, had dinner and went to bed early.

One of our favourite activities was going to the pictures, now called movies, on Saturday afternoons. We were enthralled by whatever the latest release was, with the Tarzan movies being very popular. A feature of these Saturdays was that the picture theatre was also the venue for swapping comic books. Kids of all ages would bring their comics and at the intermission there would be frantic activity in swapping to get your favourite comic books to read. The Phantom comic books were very popular.

The currency was pounds, shillings and pence and we were given six pence each if Mum had the money. This would enable us to buy a choo choo bar or a cream bun for three pence, and maybe an ice block or some lollies. Choo choo bars were very popular and it could take the whole movie to suck them to completion. This may be one of the reasons why most of the siblings required many fillings in their teeth in their teenage years.

The annual show generated great excitement for adults and kids alike. Jimmy Sharman's Boxing Tent was a big attraction. Us kids all loved sideshow alley. Travelling circuses also came to Parkes quite regularly.

The weather conditions in Parkes were extreme. The summers were very hot, and the winters were very cold. The summer heat was exacerbated by a lack of any relieving breezes. Frequent locust and mice plagues added to the harsh environment.

Through those early years in Parkes Mum and Dad went to English speaking classes and picked up their new language quite quickly, although they both retained some of that distinctive Dutch accent for the rest of their lives. We discovered later they had made a deliberate decision to speak English at home so that is the only language I have ever known. This contrasts with many of the migrant families who spoke their native language at home and English everywhere else. The kids in those families became bilingual, very naturally, and spoke both languages fluently. In hindsight it may have been better for us to have learnt the Dutch language. On the other hand, Mum and Dad assimilated into the Parkes community much quicker due to their willingness to speak English and become part of the town.

Dad was a very good soccer player in his youth. He was 17 when World War II broke out and this ended any aspirations he may have had for a professional soccer career. We were told later by the family and friends in the Netherlands that Dad was a very, very good goal scoring shooter and would have had a chance of playing in the top league in the Netherlands, but for the war. Dad eventually started playing soccer with the Parkes team in the local competition and became a leading goal scorer, even though he would have been in his mid-thirties by then. We used to go to the games to watch Dad play. The country boys were tough, and Dad got tackled one day because he scored too many goals.

The sixth child, Dianne, was born on the 29th of December 1957, and the seventh, Terry, was born on the 31st of October 1959. I was six years old when Mum was in hospital for Terry's birth and recollect that Dad had to feed us for about a week. I had hot chips, from the fish and chips shop, every day that Mum was in hospital. I couldn't eat them for some time after that.

The age gap between Dianne and I was four and a half years, which was by far the greatest gap between any siblings. Dad regularly worked away from home during this time, often spending a few weeks at a time in the bush. On the other hand, the gap between Renee and I was only thirteen months old, making us the closest in age of the siblings. Mum told me later in life that she had to have Renee out of nappies before I was born as there was only enough nappies for one baby. They were all cloth nappies then; disposables were still many years away. Mum also told us she used to put Renee in the pram, behind the back fence, if he was crying or whingeing too much when I was the newborn.

It appears that Mum practised enough tough love to ensure that we could look after ourselves as quickly as possible. You can probably already see how the seeds of our resilience and independence, which are common characteristics of the nine siblings, were being sown from the minute we were born.

Going to the council pool was a favourite activity for all the kids, especially during the long, hot summers. John and Hans were good swimmers and entered the local races at the pool every Friday night. We walked to and from the local pool even if it was dark.

The kiosk at the local pool was run by one of the Dutch migrant families, the Van Hoorn's. They lived a couple of houses down from us in Pearce Street and the families became great friends. The Van Hoorn's started Toni on her babysitting career after their third daughter, Yvonne, was born in April 1957. Mrs Van Hoorn had to go back to work straight after Yvonne was born. On non-school days, they would collect Toni from our place and take her to the pool with them all day. Toni then looked after Yvonne the whole day while the parents worked. Toni only had a break when Mrs Van Hoorn came to feed Yvonne.

Toni was only nine years old then. This babysitting role started her on what virtually became her vocation in life, looking after babies and little kids. She virtually raised the four youngest siblings, Dianne, Terry, Adrian, and Steve and later became a mother herself at the age of nineteen.

It is hard to describe what Mum's life would have been like in those years without feeling emotional about it. She was continually cooking, washing, cleaning, and raising children. Despite the hardships it was rare to see Mum sad or angry. While she was a naturally amiable person, she was also very tough and resilient. She just kept getting everything done day after day. There was a hot meal on the table every night. The only take away food available in town was fish and chips and that was a rare treat for us.

Similarly, Dad worked extremely hard and would often spend days or weeks away from home if they had a job in the bush. Dad also kept getting it done day after day. Hans recalled a time, when he was eight or nine years old, when he went to work with Dad for a day. They got stuck where they were because of a flood. They got home two days later. I have fleeting memories of going to work with Dad and going to the toilet while sitting on a round piece of copper pipe behind the nearest tree.

Our Catholic upbringing was a significant influence in our lives in those Parkes years. Mum and Dad were quite strict Catholics. We went to Mass every Sunday. During Lent, which is the holy period of forty days prior to Easter Sunday, Mum sent the older kids off to Mass every day. This started with Toni and John, and later included Hans as well. They had to walk two kilometres to church, go to Mass, and then go to school. They couldn't have breakfast first due to the fasting period required to be able to take communion at Mass. The nuns quickly saw that the Lambert kids were attending Mass every day. They decided that they would take them back to the convent after Mass, feed them breakfast and then send them off to school. If it was raining and the kids got wet on the walk to church the nuns would take their clothes off and dry them in front of the fire while the kids had their breakfast.

Not long before we left Parkes a terrible kidnapping, which would become famously known as the 'Graeme Thorne kidnapping" occurred. Graeme was an eight year old boy whose parents had just won the Opera House lottery. This was the country's first well known kidnap for ransom. It caused massive shock at the time and attracted huge public attention. I was seven years old then and heard Mum and Dad talking about it. I was very interested and had a sense that Australia had lost some of its innocence. It held the nation's attention for about six weeks until the body was found. It eventuated that he had been murdered within one day of being kidnapped.

The 1960 economic recession severely affected Dad's building work in the bush so he went to Wollongong to find work. He got a job as a carpenter on the construction of the Coles building in Crown Street, Wollongong. He did this for a few weeks, staying in a boarding house at Port Kembla, and going back to Parkes on weekends. Mum and Dad then decided to move the family to Wollongong as it was a much bigger town, with more building work opportunities for Dad. They started planning for the sale of the house and the big move.

CHAPTER 3

SHORT STOP IN UNANDERRA

— 1960 TO 1961 —

In September 1960 Dad hired a big black sedan to drive the family to Wollongong. Mum and Dad, seven kids and Muska all squeezed onto two bench seats. There were no seat belts in cars at that time. This trip took less than one day, and I recall the feeling of setting out on a new adventure. Everyone was happy and excited. The car broke down during the trip on the steep descent down Bulli Pass, but I don't recall even that dimming our sense of excitement about what was to come.

Wollongong is situated on the Pacific Ocean, around eighty kilometres south of Sydney. The prospect of living in a much better climate also influenced Mum and Dad to choose Wollongong.

For most of the descendants of Mum and Dad reading this book the decision to live in Wollongong is the reason you are all here today. Eight of the nine Lambert siblings met their future spouses in the Wollongong area. The exception was the youngest, Steve, who met his partner, Justin, in Brisbane.

We first moved to a rented house at Minnamurra, around thirty kilometres south of Wollongong. It was a very short stay of only two weeks. The house was situated on the river, which would be considered a premium position these days, but the sand flies were so bad that we had to move again. This was after we had all been enrolled in the local catholic schools in Kiama.

Dad then found a house to rent in Unanderra, which is situated around six kilometres south of Wollongong. The main road, the Princes Highway, went straight through the middle of Unanderra. Our house was on this main road just north of the town shops. This house was demolished many years later and that block of land now has a Kentucky Fried Chicken on it.

It was a very old house with a big yard. I slept in one double bed with two of my brothers. Living in this house is where my first strong, continuous memories commenced.

The local catholic primary school, St Pius X, only went to second class so I was enrolled there. John, Hans, and Renee went to Unanderra public school. Toni was in high school and went to St Mary's catholic college in Wollongong. Mum must have organised three different schools utilising public transport or walking, with two kids, Dianne and Terry, still at home. Mum did not have a drivers' licence and never got one.

Despite living on a main road, we were free to come and go. We quickly became familiar with Unanderra, which wasn't as interesting as Parkes. The big discovery for all of us kids was the beach. The nearest beaches were North Wollongong and South Wollongong. Sometimes Dad would drive us four older boys to the beach in the morning and pick us up late in the afternoon. We would buy hot chips for lunch and collect bottles which you could cash in for a few pence. We would swim or play all day. This is an interesting memory for me as I didn't learn to swim until later in life. I must have stayed close to the shore at the beach.

I can remember at least two occasions when we walked to the beach from Unanderra as Dad must have already gone to work. This was a good six kilometre walk and I was seven years old. Renee also recalls these walks and that we stopped at the Cobblers Hill service station along the way. The walk would have taken us at least ninety minutes. Dad picked us up in the late afternoon so at least we didn't have to walk both ways. This is a stark example of the different lifestyle then compared to today in 2022. Today it would not be considered safe to let a seven year old go for a walk in their own street unsupervised.

One of my most significant, impactive memories occurred while we were living in Unanderra. I had started to pick up on Mum and Dad having financial issues and the stress that came with this. One evening after dinner I walked into the kitchen while Mum and Dad were talking and doing the dishes. They were deep in conversation. Mum was startled by me walking in on them and she dropped the pan that she was drying. I saw that happening and caught the pan before it hit the floor. Mum was very happy that I managed to catch it and it broke the mood a bit.

Then I think that I exhibited for the first time an ability to ask the right question at the right time. As it was obvious to me that Mum and Dad had been having a stressful conversation, and perhaps arguing, I asked them why we never see them argue or have a fight? They both said that they had decided when they got married that they would never argue in front of the kids. They added that they would talk privately to try to make sure the kids were unaware of the problems or issues they were discussing.

Mum and Dad talked with me for a while that night in what was the first serious conversation I had ever had. It really stayed with me. Mum and Dad did stick to that while we were growing up. They were very good at always staying strong as a husband-and-wife team. Dad however always loved to have a rigorous discussion.

Mum became pregnant with her eighth child while we lived in Unanderra and Dad purchased a block of land at 20 Kaylaur Crescent, Albion Park Rail. Once again he started building the family home while doing other building work in order to keep earning an income.

Us kids lived much the same as in Parkes. We went everywhere in the town and would find something to do. There were many more cars in Unanderra, so one game we made up to play was to write down number plates of cars and see who had the most written down at the end of the day. It was a very simple game, but it kept us occupied.

On one occasion we were playing in a field, and I stepped onto a pile of broken glass. I was barefoot which was normal for us. I cut my foot quite deeply and went straight home to show Mum. She cleaned it up, bandaged it and I did not go to the doctor. I don't think Mum could get me to a doctor, so she just did it herself. I limped around for a few days, and it healed up quite well. I still have the scar from this cut. It measures over three centimetres so today I imagine it would have required four to five stitches, with a tetanus shot.

The house at Unanderra also produced my first memories of the pan toilet. This was a dunny can toilet in a small outhouse in the backyard. The dunny can was a big round black tin that would be placed under the toilet seat. Everyone would go to the toilet on it until it filled up. Thinking about it now, sitting just inches above the accumulated excrement from yourself and your family over the past week, breathing its vapours and inhaling its odours, seems like a health disaster waiting to happen. But it didn't and I lived like that until I left home at the age of 23. With so many kids we had two pans for each week. When the first pan got full Dad would clamp a lid on top of it. It would stay in the outhouse for the rest of the week, until the dunny man came and changed the cans.

On one occasion both pans were full, and the dunny man wasn't due for another couple of days. The pan we were using was overflowing and the smell was overpowering. I started to jump the back fence to go to the toilet in a service station that was close by. I don't know how Mum coped with it, but it must have been very distressing.

I enjoyed my brief time at the Catholic school. I did my first Holy Communion during that time and that was a big occasion. I made my first close school friend, Timmy Heenan, at that school and I had my first sleepover at Timmy's place.

Just before we left Unanderra the 1961 earthquake hit. It occurred on the 22nd of May 1961. I remember the ground shaking and all of us running outside. I had no idea what had happened until Mum told me. It passed quickly with no damage to the house. We found out later that this had been a significant earthquake with a Richter magnitude of 5.5. It caused significant structural damage not far from Wollongong.

CHAPTER 4

MOVE TO ALBION PARK RAIL

— 1961 TO 1962 —

We moved to Albion Park Rail, situated 22 kilometres south of Wollongong, in June 1961 after Dad had completed building our forever family home at 20 Kaylaur Crescent. It was a three bedroom, one bathroom fibro house with a large combined lounge and dining room, and a small kitchen. The laundry was just outside the back door and the toilet again was the outside "dunny". It was smaller than the Parkes house that Dad had built. It was on a large, 905 square metre block of land.

The house was very clean and fresh, with a new carpet piece in the lounge room and linoleum on the kitchen floor. The remaining floors were basic timber, and it was many years before Mum could afford any additional floor coverings.

Mum and Dad lived in this house for the next forty-two years, after which they moved into an aged care home.

Mum and Dad had one bedroom to themselves, but not for long. Toni, Dianne and Terry were in the middle bedroom. Us four older boys shared the back bedroom. It was quite large and had an external door. There were two double decker beds and a small wardrobe. We somehow managed to have our own private areas where we could keep our stuff. We generally got on quite well and we were all good sleepers despite being in a room with three other people. I lived in this bedroom until I left home at the age of twenty-three.

I immediately loved the house, the street, and the town. There were only about seven to eight other houses in the street. There was plenty of land, creeks, and forests nearby for us to explore and play in. Us older kids were soon roaming the town as freely as if we had lived there forever.

Albion Park Rail was quite a small town, with a population of a few thousand people. Like Parkes the houses were set on large blocks of land. The residents were very friendly and helpful to migrant families like the Lamberts. There was a small group of shops set along the main highway and we were soon tasked with going to the shops to get the groceries for Mum. There was a grocery store, a butcher, a greengrocer, a fish and chips shop and a newsagent, which was to become an important part of my life a few years later.

Toni continued to catch the train to St Mary's College in Wollongong, and John caught the bus to Dapto High school. Hans, Renee, and I were all enrolled in St Paul's catholic primary school at Albion Park. We caught Barry Brownlee's bus to and from school each day.

The eighth child, Adrian, was born at Kiama hospital on the 5th of July 1961, soon after we moved to Albion Park Rail. He was born a few weeks premature. He was transferred straight to Wollongong Hospital as he had breathing difficulties and was quite sick. He remained in Wollongong Hospital for three weeks. Adrian was called Ari from then on.

There is quite a story as to why Mum and Dad waited until the eighth child to name one after them. A heavily pregnant Mum was walking up the street one day and started chatting to one of the neighbours, Jack Sanders. Jack informed Mum that if they named this child after either her or Dad then this would be her last child. So that is what they did. It obviously didn't work as Steve was determined to come along and be the last child.

Now to be fair to Jack he would have known it was an old wives' tale and the context of the comment was probably a discussion about this being Mum's eighth pregnancy. Steve has reminded me that Mum in fact confirmed this story at her 80th birthday celebration, which was also Steve's 40th birthday celebration. During her speech she recalled the story and told Steve how lucky he was to be here. Mum still thought it was very funny as she couldn't stop laughing during this part of her speech.

I went into third class and quickly settled into school life. I was quite diligent and soon emerged as one of the brighter kids in the class. I have very fond memories of my four years at St Paul's although it was very strictly run by the St Joseph's nuns.

We sat at wooden desks, with a storage hutch under a lid. We had an exercise book for each subject, which we were expected to maintain very neatly. Writing materials were fountain pens and pencils. There was an ink well on each desk to keep a bottle of ink for refilling the fountain pen when required. Blotting paper was also a necessity to mop up any excess ink on the paper or any ink spills. The presence of ink was often a temptation for kids to use the ink for uses other than what it was intended for, resulting in an occasional inky mess. We were not allowed to use ball point pens.

I made lifelong friendships with three boys from that third class, Ken McInerney, Ian Pearson, and Tony Bulters.

A school milk program was in operation. The program had been introduced many years earlier to ensure that all Australian children would get fresh milk and a good dose of calcium each day. At play lunchtime (which was like morning tea) we were all given a small bottle of milk to drink, and we were expected to drink it. Most of the time the milk was cold and delicious. However, in summer it was sometimes warm by play lunchtime and the milk would be off. We were still expected to drink it. I think some kids were put off milk for life by the milk program. Occasionally we received either chocolate or strawberry milk.

Sport was a big thing, with rugby league and athletics the most popular school sports. A significant event occurred in my second year at St Paul's. I was playing in the grounds one lunchtime and some kids came to find me. They told me to rush to the high jump bars as my brother was jumping. I ran there as fast as I could and there was a big crowd of kids gathered around the bars. I squeezed my way to the front, using the "he's my brother" line to get through.

There I saw that my brother Hans, who was in sixth class, was the last one left jumping. He was jumping so high that he had reached above the height of the high jump sticks. A couple of teachers had noticed what was happening and were holding the bars at higher levels than the high jump sticks to see how high he could go.

Everyone was talking about Hans's high jumping, and I felt very proud and happy that day. Hans was one of the best athletes at the school at that time. He continued to be the outstanding athlete in our family for the rest of his life.

The school also had dunny can toilets. They were generally smelly and unpleasant to use. A girl who I went to school with told me years later that she would not use the girls' toilets. She waited until the end of the breaks and then went behind the toilets when all the other kids were back in the class.

It was around this time that my family and I became very interested in all types of Australian sports. The Melbourne Cup, a horse race run on the first Tuesday of November each year, quickly gripped our family's interest, just like the entire Australian population. There were so many of us that we could have a sweep, where everyone made a bet and pulled out a horse's name from a hat, within the one family. This became a very enjoyable annual tradition for us that would carry on in our family for many years.

The first year I was in a sweep was 1961, so I was eight years old. Mum organised the sweep the night before the race and I think it cost one shilling, or ten cents in decimal currency, per horse to enter. Whatever it was Mum must have put most of the money in anyway.

I won the sweep with the horse Lord Fury and I remember feeling quite rich with my winnings. I can't recall what I did with the money, but I hope I paid Mum back for putting me in the sweep in the first place!

John started a part time job selling newspapers, after school, at the Oaks Hotel. This started a trend for all the Lambert kids getting jobs while still at school.

Dianne started school at the beginning of 1962 after she had turned four just a month earlier. I was entering fourth class. Dianne was a full year too young to start school, so she was much smaller than the other kids in her class. Mum had somehow managed to enrol her and must have been keen to get Dianne off to school as she had two other boys at home aged two and six months respectively. Dianne didn't understand the whole school thing, so every play lunchtime and lunchtime she would come straight to wherever I was playing and stay by my side.

She always held my hand and was clearly too scared to do anything else. I sat with Dianne during those breaks watching the other kids play. This went on for several months until one day one of the nuns came and took Dianne by the hand to where the kids from her class were playing. They stayed with her until she got used to it and Dianne was fine from then on. The nuns had noticed what was happening and thought it was time both to let me play and for Dianne to become more independent.

Dianne and I have always had a very special brother-sister relationship and I think those few months provided the solid foundation for this. Dianne repeated kindergarten and then never looked back. She had to call on all her reserves of independence and resilience later in life when she unexpectedly became a single mother to four children. Based on the strength she exhibited then I think it was a master stroke by Mum to send her to school at such a tender age.

Dianne recalls that she went to school thinking that her name was Dianne, as everyone was calling her Dianne. She copied how to spell her name from another girl named Dianne in her class. She did not know her real name was Diana until she got her birth certificate when she was about 18 years old. She continued to be Dianne until she legally changed her name back to Diana when she was 64 years old.

Our new house in Wollongong had a very large backyard. Before long Dad, John and Hans built cages for chooks and pigeons. Pigeons were a very popular pet in the Netherlands and Dad knew a bit about training homing pigeons. John became very interested in pigeons and went to the local pigeon club. Hans became very interested in the chooks. His life-long love of chooks started then.

The animals quickly expanded to include another dog (though Muska remained 'top dog'). We also had a cat, rabbits and guinea pigs. Mum cultivated a large vegetable garden. Most of our vegetables, and all our eggs, came from the backyard. If we were hungry, we dug up a carrot out of the garden.

The chooks were both the source of our eggs and our roast chicken dinners. Mum always had a rooster, so the chooks kept multiplying. She would occasionally pick one or two for dinner. One of us would have to catch them, chop their heads off with an axe and place them into the laundry tub. Mum would pluck them and prepare them for cooking. Hans seemed to do this most of the time and he was very efficient at it. Sometimes we let the chicken run around after we had cut its head off. Mum was not happy if we did that.

The laundry was a very cold room, with a bare concrete floor. Mum spent hours there doing the washing. She had a wringer washing machine, which required all the clothes to be individually pushed through a roller wringer after washing. This would take quite a long time and the older kids helped Mum with the wringing process. Mum started washing at 6am almost every morning and I'm sure would have celebrated when she got her first fully automatic washing machine in 1970.

The laundry was also where the dogs and cats slept and had their babies. They were always having pups or kittens. Noticeably whatever cat we had only ever had one kitten most of the time. We didn't know why until years later. If Mum was quick enough and noticed the birth happening, she drowned all the kittens except one. Mum did this very humanely by using chloroform to put the kitten to sleep first. This was a necessity for Mum as she couldn't feed all the extra cats and she had to keep the number of animals to a manageable level. Desexing animals wasn't as available or affordable as it is today.

For the first year at Kaylaur Crescent our only electronic entertainment was an old radio that was positioned near Dad's chair. The reception was always very crackly. We would listen to whatever Dad had on, particularly the news. We had this radio for many years. I recall all of us gathered around it listening to the Australian aboriginal boxer, Lionel Rose, defeat Fighting Harada, of Japan, on the 26th of February in 1968 to become the world bantamweight champion. Boxing was a very popular sport then, and this was a huge occasion. The radio reception for the fight commentary was very poor and hard to understand and Dad kept trying to keep us quiet so he could hear it.

Sometime during the first year in Albion Park Rail Mum befriended a lady, Regina Mozart, who lived a couple of houses away. Her husband was a very big, unfriendly man who we were all a bit scared of. They had a television, and we would go to their place after dinner on Friday nights to watch 'Bonanza'. This was a very popular American show about a rancher, Ben Cartwright, and his three sons. They had a very small house, and we would all squeeze onto their bed, or sit on the floor, to watch the television. I think I have seen every episode of 'Bonanza' ever made and it still airs on Foxtel today. It was a good sign that we feared Mr Mozart as we were told he spent time in jail several years later.

We got our first telephone sometime in 1962. It was a landline with a rotary style telephone. The telephone was almost a necessary evil when we first got it. It was very expensive to make calls. None of us were allowed to make a call unless we put the money in a special money box situated next to the telephone.

Looking back now there were only landline telephones for the next thirty years and they remained quite expensive the whole time. When I got married in 1977, we did not have a telephone at home for the first six months until someone I was working for paid for one to be installed. He wanted to be able to contact me more easily. I don't think it ever got cheap enough, like it is today, for Mum and Dad to make regular calls to their siblings in the Netherlands.

Dad was an avid reader. He loved the daily newspapers, and he was always reading books. He found the local library which was situated in the Centenary Hall, Albion Park and we developed a routine of going there every Friday night. Dad would take us five older kids, and we would all get as many books out as we could. We all went through a phase where the "Bobbsey Twins" books were our favourites. In winter when we got home from the library, we would all sit around the fire in the lounge room, and voraciously read our books while Mum made hot milos. This was a big treat and Friday became my favourite night of the week.

Most of the Lambert siblings have continued to be avid readers of newspapers and books all their lives, particularly Renee who could read through the night if he was onto a good book.

John transferred from Dapto High to Christian Brothers College (CBC) at the beginning of the 1962 school year. It was situated right in the heart of Wollongong, at the corner of Crown Lane and Regent Street. This was an all-boys school and was quite a culture shock for John. It was very strictly run by the brothers and wasn't a place for the faint hearted. It also marked the start of the Lambert family's lifelong friendship with Brother Vic Bell, one of the teachers, who taught all seven Lambert brothers.

Many years later a gala dinner was held in Wollongong to celebrate Brother Bell's 50th anniversary as a Christian brother. I flew down from Queensland to attend this dinner and most of the Lambert siblings were there. After dinner Brother Bell got up to make his speech and started it off with something like, "Well I have been asked tonight what are the highlights of my 50 years as a brother? I can talk about the students who have become sports stars, like Mick Cronin and Geoff Shaw, and students who have excelled professionally but one of the greatest highlights for me was teaching those seven Lambert boys," and he pointed to us in the crowd. It was very emotional.

Another highlight of 1962 was our introduction to Cracker Night. A tradition to celebrate the annual Cracker Night, held on 24 May each year, had already commenced in Kaylaur Crescent before our arrival. This involved most of the adult residents and the older kids, getting together and building a giant bonfire on a big vacant corner block. All the kids would prepare by spending the weeks before doing any jobs they could to earn money to be able to buy crackers, skyrockets, and many other forms of fireworks. The shops had a huge selection of fireworks for sale.

The festivities commenced as soon as the fireworks became available in the shops, which was several weeks before Cracker Night. We bought as many crackers as possible and let them off all over the place. I think we were conscious of getting some distance from the house as they were very loud and would wake up any of the little kids if they were sleeping. The crackers were seriously explosive and quite dangerous. The penny bunger was the most common cracker, and it could do some damage. The tuppenny bunger was the most potent cracker. The naughtier kids caused property damage, including blowing up letter boxes, with the tuppenny bungers. They were called tuppenny bungers because they cost two pence each to buy.

One of the kids at school got caught one day with a tuppenny bunger that went off in his hand with his fingers wrapped around the bunger. He may have had a bunger with a short fuse. He suffered a severe laceration that required many stitches and took weeks to heal properly.

Cracker Night was a joyous night where everyone was happy. The bonfire was lit and the adults gathered to talk over food and drinks. The boys were busy letting off crackers, including having cracker fights. The girls were playing with the non-explosive fireworks like catherine wheels, roman candles and skyrockets. You had to be careful to protect your bag of crackers from sparks. There were times one of the kids would lose their entire bag of crackers early in the night due to an errant, or perhaps deliberate, spark letting them off.

Remarkably there were very few, if any injuries, at our annual cracker night celebrations and they were a wonderful example of neighbours coming together. We were always up at the crack of dawn the morning after to scour the bonfire and surrounds for any unused crackers. I loved the smell of the extinguished fire and used crackers, which lingered for days after.

Dad had stopped playing soccer after we left Parkes but still loved the game and followed it very closely. There was a team, South Coast United, from the Wollongong area who competed in the premier soccer competition in New South Wales. Their home ground was at Woonona, a suburb north of Wollongong. Dad went to watch their games as often as he could. We, the four older boys, would usually go with him. While we would just run around and play while Dad watched the game it gave me my first real taste of high-level sport and the passion of spectators. Wollongong had a very ethnic community, and the men loved their soccer. The crowd heaved with cheering and jeering. The referees must have been brave men because they copped it if a decision went against the home team.

Dad's two other loves were table tennis and chess. He taught us all to play chess using a chess set that he had hand made in the Netherlands in 1941. Dad was a very good chess player and he told us that he had won a few regional competitions in the Netherlands. We all picked it up quite well and there were many long, competitive games of chess played. I can't recall ever beating Dad in a game.

Dad was also an excellent table tennis player. I'm very thankful that he introduced me to this game as it was probably the sporting activity that I was best at later in life. Dad built a table tennis table, top only, that could be laid over our large dining table. He taught us to play although the table tennis top would only come out on special occasions.

Not long after we moved to Albion Park Rail, Dad went into business with another Dutchman, John Bulters, and then met a few other local Dutch families. Once again, the local parish priest played a part as he introduced Dad to John Bulters and encouraged him to assist Dad to get some building work.

Mum and Dad invited the other Dutch families over occasionally for a social night. They were very happy nights and one of the few times that I saw my parents drink alcohol. Dad set up the table tennis table and us kids were allowed to play a few games. Later in the night the men played. It generally ended with a game between Dad and Peter Naus. Dad usually won in very competitive, high-quality games.

Dad would be thrilled that my grandsons, and his great grandsons, Luka and Levi, both love soccer and chess. They are soccer mad and play chess competitively at school. To top it off, my granddaughter, and his great granddaughter, Evie, has started playing soccer as well.

It is interesting that soccer skipped a generation as none of the Lambert siblings played soccer, despite it being in the genes. This was largely because soccer was an uncommon sport for kids when we were growing up. It was not a school sport, and we never got the opportunity to play it.

Toni completed third form at the end of 1962, obtained her Intermediate Certificate and left school at this time, at the age of fifteen. Back then the only kids who went through to fifth form were those who wanted to get a university degree. Toni immediately started work at Robinson's garage in Albion Park, where she worked until she got married a few years later. Toni had already been doing babysitting jobs for several years and kept doing these as well.

When Toni got her pay each week, she handed it all over to Mum. Mum did not ask Toni for all of it, but Toni knew that Mum needed the money. Toni only asked for one thing in return for handing over all her pay. She asked Mum if she could get her teeth fixed up out of the money. Mum agreed and Toni went to the dentist at Dapto every week to get many fillings that she had needed for some time. Mum paid the dentist off with small weekly amounts.

CHAPTER 5

THE FAMILY IS COMPLETED

— 1963 TO 1964 —

Mum and Dad must have continued to love each other, if you know what I mean, as the ninth sibling, Stephen (Steve), was born on the 14th of March 1963, nine days after Mum's fortieth birthday. Talk about saving the best for last! Steve became the first and only sibling to become a dux and school captain.

This was another very difficult birth for Mum and she was bedridden for three weeks after the birth. Toni was fifteen then and started looking after Steve as soon as he arrived home. Dad pitched in to help with meals and Mrs Sercombe, our neighbour across the road, also helped. It was a real team effort to get Mum back to full health.

During this time several of us kids were billeted out to other Dutch families who looked after us while Mum was in hospital, and then recuperated. Adrian and I went to stay with the Van Krevel family in Oak Flats. Their son Jack was in my class at school, and we were already good friends. I enjoyed our little holiday there as I was always playing with Jack and his friends. Adrian was almost two and was a very cute, charming toddler. The Van Krevels were besotted with (and thoroughly spoilt!) him. I recall how delicious and plentiful the food was at the Van Krevels.

Much later the Van Krevels were to become one of the most infamous families in Wollongong's history. Jack's son, Mark Valera, became a double murderer and Jack himself was murdered by his daughter's boyfriend. It was a very eerie experience for me reading a book that had been written about these murders.

Following Steve's birth there were eleven people in three bedrooms. Adrian and Steve had a cot each on either side of Mum and Dad's bed. In the middle bedroom Toni had a single bed while Dianne and Terry slept on a narrow fold out sofa bed. The four oldest boys were still in the back bedroom.

When Steve was about one Mum and Dad decided they wanted a bedroom to themselves, so the nine kids were squeezed into two bedrooms. Steve replaced Terry in the middle bedroom, and he slept there with Toni and Dianne. An extra double decker bed was placed into the back bedroom, in front of the window. The six oldest boys were in this bedroom on three double decker beds. Fortunately, this was quite a large bedroom, and we all still managed to find a little spot for our own things.

We were all good sleepers, and the six of us settled into the back bedroom as if that was completely normal. The only regular interruption to our sleep occurred when Dad came in every night and sprayed the room with a Mortein fly spray can to kill any flies and mosquitos.

After her difficult birth with Steve, Mum's doctor advised her to stop having children. He also advised her to take the contraceptive pill which had become available at that time. My sister Dianne recalls that Mum told her later in life that she was concerned about taking the pill as it was forbidden by the Catholic church. Mum decided to catch the bus to the Catholic cathedral in Wollongong and asked to see a priest. She told this priest that her doctor had advised her that she should take the pill for medical reasons and wanted to obtain permission from the church Fortunately, Mum had found an understanding priest. He told Mum that she was allowed to take the pill as it was based on medical advice. Interestingly Mum chose not to discuss this matter with the local parish priest. This story highlights the significant role that religion played in Mum's life and in society at that time.

I guess it was always meant to end with nine siblings with Toni as a typical eldest child, me as a typical middle child and Steve as a typical youngest child.

Hans commenced high school in 1963 and went into first form at Christian Brothers College in Wollongong, joining John at that school. I commenced fifth class and experienced the impact of religion in a different way. During our bus trip to school each day we would drive past Albion Park Rail State School. Some kids would lean out the bus windows and yell out at the public school kids, "pubby wackers, pubby wackers."

Whilst it may have been just name calling, and names would come back from the public school kids, it was a sign of the subtle sectarianism that existed between Catholic and public schools at that time. We didn't mix with any kids from the public school until years later when we all started playing sport for the town teams. Fortunately, this sectarianism dissipated through my school years and I didn't notice it much through high school.

In 1963 I played rugby league in the school team for the first time. I played in the 5 stone 7lb division whereas my brother, Renee, who was in sixth class, was playing in the 4 stone 7lb division. His team became legends of the school as they won the competition undefeated without having a point scored against them all year. They had a few star players, including Mario Kecely, Garry Hughes, Vernon Feeney, and Paul Graham. Whilst Renee doesn't think he contributed much to the team's success I recall watching them play a few times and he was an effective, fearless tackler.

I was virtually a spectator in the 5 stone 7lb team. We were an average team, but it was still the case that only the best players got the ball, and most of us just made up the numbers. My school friend, Ken McInerney, recalled one game that we played in heavy rain, and it was very muddy. At the end of the game, I was the only player who was as clean as we were when we ran on. I obviously did not get the ball or make a tackle in the whole game.

Nevertheless, I started to develop a keen interest in rugby league, and I started to follow the Sydney competition. Dad always bought the newspapers, so I read all the news about the Sydney rugby league teams. I also started to listen to the games on the radio. I followed the Canterbury-Bankstown Berries, mainly because my favourite player was their dynamic fullback, Les Johns. John was an avid South Sydney Rabbitohs fan, and still is, while Hans also supported the Berries. The Berries became the Bulldogs in 1978.

As I reflect now as a grandparent, and keen spectator at my grandkids' sports games, it occurs to me that Mum and Dad never watched any of our school sports. Dad was always working, and

Mum did not drive. We always got picked up by one of the other parents to go to the game. The only parents who went to the games were the regulars who drove the kids there. Dad did make up for lost time years later when he came to watch us play rugby league after we left school. He was a very vocal spectator.

Us four older boys found many things to do in Albion Park Rail and Albion Park. John and Hans had picked up Dad's building skills. They made billy carts by using a wooden box (obtained from the greengrocer) and old, discarded pram wheels with a rope for steering. We raced the billy carts against other kids. They provided many hours of fun and entertainment. As with many other things we did, it is a miracle that there were no bad accidents or broken bones.

We built many cubby houses, again utilising John and Hans's building skills. These developed into substantial ones built in the local forests. They were so good that they became meeting places for the local kids and sometimes we slept in them overnight. There were huge tracts of vacant land at the end of Kaylaur Crescent, and across the railway line. We were free to roam and explore this land. We did not know if anyone owned the properties, and we were never chased off a property. We found a few grassy hills we could slide down on pieces of cardboard or bags. We regularly spent hours playing like this - finishing with competitive races down the hill.

There were lots of blackberry bushes growing in the wild. We picked blackberries all day and came home to present Mum with buckets full of blackberries. This was hard, tricky work as the blackberry bushes were very prickly and it was very easy to get nasty cuts and stings from them. We ate the blackberries raw, and

Mum also made blackberry pies from them. There were times that they were an important source of food for Mum.

We made up our own games to play at home. We made "guns" using a match box, clothes pegs and elastic bands. They were set up so we could fire the elastic band, as the bullet, at each other. We then split into teams and played war games. We progressed from these elastic band guns to making slingshots, that were called shanghais. We made these using a forked tree branch and the rubber from a bicycle tube. Small pebbles would then be used as the bullets fired from the shanghai.

We turned our back bedroom into a ghost house as another game. We blacked it out and placed obstacles everywhere. This included plenty of marbles spread across the floor. Each kid had to make their way through the bedroom with the others trying to prevent them getting through. Mum was not happy with the aftermath from the game as the room was often left with stuff everywhere and I think she gave up on trying to clean our bedroom. She changed the sheets but otherwise largely ignored the mess - I guess with so many children to look after there was only so many hours in the day!

The nearest beach to Albion Park Rail was Shellharbour, located about seven kilometres away. Shellharbour also had a harbour and an ocean pool right in the middle of town. Dad dropped us older kids off at the harbour in the morning and picked us up in the afternoon. We swam across the harbour, walked around the harbour, went to the pool, searched for crabs in the rocks and played games in the park which adjoined the harbour. There was a fish and chip shop located between the harbour and the pool. If we had money, we would buy hot chips for lunch.

I had my first and only swimming lesson on one of these days when I was about nine years old. We were swimming in the pool. I was in the shallow end when a couple of my brothers decided that it was time for me to learn to swim. They took me up to the deep end (which was well over my head) gave me some quick instructions on how to tread water and then threw me in. Somehow, I came up and made it back to the side of the pool. I never had any proper swimming lessons. I remained quite a poor swimmer through my school years.

We also sunbaked on these days. There was no sunscreen protection, and it was normal to lay in the sun to dry off or to have a rest. We also spent the long, hot summers virtually shirtless. We got sunburnt many times and developed deep tans every summer. It was a regular occurrence for our skin to peel after a bad bout of sunburn. Melanoma was not a commonly known disease, and we had no idea that we could be compromising our long-term health.

We kept going to the harbour and pool for many years and later in life we rode our bikes there. This resulted in some very dangerous riding home down the steep hill on Pioneer Drive, Oak Flats, where it was impossible to stop the bike gathering full speed. We just hung on for dear life until we reached the bottom of the hill. Bike helmets hadn't been invented yet so an accident could have been catastrophic.

Mum, Dad, Toni, John, and Hans were all naturalised as Australian citizens in 1963.

1963 was a big year for the Lambert family as it was also the year we got a brand new television. The television was black and white, had three free to air channels, with limited broadcasting hours. It would be many years before morning or all night television would become available. Having that television was an incredible feeling. I knew from school that most families already had a television, so I felt like we were a bit more like everyone else finally. We all loved watching anything that was on. Dad was continually telling (or perhaps yelling!) at us all to keep quiet so he could hear the television. I particularly liked Bob Dyer's 'Pick a Box' which was a game quiz show. I have liked quiz shows ever since.

Over time the older boys managed to get second hand bikes and we took any opportunity to ride them around town. We gradually built up a circle of close friends and the vacant block next door to our house became a central point for all types of sport and games. We mowed the block and used it for cricket, rugby league and all the usual games of the day. We managed to break the laundry window so often with an errant cricket shot that Mum stopped repairing it.

One game all the kids played together was hopscotch. We drew up the hopscotch court on the concrete path outside the laundry. It was a simple game where you would draw up numbered squares from one to nine. You would have to throw a rock into each square, starting from one, and then hop through all the squares but missing the square that had the rock in it. First person to complete all the squares was the winner. This area also became our handball court which was another popular game for the boys.

We played plenty of indoor games, including board games, cards, and a game that I think we invented for our own use, called "boy girl". This involved someone randomly selecting a letter of the alphabet. Then all players had to write down a boy's name, a girl's name, a thing, a place, an animal, a song, and a colour commencing with that letter. As soon as someone finished everyone had to stop and scores were tallied. Mum loved all these games and always played them with us.

As I think now about these games, I realise that we all had a healthy competitiveness that we carried through our lives. We all liked to win but generally maintained the right spirit and didn't get too despondent if we lost. It would be remiss of me however not to mention our cricket loving oldest brother, John, who would insist on batting first whenever he joined us for a game. He would then make up some excuse as to why he had to leave and would stop playing after he had had his bat. I should be fair and point out that John did only ever play and have a bat because we continually asked him to, knowing that he didn't want to. We loved having that time with our big brother.

I, and my siblings, have carried this love of games right through our lives. I'm a regular trivia player now and still like to organise a game of charades or spoons whenever the opportunity arises. I have now started playing "boy girl" with my grandkids. Pleasingly they love it and exhibit the same competitiveness that we all did at those ages. One of the categories now is celebrity so I am learning the names of influencers and you-tubers, who are the modern celebrities.

We used to enter the various competitions that were in the kids' sections of the Sunday papers. Most of these were colouring in competitions, which I was never going to win, as I was too untidy. For some of the competitions you had to be ten years of age to enter, so I was very keen to turn ten. I loved turning ten in 1963 and thought I was a big kid then.

John was completing second form when Mum and Dad decided it was time for him to leave school. John's recollection is that he had to leave school to assist the family financially. It was also obvious that he would be a good carpenter so they thought he may as well leave and get on with it. He left school in August 1963, just before he turned fifteen. He is the sibling with the least amount of formal education, yet he went on to be the sibling who successfully ran their own business.

John also started paying board to Mum as soon as he started work. He recalls that he gave his whole pay packet to Mum, and she would give him back some spending money for the following week. By the time I started work the normal board was fifty per cent of your pay. We accepted that quite happily as Mum and Dad clearly needed the money. I don't think any of us realised until years later that plenty of kids didn't pay any board at all.

By this time, us kids had settled into routines for household chores. Saturday mornings were allocated to do all the chores. We cleaned floors, mowed lawns, tidied up the gardens and went to the shops. Two of us were selected to do the weekly shopping trip. Mum compiled a list each for the grocery store, the butcher, and the greengrocer. We took Mum's shopping trolley and walked around one kilometre to the Albion Park Rail shops to do the shopping. It was a big shop and we used to stop halfway home for a rest.

By the end of 1963 the Beatles phenomenon had hit Australia. I first became aware of the Beatles when I saw one of our school friends, Peter Graham, at church one Sunday. He had a new haircut which was very different. I found out that it was the mop-top haircut worn by the Beatles. They were a pop group from Liverpool, England. They had taken the music world by storm with a succession of number one hits. Their concerts were always sold out and were featured by hundreds of young girls fainting from the excitement. The Beatles would later be recognised as brilliant songwriters and musicians, but at that time they were treated as brash, drug taking youths who were upsetting the established status quo.

Financial issues were always in the background. One day they came to a head when a council notice appeared in our front yard stating that the house was to be sold to recover unpaid council rates. John and Hans were very upset by this. When John got home from work and saw the notice he went straight to it, shook it loose and laid it down on the grass. He didn't want anyone to see it. This issue was resolved, although I'm not aware how, and that was probably the closest Mum and Dad ever came to losing the house.

At home our menagerie of animals kept growing and Renee and I started to take an interest in breeding guinea pigs. We built up the numbers to the point where Dad built three big enclosures inside the garage, and we could have up to thirty or forty guinea pigs in each enclosure. We left them in the garage at night. Sometimes we put them outside in the daytime in grassed areas fenced in by wooden boxes. We picked a few bags of grass after school every day to feed them at night.

By 1964 we had settled into life as a family with nine kids. Renee had started high school at Christian Brothers College, and Toni and John were settling into their working lives. Toni also took up the role of looking after the "little kids", Dianne, Terry, Adrian, and Steve. She bathed them, clothed them, played with them, and read them books. I have seen Toni do much the same later in life with my grandkids. She just takes charge, and the kids respond to her very willingly. Our backyard was taking shape, with the animal cages and vegetable gardens well established.

One of Mum's biggest jobs was cooking for eleven people every night. A standard meal was sausages, potatoes, carrots, and beans. There were usually plenty of vegetables, as they mostly came from our garden. We did not have meat with every meal. Sometimes Dad would get a piece of meat and we would only get the sauce from the meat, called shu. A standard Dutch dish that Mum made was Hutspot which was potatoes, carrots, onions all mashed and covered in shu. This was the whole meal.

My favourite dish was Mum's Dutch vegetable soup with meatballs, called Groentesoep. Mum would make up a very big batch of this and we had it, with bread, as the meal. There were generally leftovers when Mum made this, and it tasted even better the next day. Mum also made a hot dessert boiled rice dish, which we used to fill up on as we were often still hungry after dinner. Another favourite was Wentelteefeefjes, which was French toast the Dutch way. Mum would spend what seemed like hours patiently making these two slices at a time in a frying pan. We then devoured them in no time.

We all sat at the table for the evening meal. It was a big table. While there was plenty of bickering, they were great times which tightened our bond as siblings, without any of us realising that was happening. After dinner we all did the cleaning up. The dishes were divided into four jobs which were, table and floor, (ie. clearing the table and sweeping the floor), washing up and two people drying up and putting away. These jobs were shared between the four older boys as Toni had gone back to work with the little kids. We had our own way of selecting who would do what by the quickest person nominating what they wanted to do after we sat down to eat. We would be starting dinner, and someone would just say "table and floor" and then everyone would pick the other jobs. That worked well although I think that Hans sat back most of the time so he could do the washing up as no one else wanted to do it.

It was quite a big job doing the dishes and Dad would be forever asking (that is, telling us!) to keep quiet so he could watch the news. Dianne was brought into the dishes group from a pretty young age as well, though sometimes her washing up efforts weren't good enough to withstand Renee's scrutiny. He wanted the dishes done properly. Looking back the enormity of Mum's cooking role over so many years is quite hard to believe. I cannot recall eating in a restaurant until I left school. We rarely had take away food, and we never had a family vacation. Mum cooked all the time and she seemed perfectly happy doing it.

I never went on a family holiday with my parents and siblings. When the school holidays came there was never any discussion or thought about why other kids at school went away but we didn't. We just treated the holidays as a holiday from school and loved being able to play and explore all day.

During sixth class my teacher was a very strict nun, who I won't name as she would have thought she was doing the right thing, and always endeavoured to teach us properly. She gave the cane out very frequently, including to any kids who admitted to not going to church on Sundays. Almost every Monday morning she would ask any kids who had not been to Mass on Sunday to stand up. She would then give them six hits or "cuts" with the cane. There were a few regular boys who always stood up and didn't seem too concerned about getting the six cuts.

One day she thought two of the students in my class had cheated on a mathematics assignment. She demanded they admit that they had cheated. They refused and so she gave them the cane - one got 52 cuts and the other one received 64 cuts. I had recalled the number of 64 cuts but didn't know how we knew the number. In preparing for this book, I spoke to the student who copped the 52 cuts. He told me we knew the number was 64 as the whole class counted out loud while the student was getting them. The nun was irate that day and only stopped the punishment when a parent came to the school to see her. The student assured me that they did not cheat.

We were used to getting the cane and the strict teaching environment but that day there was a sense of disbelief in the classroom; the class knew this was too much punishment and just "not right". Some students had already rebelled in their own way against this nun prior to this incident. I was told later that one student once threw the nun's cane into an incinerator and another one hid the cane on top of a cupboard in the classroom.

There were still plenty of good times and lifelong friends made in primary school. I was quite studious and enjoyed the academic side. However, I was a disappointment to the nun at the end of sixth class. By then I was one of the "brains" of the class and was expected to score four A's in the primary final examination. I scored two A's and two B's. I still topped the class, but it was made clear to me by the nun that I had under performed. This was one of the factors that drove me to work harder and live up to my academic potential in high school and at university.

Our back boundary adjoined that of the local pub, which was the Oaks Hotel and Motel. The Oaks Hotel is still there today in a more condensed version and the motel was demolished many years ago. There is now a large McDonalds store on the motel site. We were always playing in the hotel grounds as there were no dividing fences. We soon came across a boy named David Tobin, who was the only child of the owners of the hotel. David became a good friend to all of us, but especially Renee and I as he was around our age.

David was quite a spoilt kid, by our standards. He seemed to be allowed to do anything he wanted to. He took bottles of Coca Cola, chocolates, and chips from the bar supplies. Through him we had our first taste of these junk food items and we loved them. Whenever we got a small bottle of Coke, we would put a couple of small pebbles in it to fizz it up and then we drank it. I don't know why we spoiled a bottle of coke by putting rocks in it, but it might explain why I never drink it now and haven't for a very long time.

Whilst the junk food was great, I think I enjoyed the meals from the motel kitchen the most. They were delicious and very Australian. I particularly loved the roast dinners which were different to the way Mum cooked them. Perhaps I was more influenced by the sheer size of the meals.

Later, when we were in high school, David introduced us to cigarettes as he also got them from the hotel. I'm not sure his parents were aware of that. Fortunately, we all treated this as just a naughty thing to do and none of us got addicted to them. I never understood the attraction of cigarettes and have never learned how to do the drawback.

By this time Mum had developed some traditions around our birthdays. She treated it as a very special day. If it was your birthday, you woke up to a series of small presents on the dining table. They were usually lollies and chocolate bars, which were very special treats as we didn't generally have them in the house. The person whose birthday it was also had two other special treats that day. They did not have to do the dishes and they could also choose the television programs to watch. This was always overridden a bit by Dad as the news was compulsory viewing every day. I recall making the lollies I received last as long as possible.

As with the house at Unanderra we had the dunny can toilet in the backyard. We again had two dunny cans which had to last for one week. Fortunately, I can't recall any overflows, but I think that Dad had to get an extra can occasionally. Us older kids would take the little kids to the toilet. This involved lighting the candle to provide light, and then waiting while they went to the toilet.

If we were lucky there was toilet paper to use. Otherwise, we used newspaper which had been cut into small pieces. While it wasn't a pleasant smell in the toilet, particularly when both pans were almost full, I generally found the outside toilet to be quite bearable

With so many boys the practice soon developed that, after dark, we would only go to the toilet for a number two. We would all do our number one's from the path onto the grass. As the years went on this wasn't such a great idea as we killed the grass and that area constantly smelled worse than the toilet itself.

CHAPTER 6

THE BLUE BIKE

— 1965 TO 1970 —

I started high school in 1965, at eleven years of age. We caught the train to school at around 7.45am and the train arrived home via the Albion Park Station at 4.30pm. As soon as we got home Renee and I would get dressed and pick a few bags of grass for the guinea pigs. They were long days.

The days were even longer for me as I got my first job, selling newspapers, just as I started high school. I got the job because we knew the proprietors of the newsagency, and as John and Hans had already started selling newspapers after school at the Oaks Hotel.

Mum got me up at around 5am every weekday morning. She did this every morning for the next five years. I rode Hans's bike to the newsagency, around one kilometre away, picked up the papers and then rode to the Albion Park Station. I got to the station about twenty minutes before the 6.10am train arrived and sold newspapers to the regular customers who boarded the train there. Newspapers were very popular and important at that time as they were the main source of the latest news and sports information and most customers bought the two main morning papers, being the Sydney Daily Telegraph, and the Illawarra Mercury.

Most of these customers were employed at the Port Kembla steelworks. They were salt of the earth tradies and labourers, "aussies" and "wogs", and collectively educated me about life for the next five years. I learnt about sports, a favoured topic of conversation, politics, hard work and people. Some of the workers loved to chat, others never did. Some of the workers were always happy and polite, others were reserved and grumpy. They were almost all men.

These workers were tough and resilient. There is something bleak about train stations that makes them seem colder than everywhere else and Albion Park particularly was very cold in the winter months. Mum knitted me a full balaclava beanie, which I wore with gloves, and warm clothing, to insulate myself from the freezing temperatures. However, many of these workers just took the cold weather in their stride. They would just throw a jumper on and happily go to work on the freezing train.

When the train arrived and stopped to pick up the passengers, about six more regular customers would lean out the windows so I could sell them a paper. I started at the first carriage and ran down the train selling as quickly as I could as the train only ever stopped for a short time. This became very hectic at times and often a couple of customers missed out, or money or papers were dropped. These men loved their newspapers, so I tried very hard to make sure they received their daily "fix". Whilst it was great for me if I sold out, there was nothing worse than selling out and leaving unhappy customers who had missed out.

As soon as the train departed, I rode back to the newsagency, dropped off any papers left over, counted the money, and reconciled it to the number of papers sold. I then took my pay from it, quickly rode home, had breakfast, got dressed and walked back to the same station to catch the train to school. This was to be my daily routine for the next five years. Almost sixty years later I still have the habit of waking up around 5am every morning and just can't seem to sleep in past this time.

I made the equivalent of around forty cents a day. That was enough money for me to have some spending money for the school tuckshop, as well as save for clothes and other essentials. This made me feel quite independent. At the start of sixth form, my last year of high school, I had a discussion with Mum and Dad, and we decided that I had to focus on my studies. I reluctantly gave up the newspaper job and really missed it, both financially and emotionally. I had really enjoyed the 'people side' of this job.

The newspaper job directly led to one of the most significant friendships of my, and my family's, lives. One day during my first year doing this job, I noticed a nice piece of fruit had been left in the pouch on my bike. I told Mum about it. She just thought someone was being nice to me and let me keep the fruit.

This started to happen regularly, and it was a different type of fruit each day. It was always a very nice, fresh piece of fruit. One of my regular customers, who I later learnt was Mr Age Van Der Zande, soon told me that he was leaving the fruit for me as he thought I was a hard-working young boy who deserved a little bit extra. He was always at the train station early and if I could talk to him I would. We soon worked out that the family backgrounds were similar as he was also a post war Dutch migrant.

One day, around six months later, he asked me if I could get my father to drive me into Wollongong on a Saturday morning as he had bought something for me that needed to be picked up. It was a big thing to ask Dad as he usually worked on Saturdays, but we somehow worked it out. Age met us at a bicycle shop. He had bought me what looked to me to be the best bike in the shop, and in the whole of Wollongong. It was a brand-new, brilliant blue Malvern Star bike. It had everything a bike could have, including gears, bells, lights, rack, front, and back brakes. I was overwhelmed and Dad was very impressed as well.

This was the first new bike anyone in the Lambert family had ever had. My older brothers were very happy for me and there was no hint of jealousy from them. They were also happy to grab my bike for a ride whenever they could.

Dad then got to know Age and before long he was a regular visitor to our home. He didn't have a car and walked from his place to our place. He became a benefactor for the family. If a Lambert kid had a birthday, he usually bought them a watch as a birthday present. He acted as a loan guarantor so Dad could buy a car. I'm pretty sure he helped Mum and Dad out financially a couple of times when things got very tough.

Age was a single, very quiet, man, who lived on his own, and we quickly became like family to him. I visited his home quite regularly, sometimes with my brothers, but generally on my own. This included sleepovers every now and again. He was a very religious man. His house was testament to this, with religious items prominent throughout the house. He did not have a television, so it was quite boring for me to stay there. I guess I felt some obligation, as he had been so good to us, but I also enjoyed some time away from the very busy Lambert household.

I reflect now that I wouldn't have let my kids stay with an older, single man and today it would not happen due to the fear that he may be a paedophile. While I was quite naïve sexually in my teens I would have known if something bad was being done to me. I'm happy to say that absolutely nothing ever happened. Age was simply a very good person. I don't think Mum and Dad were ever concerned about us staying at his house.

He taught me a bit about life as well. One day we were talking, and I asked him why he had never married. He smiled and said to me: "Gerald, it doesn't matter what size the pot is, there is always a lid to fit it," meaning he had not given up hope and would like to get married one day. Sure enough a few years later he met a widow, Doris, and they married when he was around 57 years old. They were very happy until his death at the age of 78. Doris and Mum became very close friends for the rest of their lives.

Toni recollects an important part of the Van der Zande story that I was unaware of prior to writing this book. One Sunday morning Age and Doris came to visit Mum. They were dressed in their Sunday best clothes as they had come straight from church. They asked Mum if they could talk to her in private. Mum went outside with them, and they framed the discussion by talking to Mum about how she had such a large family whereas they had no children but had the means to raise a child. Then they asked Mum if they could take Dianne to live with them. They thought they would be helping Mum out by taking one child, and they would benefit by having their own little family. Mum politely and quickly rejected this request. She must have done it very diplomatically as the friendship remained as strong as ever. I don't think anything like this was ever discussed again.

Age had developed dementia by his mid seventies and spent his last years in a nursing home. I was living in Queensland by then and on one of my trips back to Wollongong I went to visit him at the nursing home, at Warilla. He was sitting in one of those sleeper chairs in that typical nursing home room that we all dread to visit. All the residents were non communicative and either asleep or staring into space.

I talked to Age for a while and didn't get any hint of recognition. My brother, John was with me and he left quickly as he didn't think Age would recognise us. Then I decided to mention the bike. I asked him if he remembered the brilliant blue bike that he bought for me and described it in detail. The biggest smile came over his face and I was certain he did remember. I left shortly after and said goodbye not knowing that would be the last time I would see him. He passed away peacefully a few months later.

I, and my brothers, tried to get whatever jobs we could during the school holidays. I got one working at a poultry farm in Albion Park Rail but lasted only one school holiday with this one. One of the tasks was to find rats and use the resident Alsatian dog to kill them. The dog had been trained to kill rats with a single bite across the neck. He could kill forty to fifty rats in a few minutes. I didn't like that part of the job. Also, the same breakfast every day of four runny eggs soon grew tiresome.

When I was 14 years of age, I got a job during the Christmas school holidays delivering parcels from the local post office, which was adjoined to the newsagency. I got this job from my newspaper job and it was full time. I started as soon as the school holidays commenced and finished on Christmas Eve. I used my bike to do the deliveries. It got quite hectic as there were always lots of parcels, being Christmas presents, to deliver and I could only do a few on each trip. I did it for three years and managed to save money from it each year. I loved this job. It continued my education through working with adults and reinforced the benefits of hard work.

Renee's first job was cleaning the toilets at St Paul's School, when he was in sixth class. He rode his bike to the school to get there by six in the morning to clean the toilets. He did not do this job for very long because it took too long to ride to and from school. He also had a job making deliveries for the local chemist.

CHAPTER 7

MY FIRST PAIR OF LONG PANTS

— 1965 TO 1968 —

In January 1965 I went into first form and joined Renee at Christian Brothers College in Wollongong. Only first and second forms went to the Crown Lane School, which was called the Junior School. Christian Brothers College was an all-boys school. A new Christian Brothers school, Edmund Rice College, had been built at Keira Mine Road in West Wollongong a few years earlier. The third to sixth form kids went to this new school, called the Senior School. Hans started there from 1965.

High school was very different from primary school with the school day organised into periods for different subjects. All students were assigned to a home class. My first home teacher was Brother Bell. He was very happy to have another Lambert brother in his class.

It was also very disciplined. We were expected to work hard and do our homework. It quickly became clear that any misbehaviour would be punished. Most of the teachers were Christian Brothers. They each had a leather strap which they would not hesitate to use as punishment. There were a few older brothers who used the leather straps frequently and as both a first and last means to control a classroom. It is fair to say that many parents at the time condoned the brothers' "muscular" approach to educating boys.

I grew up quickly in that first year of high school. The school grounds at the play lunch and lunch breaks were no place for the faint hearted. Boys being boys, boys going through puberty, boys playing sports and boys looking to cause trouble produced plenty of tense, uncomfortable situations. Fights between kids were common and further tensions arose if the teachers stepped in to quell the situation. On one occasion one of the students had a full-on fight with one of the brothers. The brother "won" the fight and the student was suspended. That student left school at the end of second form.

Sometimes these tense situations occurred because of the different nationalities and cultures at the school. The Wollongong area had become very multi-cultural due to the high number of post war migrants that had settled in the area, after being attracted by the employment opportunities. There were plenty of Italian, Yugoslav and other European kids who were often collectively referred to as "wogs". I was sometimes included in the "wog" category but generally I was left alone as I looked Australian and my name appeared to be quite Australian too. There were many times that these kids were picked on cruelly and unfairly. There were also many times when the "wog" description was more about name calling and teasing in a more light-hearted fashion.

Bullying was also an issue. The weaker kids were picked on, sometimes mercilessly. Some of the brothers did try to stop it, but the bullies would find a way. I was never bullied at school, but I did have a brief, nasty bullying experience on the school train in my first year of high school. There was a youth who boarded the train at Kiama who took a disliking to me. He was working and was probably around eighteen years of age. He would walk past me, sneer and make comments and then one day he punched me in the stomach. It was a very hard punch and it hurt me. I had never talked to or provoked this youth, and he didn't tell me why he punched me.

I was very upset and when I got home, I told Mum and Dad. Dad came with me the next day and boarded the train. The youth was on it and Dad found him and took him aside for a chat. This was a very quick chat as Dad didn't stay on the train. Whatever Dad said to him worked a treat as he never came near me again.

While I did not get bullied at school, I did get teased quite a bit when the kids at school found out that I had Maria as one of my middle names. The hit song "Maria" from the musical, West Side Story, was very well known. It was sung to me many times on the school train or in the playground.

There were also many happy times experienced in the school playgrounds. Most of the kids, including me, played sports or games during the breaks. Handball, cricket, rugby league and touch football were very popular. Disputes, ripped shirts, constant sledging, innocent cheating and that constant desire to win were all part of a vibrant environment from which genuine mateship emerged. As the high school years went on, I sensed that we all subconsciously knew that these were very important, formative years in our lives. It soon felt like the whole class was on that journey together.

Classrooms were the location of both good and not so good times. The teaching standards were quite good. The teachers were generally encouraging and knew their stuff. I liked the greater variety of subjects and performed well academically (albeit with repeated commentary on my report cards that I could do better!). However, I did not enjoy the work in the science laboratories. I never really understood the experiments and I laboured through science right through high school.

There were many unfortunate experiences when kids got into trouble either innocently or not so innocently. Talking or mucking around in the classroom was dealt with quickly and severely with several hits with the strap, which could really hurt. We became quite used to it as some kids were constantly naughty and some brothers dished the strap out very regularly.

There were also occasions when kids were punished for innocent mistakes. One day in first form we were doing comprehension and every kid had to read a paragraph from a book aloud to the class. During one kid's turn he was reading very slowly and pronounced the word carcasses as two separate words "car cases". This brought howls of laughter from the class as everyone could see the paragraph that he was reading and that he should have said carcasses, as in animal carcasses. I'm ashamed to say that I joined in the laughter. The teacher was critical of the student, rather than supportive. That poor kid was so embarrassed, and it could have been handled much better.

High school brought together many kids from all the catholic schools in the Illawarra and South Coast regions. Only about six kids from my primary school went to Christian Brothers College so there were plenty of new friends to make. This started on the school train when the kids from the same class gradually came to sit together. I developed great friendships with a group of kids from Kiama including Mick Warren, Peter Cooney, and Colin Devenish, and from Dapto including Steve Long, Tony Day, and Mick Bickerdike. I enjoyed the train trips as we generally played cards, with euchre generally the game of choice. We also took the opportunity to do homework or study if we had to. Mick Warren told me after we left school that he only passed French because I used to help him with it on the train.

Another big change in high school was how many books we had to have. This included many heavy textbooks and an exercise book for every subject. We carried the books in our school ports, which were sturdy cardboard cases. These were always hand me downs in our family. I only used two school ports during my 6 years of high school. Whilst we only took the books home that were required for homework, my school case was always heavy. Carrying it in one hand may have contributed to the back issues I had later in life.

Mum made us a couple of jam or peanut butter sandwiches for lunch, with a piece of fruit for play lunch. I always took the piece of fruit that Mr Van Der Zande had given me that day. The sandwiches became very hot, tasteless, and hard to eat by lunchtime. The sandwiches were kept in a brown paper bag in our school ports and the heat got to them by lunchtime.

The school tuckshop was a big treat. We sometimes got tuckshop money from Mum, but not very often. I also sometimes used my newspaper money to get tuckshop food. Meat pies and sausage rolls were the favoured purchases whilst sandwiches were also available. There was also a wide range of lollies available. Kids bought them to eat during class, even though that was not allowed. The tuckshop food range was a dentist's dream.

We were always ravenous when we got home from school. Mum made a sandwich covering called lecradinger, which was cocoa mixed with sugar. I think the name given to this mixture by Mum came from the Dutch words for "nice things". If there was bread available, we ate a few slices of bread with lecradinger, before heading out to play. It was not the healthiest thing to put on a sandwich, but it tasted great. Sometimes we had a plate of Weet-Bix and milk as that was also quite filling. For Renee it was always a plate of scrunched up rice bubbles, his favourite cereal, without milk.

Dad had a blue Holden utility. On Sundays, when he could, he took the whole family for a ride to get an ice cream. He usually drove to Wollongong on the back road, through Warilla and Warrawong, which was a single lane road then. Dad drove quite slowly with so many kids in the front and back of the utility. Almost invariably a very long line of cars formed behind us, with drivers getting frustrated because we were going so slowly, and they couldn't get past.

I recalled this story at Dad's 80th birthday celebration and twisted the story a bit by saying "Dad was such a good driver that all the other cars used to follow him." Dad laughed so much at this that we had to stop the recollections for a few minutes.

During my first or second year at high school there was a significant disruption at home when the fridge broke down and stopped working. We only had one fridge back then so it was a significant inconvenience. The financial situation was very tight when this happened and it was several weeks before the fridge was repaired. Replacing the fridge was simply unaffordable at that time.

Mum's resilience was again demonstrated through this time without a working fridge. She would have been quite distressed by it but just kept on going. There was still a cooked meal on the table every night.

Us kids developed a routine where one of us would walk to Joe's BP service station each morning to get a few bags of ice. This was a short walk as you could access the garage from the end of our street. We would bring the ice home and pack it throughout the fridge in an attempt to keep the food cold for as long as possible. By the time we returned home from school the ice had completely melted and we repeated the whole exercise again. Despite our best endeavours, food and drinks became warm quite often. Having rancid milk on my cereal for breakfast remains an unpleasant memory.

On the 14th of February in 1966 Australians woke to a brand new currency. Our currency changed from the English based pounds, shillings, and pence to a decimal currency, comprising dollars and cents. This affected me on my paper run as I had to adapt to the new currency very quickly. Australians embraced the new currency.

Toni was enjoying her work life and fewer responsibilities at home as the little kids were getting older and more independent.

She met a man named Malcom Yates when she was 18, and after a whirlwind romance, they were married on the 19th of March 1966. Her wedding, at the Albion Park Catholic Church, was the most important event I had ever attended. The wedding reception was held in the Albion Park Rail Progress Hall, with plenty of food, drinks, flowers, and trestle tables. This was a very exciting day for all the Lambert kids.

Malcolm was a good addition to the family. He loved a chat and was very different to us. He was very handy. Malcolm repaired one of the cars, or something mechanical in the Lambert house, on many occasions.

Toni's first child, Tracey, came along on the 7th of August 1966, just after Toni's 19th birthday. With Malcolm working long hours so they could save money for a house, Toni was often at our house with the new baby. Tracey was only three years younger than Steve, so she virtually became the 10th Lambert child. Poor Mum did not get much of a break between parenthood and grandparenthood.

A significant incident occurred when Hans went away to a school cadet camp. It was compulsory for students to join the cadets from third form to sixth form. Hans was in fourth form and 15 years old at that time. The annual cadet camp was held at Singleton, near Newcastle in New South Wales. This camp comprised a week of intensive military training, which included learning how to shoot a 303 rifle. Every student was given a rifle which they had to maintain for the week. Everyone slept in tents; six students to a tent.

We are not sure how it happened, but Hans got shot in the knee with a blank bullet from point blank range. Blanks were still quite powerful rubber bullets. They were meant to be fired, with caution, from a distance. It caused a severe injury to Hans's knee. He was rushed to the local hospital and spent the next week there. One of the brothers stayed behind to ensure Hans was looked after and to accompany him home.

It wasn't possible for Mum or Dad to go to the hospital as it was at least a four hour drive to get there. The brothers called Mum and Dad with regular updates on Hans's condition. He returned home and recovered from the injury reasonably quickly, but it took quite a long time before he was running normally. It would have been a catastrophic injury if it had been a real bullet so in that sense it was a fortunate outcome.

Hans was a very fast runner both before and after this incident, but I always wondered if he would have been even faster had the injury not occurred.

In mid-1966 the Lambert family's lives changed dramatically when Dad's building career came to a sudden and unexpected end. He was working on a building site in Kiama when he fell into a septic tank pit and badly injured his knee. This led to an extended period of almost three years when Dad did not work. The injury affected Dad both physically and mentally and it took him a long time to find the motivation to change careers. During this recovery period he waited for compensation for the injury to be paid, and although we would learn later he did receive some compensation, it was much less than he expected.

Dad's injury placed a tremendous strain on the family's already poor financial position. Mum decided to find a job. Fortunately, the owners of the Oaks Hotel and Motel were happy to employ Mum and she started work as a cook and a cleaner. It was only a two minute walk for Mum to walk through our backyard to the Oaks' kitchen. She started work at six o'clock each morning to prepare breakfasts for the motel guests. She then cleaned the rooms that had been occupied the previous night. Her hours were generally from six until eleven each morning but that varied depending on the number of motel guests exiting the property that day. Dad took over the morning duties at home including getting all us kids off to school.

Mum's workload had become herculean. She kept doing the main household work, including the washing and cooking. Toni had left home. Dad did more at home, but he was limited by his injury. I think we all lifted and helped, but Mum always had the pressure of running the household.

Dad's injury, and his extended period of not working, cast a pall over the Lambert household. Although we had always lived frugally, we were always generally happy and enjoyed our lives. The stress of Dad not working created a household atmosphere that was gloomier and more subdued during this period.

Our resilience, both individually and as a family, gradually got us all through these tough times. John continued to succeed in his work and was able to contribute to the family's finances. Us older kids tried to get whatever jobs we could, and quickly became more independent. Dianne and Terry used to help Mum clean the motel rooms. Dianne cleaned the bathrooms and learnt how to make the beds properly. Terry became very good at placing the paper strip around the cleaned toilets. Dianne and Terry were 11 and 9 years old respectively at this time.

Renee and I kept breeding the guinea pigs and sold them regularly to a few pet shops. Dad would take us around to the pet shops with the baby guinea pigs until we found a buyer. One of our jobs with the guinea pigs was to get fresh sawdust for their cages. We rode our bikes to the Albion Park Building Supplies, which was on the highway a few kilometres away. We checked in with the office and then were allowed to fill as many bags as we had. We usually filled up five or six bags. Then we waited on the side of the highway for Dad to drive past. He would stop and we would throw the bags in the back of the utility. Sometimes we waited there for several hours for Dad to arrive. Fortunately, we only had to get sawdust every couple of months.

This lasted for a few years until one hot summer day. We had put the guinea pigs outside in the morning, only to come home after school and discover they had all died in a heat wave. At that point we were winding down and we only had about a dozen of the older breeders left. While it was a sad way to end, it was time as they were a lot of work for not much return. At one stage we had 180 guinea pigs to care for!

Hans left school at the end of 1966 after he had completed fourth form. He started work as a commercial trainee at Australian Iron & Steel, Port Kembla.

I moved to the Senior School at West Wollongong at the beginning of 1967 and the start of third form. This was another big change for me in terms of my school environment. It was a very modern school with much better facilities including a large, well-stocked library. There were more lay teachers. The school grounds were very large and included access to two sporting ovals.

The hard work and discipline continued at the Senior School. The strap was still used, although the frequency decreased as high school advanced. The school atmosphere was lighter and happier compared with the Junior School. The expansive school playgrounds had a lot to do with this. The kids were much more spread out and there was less conflict. The banter against the "wogs" had virtually disappeared. We all knew each other by this time and there was a greater sense of camaraderie as we settled into the more serious high school years.

Starting third form was very significant for me as the uniform included wearing long pants. I had worn short pants to school through primary school and high school to date, even during the cold winter months. Mum bought me a brand new pair of long pants to wear to school. I was 13 years old, and this was the first new pair of long pants I had ever had. Any previous long pants I had were hand me downs from my older brothers.

In third form I had the first and last fight in my life. I had a very good friend from Dapto, Steve Long, who I travelled with on the train every day. One day we were on the train trip home, and we were niggling at each other. Then we started to fight, which comprised only wrestling and grappling. We didn't punch each other and neither of us got hurt but I did lose all the buttons off my school shirt. That upset Mum more than the fact I had had a fight. We started fighting at Unanderra and finished when Steve got off at Dapto, just over five minutes later. We were best friends both before and after the fight. Later we could not recall why we had the fight.

Other activities also became more prominent in school life. I joined the cadets. We had to dress up in full military uniform, which was provided by the army. The uniform had to be spotless. This involved me polishing boots and badges and Mum washing and ironing the uniform. Cadets were held once a week with half a day allocated for cadet training and exercises. This was very physical, intense training with many field exercises. We learnt to carry weapons and how to shoot a 303 rifle. We also had to march in the Anzac Day parade in Wollongong every year.

I persevered with cadets simply because I had to. It did not suit me, and I never liked it. I attended one cadet camp, which was one week away at an army base in Singleton, NSW. I did not enjoy this camp at all, but particularly disliked the 303-rifle training. I was influenced by Hans's injury. I felt quite unsafe both with the rifle in my hands and so many loaded rifles in the vicinity. I did whatever I could to get out of going to another cadet camp. I think that I was able to use my newspaper job as an excuse not to go. I never went to another one. I should note that I was the exception here; most of the school kids liked the physical aspects of cadet training.

The main school sport was Rugby Union and I started playing for the school in third form. Once again, I was just making up the numbers. Swimming in summer and athletics in winter were the other standard sports activities. I never learned how to dive properly so that limited my swimming prowess. I enjoyed athletics, particularly the running races.

Renee left school at the end of 1967 after he completed fourth form. He was very happy to leave school. He started work as a commercial trainee, joining Hans at Australian Iron & Steel in Port Kembla. He commenced in the invoice department. One day a guy, who he worked with in this department, told him he looked like Fuji, a character from the TV show, 'McHale's Navy'. Another guy overheard this, and they called Renee Fuji from then. This quickly became his nickname for everyone. Later in life Fuji became possibly the best known nickname in Wollongong, such was his popularity.

During his first year of work Fuji managed to save some money. When he noticed Mum hinting that she needed a decent freezer he used his savings to buy her one. I would not learn this until many decades later.

During Dad's period off work, he became very curious and was constantly thinking of things to invent. He produced a beach chair and a multi-level comb. He also tried to invent games. Dad dreamt that one of these inventions would turn into a big money earner but unfortunately that never happened. Dad also read a lot through this period.

Hans had started playing tennis and joined Albion Park Rail tennis club. Renee and I soon started coming with him and we all started playing regularly. This started a pattern for me with Hans. He would start a sport and I would follow him. We had very similar sporting interests, albeit he was always a couple of grades higher. Later in life Adrian also followed us into cricket.

We were all settled into Albion Park Rail by this time. Our place was often the meeting spot for the neighbourhood kids, mainly because we had the vacant block of land next door to use. We were free to go wherever we wanted to on weekends, and we were usually out most of the day. Swimming in Macquarie Rivulet was a popular pastime.

By 1968 the little kids were old enough to understand and enjoy Christmas. This became a joyous time of the year for the Lambert family. Us older kids were all earning some money and by then it was customary for each older kid to buy presents for every sibling, as well as Mum and Dad. Mum and Dad always managed to buy one special present for each kid, as well as several smaller presents. As you could imagine there were a lot of presents to hand out. Mum handed them out one by one and that took at least an hour. That hour of being in a circle while the presents were being handed out was the highlight of Christmas for all of us. It was just as enjoyable as playing with the presents later.

One year the special present for us four older boys was a pogo stick each. They were all the rage at the time. We played on them continuously and were soon organising competitions between us. One of them was who could do the most consecutive jumps on a pogo stick. I can't remember who won this, but the winning number was around four hundred.

Christmas lunch was another highlight. Mum always cooked a roast chicken meal with all the vegetables and trimmings. It was delicious and made the day perfect.

Towards the end of 1968 I was approaching the end of fourth form. This was the year that both Hans and Renee left school to get a job and contribute to the family's finances and it was a given that

I would leave school and do the same. However, one of the brothers, Brother Barnes, took me aside and told me that they would like to speak with my father about allowing me to stay at school so I could complete fifth and sixth forms, and hopefully go on to study at university. This proved to be a life changing discussion.

Brother Barnes said that firstly I had to go and speak with several of my teachers and ask them if I should be given the opportunity to complete fifth and sixth forms. Most of the teachers were supportive of the brothers assisting me to stay in school and felt I had the academic ability to matriculate into university. However, one of the brothers, Brother Barrett, told me it was a waste of time for me to keep going as I was too lazy and not working to my potential. He told me I wouldn't amount to anything, and I may as well go and get a job now. That certainly fired me up as I had achieved reasonably good results and thought I had developed good study and homework habits. Little did I know that this was a set up to spur me on in those last two years. The set up worked.

Dad came to meet with the brothers. They explained I was performing well academically and should complete high school so I could go to university and embark on a professional career. They also told Dad they would waive school fees totally for my last two years of high school. Dad and Mum agreed to let me stay at school. This was not an easy decision for them to make financially. I was very grateful and became determined to work hard to justify the faith shown in me.

So once again I was the fortunate one of the Lambert siblings by being the first one afforded the opportunity to complete high school. Like the reaction when I was given the blue bike by Mr Van Der Zande, I experienced complete support, and no jealousy, from my siblings. They were happy for me, but I did cop some ribbing for being a bit too studious in those last two years.

I completed the School Certificate at the end of fourth form, in 1968. I obtained 6 A's, advanced levels, in all subjects. As it turned out I won a State Bursary which paid my school fees for those two years.

CHAPTER 8

TAKING MY OPPORTUNITY

1969 TO 1970

I commenced fifth form in 1969 with a much smaller class group. The kids who were going to become tradesmen had left school at the end of fourth form. All the kids from Kiama had left school and there were only about five or six of us by then catching the train. The mood at school shifted as the students who stayed on were all reasonably serious about studying and doing well in the Higher School Certificate. There was much less mucking around and school yard fights were rare. We also got to know our teachers better in those last two years of school. I ended up appreciating them more.

My curiosity led to a life changing conversation for me one day soon after we started fifth form. I had the same teacher for both science and religion and those periods followed each other. One day in science he taught us about Darwin's theory of evolution, which inter alia espoused that we, the human species, evolved from apes.

At the commencement of the religion period, I raised my hand and stood up for a question.

"You have a question Mr Lambert?" the Brother said.

"Yes brother, you have just taught us about Darwin's theory of evolution and I'm having trouble reconciling that theory with the religious teaching that we all came from Adam and Eve," I started.

I didn't get to ask my question.

"Sit down and shut up Mr Lambert, that's science and this is religion!" he barked.

That was the end of that conversation, forever, with that brother. For me it was life changing in a good way. It didn't make me an instant non-Catholic or dramatically change my religious views, but it certainly made me think differently about them. I guess it was a bit like when you find out that Santa Claus doesn't exist as a real person. A practical part of the Santa Claus story may have been historically formulated a certain way but that didn't mean that the concept of Santa Claus was any less important and meaningful.

I studied very hard from the commencement of fifth form and was doing homework and studying for three to four hours every night, plus more on weekends. I was one of those students to whom the saying "the harder you work the better you get" applied. I was not naturally intelligent, like some of the other kids who seemed to get through with minimal study.

I experienced a close death for the first time in February 1969. One of my close school friends, Ian Pearson, lived on the highway near the shops in Albion Park Rail. I often went to Ian's place, and we usually ended up playing cricket with his older brother, Joe. Joe was a good friend of my brothers, John and Hans. He was a very good cricketer and rugby league player. He became ill very suddenly after contracting encephalitis and passed away several months later.

One of the brothers drove me and a couple of Ian's other friends from school to the funeral. It was a massive funeral as Joe was a very popular young man and the Pearsons were a multi-generational family in the area. Joe's death rocked the small Albion Park community.

Joe's death made me more aware of the frailty of life, and how insulated us Lambert kids had been from death due to not having relatives in Australia. That would not have been the case for Mum and Dad however, who were regularly informed of family members' deaths and mourned quietly from afar.

One day in late 1968 John was at a working bee with a few of his mates from the Dapto Young Christian Workers (YCW) group. They were cleaning up the Albion Park Catholic Cemetery, an old cemetery situated directly behind the Catholic church in Flinders Street, Albion Park. The parish priest, Father Michael Bach, was directing the working bee. During a break the mates were talking about the fact that there was nothing to do for young people, around their age group, in Albion Park. Father Bach, who was a progressive, young priest said to the group, "Why don't you do something, like run a dance?"

The group was energised by Father Bach's prompting, and they agreed then and there to do it. They decided they would hold the first one in the Centenary Hall at Albion Park. They would connect with a band promoter, with the objective to run a dance once a month. Further they decided on the lofty ambition of hiring the band who had the number one hit in the country at the time. This group of mates had no fear and did not consider the things that could go wrong or obstacles they may encounter. This group included my brother John, Mick Keys, Geoff King and John and Gerard Bulters.

At that first impromptu meeting they decided they would need a name for the dances. They threw around some ideas. They decided that they wanted to be different and didn't want to be part of the "in set". Someone then said why don't we call ourselves "Outset?" The "Outset Youth Dance" was created and quickly became a phenomenon in the broader Wollongong area.

The dances started early in 1969 and became very popular, very quickly. They stuck to the plan of hiring the top bands. On the 28th of March 1969, the Executives came to the humble Centenary Hall in Albion Park. They had already had several number one hits and regularly appeared on television. The dance sold out with standing room only. The Executives played all night, and they brought the house down.

Interestingly Ian Pearson, my school friend, was there and met a girl, Kathie Johnson, at this dance. They were both 16 years old at the time and they have been together ever since.

The dances were alcohol free. The age limit was 16 and above, correct dress was essential, and the admission price was eighty cents. I was lucky to be able to go to a few dances before I turned 16 as I worked in the ticket booth. A few of the parents and some of the church elders came and performed the roles of bouncers and supervisors. They were required at times as trouble sometimes occurred due to drunk kids trying to get in or general youth exuberance. It was always the male youths in trouble.

Mick Keys' father, affectionately known by all as Chief, was the undoubted leader of the bouncers. He was a tough man, hardened by many years of running the family dairy farm, and he dealt with any troublemakers quickly and decisively.

The dances became more well known and popular through 1969, with almost every dance being a sell out, which was around seven hundred people. There were always many more people outside the hall. The small town of Albion Park came alive on those Friday nights. Some of the top Australian bands that played included Flying Circus, the Atlantics, Jeff St John and the Copperwine, Autumn, Aesop's Fables and the Dave Miller Set. The Dave Miller Set left a lasting impression on the town as they caused a blackout of Centenary Hall and parts of Albion Park. They were very loud and overloaded the electricity substation. Some of the residents were not as happy with the Outset dances as the youth of the day were.

The Outset group became more ambitious towards the end of 1969. They decided to hold a Pop Spectacular at Wollongong Showground on the 28th of December 1969. This was an afternoon pop concert featuring Russell Morris and many leading bands and was compered by Donnie Sutherland. This concert was a failure. The crowd was poor, and they lost money for the first time. This concert would be the last Outset dance. The group of mates were jaded and not all of them wanted to continue running dances. Most of them were settling down with girlfriends and their careers and didn't have the appetite for the hard work and time commitment required.

The Outset Youth Dances ceased as quickly as they had commenced. These dances were held charitably and the excess funds were donated to worthwhile charities.

John was not jaded and had developed a keen interest in the music industry. He had been responsible for booking the bands for the Outset dances and he wanted to keep going.

The impact of these dances on my life was profound. I was introduced to the world of live music, and I loved it. Music had changed dramatically in the 1950's and 1960's with the emergence of Elvis Presley and the Beatles, together with many more bands and artists. They introduced the world initially to Rock and Roll music in the 1950's and to Pop music in the 1960's. Music was loud, catchy, meaningful, and generally frenetic.

Along with the new wave of music, dancing changed dramatically. Dancing became wild, uninhibited, and individual. Girls loved to dance. The days of girls waiting for a boy to ask them to dance at a formal dance were over. The kids loved it, but the parents were more guarded about the new trends.

There was still the usual boy/girl shyness and girls preferred to be asked to dance by boys. However, if they didn't, they would just get up and dance in groups. This new wave of music led to significant cultural change around the world in the 1960's. People were more outspoken and non-conformist. The younger generation did not want to follow in their parents' footsteps.

This new found freedom in the 1960's had some dramatic side effects including the emergence of a drug culture and the hippie generation. Psychedelic drugs became common and there was a sense of rebellion in the world. Smoking was commonplace with advertisements on television extolling the pleasures and virtues of smoking. Millions of people around the world were enticed into an addictive habit which would, within a few decades, be proven to have extremely detrimental long term health impacts.

We were passive smokers as children. Dad was a heavy smoker of cigarettes and cigars until he reached the age of 70, when he gave up smoking. He smoked in his lounge chair. The ceiling above Dad's chair was blackened by the cigar smoke.

I, like most kids of the time, loved Elvis Presley, the Beatles, the Rolling Stones, the Bee Gees and Johnny O'Keefe, the king of Australian Rock & Roll. We eagerly awaited the release of the Top 40 songs each month, which you could obtain from one of the record shops. I listened to an old radio in my bedroom to hear the latest music as we did not have a record player at home. I memorised the Top 40 songs each month.

I saw Johnny O'Keefe sing live a few times in the 1970's. He was very magnetic and charismatic. At one concert he came out, did not say anything, and launched into "Move Baby Move" as the opening song. It seemed like every woman in the place got up to dance simultaneously as soon as he sang the first word. The atmosphere was electric, and the women danced all night.

In June 1969 Toni was heavily pregnant with her second child and went to the doctor for a check up. Dad drove Toni to the doctor because Toni's husband, Malcolm, was at work. He and Mum looked after Tracey in the car while Toni went into her appointment. She suddenly started having severe contractions in the waiting room. They put her on a bed and called Mum in. The doctor didn't want Toni to push, but Mum told her to push if she had to. Toni did and Mum delivered Melissa while the doctor was in another appointment. He came in a couple of minutes later, cut the cord and then organised an ambulance for Toni to go to hospital. It was a fifteen minute labour with the scheduled appointment being at 4.20pm. Melissa was born at 4.35pm on the 11th of June. The doctor did not miss his next appointment and Mum could now add midwife to the jobs she could do! Melissa was wrapped in Mum's cardigan for the ambulance trip.

Dad made a significant move back to the workforce towards the middle of 1969 when he was 47 years old. His days as a builder were over and he decided to become a life insurance salesman. Dad joined Colonial Mutual Life (CML). After considerable training he commenced work at the CML building on the corner of Crown and Keira Streets in Wollongong.

It must have been quite daunting for Dad to make such a dramatic career change. The training was very complex, and he was still adapting to the English written language. Dad was quite determined, and his natural intelligence was an asset as he completed the training. He became successful reasonably quickly and kept this job until he retired.

I joined Albion Park Rail Tennis Club and tennis became my main sporting interest and activity outside school hours. By this time (1969) I was playing in three competitions, under 16 boys on Saturday mornings, C grade mixed on Saturday afternoons and C grade men on Sunday mornings. The club also held a tournament every Saturday night, which Hans, Renee, and I played in. While I loved tennis, the best part of the Saturday night tournament was the supper with scones, lamingtons and sandwiches made by the tennis ladies. This food was a real treat.

I could only keep up with my tennis workload for a short time and by the end of 1969 I was only playing in one competition, the under 16 boys. Our team comprised Bob Pearson, Michael Bennett and I. We were reasonable players, but not the best juniors in the club as they were playing higher grade men's competitions.

Nevertheless, we performed well and qualified for the final against Kiama. As the number one player in our team, I was up against one of the best junior players in the district in the first singles game. He was a much better tennis player than me and was expected to beat me convincingly, on his home court. There was no coach or manager, we were left to ourselves to try to win.

As the game commenced, I experienced an odd feeling that I would describe as instinctive. I became very calm and focused. I then adopted tactics to try to beat him without thinking too much about them. I slowed my game right down and concentrated on the placement of each shot. I kept him running and guessing as much as I could. He soon became very flustered as he was unaccustomed to both the slow pace, and not being the dominant player. I won the set 6-1. The whole team then played very well, and we won the final convincingly. We were euphoric.

I don't think I would ever have beaten him again as he would have been ready for my tactics. The win taught me the importance of tactics and planning. I took this lesson into my table tennis career later in life, when I had several good wins over more skilled opponents by out-thinking them. The win also fuelled my desire to play competitive sports, particularly in a team environment.

Hans was quickly developing into a good tennis player and was playing in the B grade competitions. Fuji was also a very solid player and had settled into men's C grade competitions. He was starting to change from being a relatively quiet person to a bit of a character. He had quite a cheeky sense of humour, which was starting to emerge.

Tennis brought more friends into the Lambert family. Hans made friends with a few guys who were playing Rugby League with Albion Park. He also worked with John Marley, who was one of Albion Park's star players. Hans wanted to join his mates and decided to play rugby league with Albion Park. We think his first full season was in 1969. He mainly played reserve grade, and quickly became a prolific try scorer, mainly due to his blinding speed.

John also played a few games of rugby league with the Albion Park reserve grade team that year. His first game was very memorable. He ran on as a substitute. He lined up to take the ball from the dummy half for a settling run. The dummy half passed him the ball and John immediately passed the ball straight back to the dummy half. Nerves had gotten the better of him and he simply forgot what he was supposed to do. It was very funny with the referee and opposing players having a good laugh. They all realised it was his first game. John recovered and went on to show that he was a very good, tackling lock forward. Around this time John received the nickname "Sticks" due to his skinny legs.

It took a while for my studying habits to reap the rewards but by the end of fifth form I received a very good report card. I was in the top three students for all, except one, subjects. During this year a Level One Mathematics class was formed and about ten students, including me, were promoted to it. Mathematics was my best subject and became my focus in sixth form.

1970 came along and I entered sixth form. I gave up my newspaper job to focus on studying and matriculating into university. I missed the money and camaraderie but I didn't miss getting up at five o'clock every morning. By this time, I was sharing the back bedroom with Fuji and two of the little kids, Terry and Adrian. John and Hans had moved into the garage which had been converted into a bedroom on one side. Dianne and Steve shared the middle bedroom and Toni had left home.

I studied each night at a small desk with a lamp in our bedroom. When the little kids came to bed they'd just come in and jump into bed, falling asleep quickly. They rarely interrupted me. Mum was very supportive in providing time and space for me to study. Despite everything she had going on she was very conscious that this was going to be a big year for me, and she made sure I had that quiet space I needed.

Dianne commenced high school at St Anne's College, Dapto in 1970. In April that year, a serious accident occurred when the little kids were playing outside just before dinner time. Dianne, 12 years old, was looking for Terry, who was hiding in some high grass next to the garage. She found him, ran, and jumped to catch him. She was barefooted and as she jumped, she trod on a piece of wood that was sticking up. She impaled her foot on the piece of wood, which was sticking out the top and bottom of her foot. Terry ran for help and as soon as Dianne realised what had happened, she started screaming uncontrollably.

Dad, Mum, and the older boys quickly came out. Dad picked Dianne up and placed her on the back seat of Hans's car, an old Morris Minor. Hans drove, with Mum in the front, and Dad with Dianne in the back. They drove to the local doctor's surgery. Dad carried Dianne in. The doctor on duty took one look and told them to take her to Kiama Hospital. He would meet them there. Dianne pleaded with the doctor, "Please don't chop my foot off?!" Hans drove very fast to the hospital and Dad had to tell him to slow down a bit through the notorious Minnamurra bends.

I was studying in my bedroom and missed the incident completely. I came out for dinner and asked where Mum was. One of my brothers told me what happened. They were amazed that I hadn't heard Dianne screaming and the urgent discussions as Mum, Dad, and the older kids decided what to do.

Dianne was immediately admitted to hospital and operated on later that night. It appeared that the operation to remove the piece of wood was successful. However, her recovery was very slow, and she remained in hospital for ten days. This was a very lonely time for Dianne; it was very difficult for Mum or any of us to get to Kiama hospital on public transport. Dad could not go every day and she did not have many visitors while in hospital.

When she arrived home her foot continued to be very painful, and she had to use crutches to get around. The doctor kept saying that it would get better. Every week Dad took Dianne to the Wollongong Hospital outpatients ward, and they treated the sore. It was a big, angry sore that was continually full of pus. The doctors must have thought that treating the sore would eventually make

Dianne better. It didn't and she spent several months at home, unable to attend school.

Mrs Sercombe, our wonderful neighbour, had a spare bed which was brought over to our house and set up in the lounge room so Dianne could watch TV and be with the rest of the family. We all played games with Dianne and did what we could to keep her occupied. It was a very gloomy time as there was no improvement and it looked like Dianne could have a permanent injury. Dianne took it in her stride. She did not complain, although she did shed a few tears occasionally.

One day, three months after the injury, Dianne saw something poking out through the sore on the bottom of her foot. It was a small piece of wood working its way out of the foot. Dianne pulled it out - it was a big splinter about two and a half centimetres long and between one and two centimetres wide! It was this splinter that had been left in Dianne's foot that had caused the severe pain and discomfort. Apparently, x-rays did not detect wood back then.

Dianne recovered very quickly after the splinter came out and she was soon back to normal. Although Mum and Dad had accepted the medical treatment she received as a normal part of life at the time, they were very relieved she was better. Dianne quickly overcame the time lost at school and passed all her exams that year.

In early 1970 my brother John and two of his friends from the Outset group, Mick Keys and Geoff King, decided to have a go at running dances and concerts as a business. They formed a company called Trinity Promotions. They all kept their day jobs.

They ran a couple of Dusk to Dawn dances at the Capitol Hall in Corrimal, which were moderately successful. They were then offered the opportunity to sign the Beach Boys up for a concert during their Australian tour. The Beach Boys were an American band who were one of the biggest bands worldwide during the 1960's. It was a tremendous opportunity as bands of that calibre rarely played in Wollongong.

They signed the Beach Boys up to do two concerts at the Capitol Hall, at 7.30pm and 10.30pm on Tuesday the 28th of April 1970. This was quite a financial risk for John, Mick and Geoff who were only aged 20 or 21 at that time. Tickets were $2, which was quite expensive at the time. Fortunately, they covered all costs and made a small surplus from the night.

This was a massive night for me as I worked in the ticket box, watched some of the songs and went backstage. The Beach Boys were fantastic, and the whole place was heaving. The girls danced as if mesmerised. The crowd was very happy and there was no trouble.

This was the last big event for Trinity Promotions. They found that the entertainment scene was changing rapidly with bands increasingly playing at hotels and clubs. John, Mick, and Geoff went back to their day jobs and girlfriends.

Sixth form saw us introduced to the dreaded (for most of us) world of formal dancing in preparation for the school formal. There was an all-girls Catholic school in Wollongong, St Mary's College, that would combine with our school to hold a school formal dinner dance. This was the school's way of introducing us to the opposite sex, and hopefully preparing us for entry into the real world after school.

There were several dance rehearsals held with the St Mary's girls. These rehearsals were intended to teach us how to dance and for us to meet the St Mary's girls, before the school formal was held. We were taught the Pride of Erin, the Canadian Three Step, and the Barn Dance. Pop music dancing was not on the agenda for the school formal.

These rehearsals were cringeworthy at the beginning with groups of boys and girls forming. There was not much interaction until you were forced to go to ask a girl to dance. They did get better and more enjoyable as we realised that we were all in it together, and as boys and girls became more familiar with each other.

The process for getting a partner for the formal was that all boys and girls had to list their top three preferences in order. If a boy and girl listed each other as their number one choice they would be partnered for the formal. This process was conducted quite strictly by the teachers from both schools.

Fortunately, I had met a girl, Robyn Harper, at the rehearsals and we both listed each other as number one choice. That was a big relief for me as I was quite shy and completely naïve with the opposite sex. As you can imagine the best looking girls received plenty of number one choices. The formal night turned out to be enjoyable, and not as stressful as I was anticipating. That was my first and last "date" with Robyn.

1970 was a good year academically. There was an outstanding student, Pat Dowdell, who was the dux of the class. Pat was both very intelligent and a very hard worker. In Level One Maths I received 252 out of a possible 270 marks in the Term 1 exam. I then discovered that Pat had achieved a perfect score in this exam. I was gutted as I thought I had beaten him this time. Pat was very generous with his knowledge, and it spurred me on trying to catch him in subjects. I never did.

Dad settled into the insurance business in 1970 and Mum was able to give up her job at The Oaks hotel. The three older boys worked and paid board which certainly helped the financial position of the family. They were also not at home much, and I had an enjoyable year with just me and the "little kids" most of the time. I studied hard all year and continued to improve academically.

Toni and Malcolm were going well raising their family. They had commenced a business called Antique Bathrooms. This was a bathroom renovation business, and they had a showroom at the end of the Albion Park Rail shopping centre. They rented the house at the rear of the showroom. Malcolm was the bathroom partner and Toni was the business partner.

Towards the end of the year, we started to prepare for life after school. Vocational training was organised at school to assist students to determine what careers would suit them best and provide some education about tertiary education and careers. My vocational training feedback was that I would be best suited to a medical career but also that an accounting career would be a good option.

I didn't give medicine much thought as I knew it would require completion of a university degree on a full-time basis. It was time for me to get to work and pay my way. I decided that I wanted to study accountancy and applied for a commercial trainee job at Australian Iron & Steel (AIS), at Port Kembla. Hans and Renee were both enjoying their jobs there and I liked the idea of working where they did. I got the job and commenced it on the first Monday after I completed the Higher School Certificate exams. Jobs were plentiful and it was quite easy for school leavers to get a job at that time.

I left school in November 1970. My last exam was a Level 1 Maths exam and there were only about eight kids in that class. This exam was held one week after all the other exams had finished, so all the other kids were gone. I finished the exam early and left the school grounds on my own, to walk to the Wollongong train station about 4 kilometres away. I remember the feeling as if it were yesterday. I felt elated, blissful, and excited but also trepidatious. I started thinking about what I would do for friends from now, and I suddenly felt quite lonely.

I achieved a good result in the Higher School Certificate, passing all subjects at the levels I had sat for. I found out later that I just missed out on being in the top 100 students in NSW for Level 1 Maths. I was still behind my classmate Pat Dowdell who finished 12th in the State. I received a Commonwealth University Scholarship though, and that paid all my university fees for the next six years.

On the 31st of December 1970 my brothers took me to a New Year's Eve party at the Bulters' family home in Albion Park. I had not touched a drop of alcohol yet and they decided it was time to introduce me to the world of drinking. I had observed a lot of alcohol consumption at our sixth form going away party at Peter

Rowles's place and had been shocked by this as it had not occurred to me that any of the kids would have been drinking already. I was as naïve as they come.

That night was a blur. I was told later I drank three or four cans of Tooth's KB beer, which was the most popular beer at the time. I then proceeded to play touch football in the backyard, with a full can of KB as the football. At some point I passed the ball to my friend, Tony Bulters, who completely missed my perfectly directed pass. The full can hit him with some force right in the middle of the forehead. It split his head open, and his brothers took him straight to hospital to get the cut stitched up.

I remembered playing touch football but had no memory of the incident with Tony or of my brothers getting me home and helping me into bed. I don't even know if I enjoyed getting drunk for the first time, but I found out that I did not enjoy hangovers.

We lived in a society at that time where drinking was a fundamental part of Aussie culture, particularly for men. My introduction to drinking was timely for both my social life and work life.

Dad's family in 1931 – (L-R) Riet, Dad's mother, Diny (on lap), Rene, Dad (Adrian), Dad's father, Nellie (on lap), Cor. Seated at front – Joop, Bert. Absent – Toni, who was not born yet

Mum's family circa 1938 – (L-R) Marga, Truus, Mum's father, Marie, Jan, Paul, Sjaan, Geirie (Piet's wife), Piet, Mum's mother, Niek, Mum (Martha). . Front – (L-R) Joop, Kees

Dad's parents, Johannes Lambert and Antonia Scheepers, date unknown

Mum's parents, Jan Van Ammers and Jansje Ruiter, circa 1938

Mum and Dad together before they were married, circa 1945

Mum and Dad's wedding - February 1946

Christmas 1953 – Lambert kids playing outside the garage at 26 Pearce Street, Parkes where the family lived for 2 years., (L-R) Toni, Renee, John, Hans

Boarding the plane for the long flight to Australia in September 1951. (L-R) Dad, Air hostess holding Hans, Mum. Front – Toni, John

Leaving the Netherlands in September 1951 – (L-R) Mum holding Hans, Dad's father, unknown person, Dad. Front – (L-R) John, Toni

Us 5 older kids in Parkes circa 1954. Back row (L-R) Toni, John. Front row (L-R) Renee, Me, Hans

Lambert family portrait circa 1961. (L-R) Renee, Hans, Mum with Terry on lap, Toni, Dad with Dianne on lap, John, Me

On the front porch of the Kaylaur Crescent house with Muska circa 1963. (L-R) John, Terry, Me

The four older boys in the front yard before leaving for Toni's wedding in March 1966 (L-R) Me, Renee, Hans, John

Lambert family at Toni's wedding in March 1966. Back row – John, Mum, Dad, Hans. Middle row – Renee, Dianne, Me. Front row – Adrian, Steve, Terry

A candid photo of Dad, Toni and Malcolm (Toni's husband), Steve (next to the guinea pig cage) and in the front Ossie (we think) circa May 1966. This is the block next door to the Kaylaur Crescent house that we played on for many years. The Oaks Hotel, where Mum worked, is in the background.

Steve, Ossie, and Terry with Muska circa 1968. Muska had done this with us older kids a decade earlier.

Dad at his desk in the lounge room circa 1969. He is dressed for his insurance job with the obligatory cigar in hand.

Candid photo of me in my school uniform circa 1969.

School class photo at the 1970 formal. I am in the third row, from the bottom, one person to the right of the boy in the centre.

Me with my partner, Robyn Harper, for the school formal in 1970.

Age and Doris Van Der Zande at their wedding circa 1971

CHAPTER 9

RUGBY LEAGUE AND THE MAGIC OF OUTSET

— 1971 TO 1974 —

In early 1971 a group of enterprising male Young Christian Workers (YCW) decided to form their own amateur rugby league competition. Most teams came from the previous Catholic Youth Organisation (CYO) social competition. The organising committee was headed up by John Lawler, from Dapto YCW, who worked tirelessly to get the competition up and running. The intention was to have a rugby league competition played for enjoyment, fitness, and social interaction.

Rugby league was the most popular sport in the Wollongong area and most of the young men who came to play in the YCW competition had previously played rugby league for their school or town teams. These competitions were generally very physical, particularly in first grade. The YCW competition was intended to be less physical, and less serious, than town rugby league. It appealed to many young men who did not want to play in the town competitions.

The 1971 competition commenced with six teams; Dapto, Wollongong, Western Suburbs, Port Kembla, Corrimal, and Outset. The Albion Park based YCW men, including my brother John, decided to enter a team based in Albion Park. They also decided to call the team Outset following the success of the Outset youth dances which had been held at Albion Park.

The Outset organising committee recruited very well and were able to attract many players who could have played first or second grade with the Albion Park town team that year. These included Paul Graham, who was being touted as an outstanding prospect, Ken Pearce, Steve Dowd, and Neil Paget who had each already played grade rugby league with Albion Park. Ron Smith (Smithy) had played first grade with Berry for many years and was appointed as captain coach.

Smithy worked on the Keys' dairy farm with Mick and John Keys. They persuaded him to join Outset for the love of the game and no payment. This turned out to be the key to our success as Ron was both a good coach and an inspirational leader. He played with no fear despite being a very skinny front row forward.

My brother, Hans, decided to stay with Albion Park and not join his brothers at Outset. By 1971 he was an established reserve grade player and had also played some first-grade games. He was also the Treasurer of the Albion Park club, and had many friends playing there, so he stayed loyal to Albion Park. This made weekends very busy as we played for Outset but also tried to watch as many of Hans's games as possible.

John told Fuji and I about the new team being formed and asked us to come to training as they were looking for players. Two of my close friends from school, Ken McInerney, and Tony Bulters, had also joined Outset and I knew most of the other players through my brothers. I had not intended to play competitive rugby league at all as I had seen many of Hans's games and I thought it was too tough for me. I was tall, skinny and weighed around 70 kilograms. I decided to play as I liked the camaraderie immediately and it didn't look like it was going to be too rough.

Mick Keys brought a couple of his cousins along to play, Ken Tate and Peter Waugh. Ken was a very, very good five eight and was one of the stars of our team. Unbeknown to us at the time Ken maintained meticulous records of our games. He wrote up some of the games like a reporter and provided his assessments of all the players at the end of the year. Ken sadly passed away in 2016 and his wife Debbie has kindly provided Ken's records as research for this book. Already they have brought much joy to the players that I have shared them with.

The Outset rugby league team changed my life. It came along at the perfect time for me as I had just left school, started work and was wondering what I was going to do both sporting wise and socially. Outset provided both of those answers.

I loved it from the start. We trained two nights a week at Keith Grey oval, Albion Park. There were no dressing sheds and we just turned up in our footy gear ready for a run. These nights became very cold and uncomfortable as autumn turned into winter. That didn't deter anyone, and we trained in all weather conditions. Smithy trained us quite hard but also made sure it was enjoyable. Whilst we were keen to improve our rugby league skills and learn about the game, it quickly became apparent that training was also about mateship. There was continual banter with everyone "putting shit" on each other.

A group of about twenty young men bursting with enthusiasm for life, girls, and alcohol was a recipe for plenty of fun and good times. After training we went to the Albion Park hotel for a few beers and further camaraderie. A real team bond formed quite quickly. Everyone seemed to like each other. Most of my closest life friendships came from that group of men.

Albion Park RSL was the 'go-to' place for the young crowd. It was split into two main areas; the public bar, which was men only, and the mixed lounge which had a restaurant. The Saturday night dances were held in the mixed lounge. The public bar had a games area where there were two snooker tables, a table tennis table, and a darts board. This area was always busy.

The RSL reflected some key elements of the social culture at that time. It was an accepted way of life for men to have a drink after work at their local pub or club before heading home for dinner. That's not to say the wives were always happy with this. Being quite naïve when I started going to the RSL I was always bemused by the phone calls that wives would make to the club demanding that their husbands come home. This was broadcast over the loudspeaker, and it was the same regulars, the biggest drunks, who kept getting the calls. Sometimes the wives would come to the club and literally drag their husbands out. It was quite sad to see this as you could feel the wives' desperation. The drunks were in the minority. Most men were quite responsible, had their few beers and went home.

The other element I observed was the poker machines and their addictive nature. This happened in our circle of friends with one of our footy mates. He went through a period of putting his whole pay packet through the pokies on pay day. When we realised this, we tried to stop him, but had limited success. Everyone was paid weekly in cash which made it more tempting for the gamblers.

After my introduction to alcohol on the previous New Year's Eve had gone so badly, I was wary of alcohol for some time. That changed during that first year with Outset. A group of us (mainly the guys without girlfriends) would regularly meet at the RSL. We went there several nights a week to play snooker, table tennis and darts. We didn't drink much on weeknights. It was more about companionship than drinking. However, the barmen did not take kindly to serving soft drink. On more than one occasion I asked for a sarsaparilla only to be told I would have to go to the local milk bar if I wanted one of those.

Later in life a friend of mine from that time would comment that the Lambert family was often the catalyst for the social activity in that broad group of friends. I thoroughly enjoyed my time at the RSL, so much so that I have a clear recollection of going there every night for 70 consecutive nights! It was during a university break and I was trying to break some sort of record, which I did.

I always gravitated towards the table tennis table. That is how I met a guy named Keith (Ocka) Eastham, as he was always up for a game. I was quite wary of Ocka initially as he was the star hockey player, wore the latest fashion as he worked at Lowe's menswear, had the flashy hairstyle and was very popular. I didn't think he would want to hang out with me. I was wrong. Ocka was very friendly, down to earth, and not "up himself" at all. We teamed up to play doubles in the RSL club championships and a lifelong friendship was formed.

Ocka was often at the RSL with his father, Fred, and his brothers Ray, Ken, and Brian. They loved each other's company and having a drink together. It was interesting for me to observe this lifestyle, which was typically Australian, as I had never had a drink with my father.

Fuji was emerging as one of the social leaders of the Outset group. He was starting to love alcohol. He quickly became an all or nothing drinker. When he did have a drink, he would usually have quite a few. He could also just drink 'Orchy's' (orange juice) all night. He was the life of the party when he drank and became very cheeky and naughty. He had a magnetic personality which ensured that he never got into trouble. His popularity quickly transcended the Outset group and it seemed like everyone in Albion Park knew Fuji.

By this time, I had attracted the nickname "Ged". This came from a popular American television show at that time, the Beverley Hillbillies. This show was about a family called the Clampetts and two of the lead characters were named Jed and Jethro. I was initially called Jethro after that character and then became Jed, which I spell as Ged. I have mainly been called Gerry at work and Ged socially ever since then.

We couldn't wait for the first game. The season started with a knockout competition on the 28th of March 1971. We won this knockout with a very close 5-3 victory over Dapto in the final. The competition started the following week and we lost to Western Suburbs. They were a strong team and defeated us twice in the competition rounds. They were the only games that we lost.

We had played a few games when one of our players, Peter Waugh, brought a friend of his along to training. His name was Ross Greenfield, and he was to have a profound effect on both the team and all our lives. Ross was a very, very good player and quickly assumed the lock forward position in the team, becoming one of our best players.

One night at training Ross called Ken McInerney, "Swampy" because he reminded him of another guy called Swampy. Ross told Ken that he had the same mannerisms as the other Swampy. We didn't know the reason for the nickname at the time; we assumed Ross had called him that due to smelling something that he thought smelt like a swamp. Ken was called Swampy ever since that day.

The formation of the Outset team led to some friendly, and not so friendly, rivalry with the Albion Park town rugby league teams. They were not happy that a lot of good Albion Park players were playing with Outset. We all drank together at the local pub and clubs, and a few of the Albion Park players were constantly challenging Outset players to play their reserve grade team. Fortunately, that game never eventuated as, if it did, it would have provided the tougher Albion Park players the opportunity to demonstrate that toughness.

Fuji started that year very strongly. He was a hard running, hard tackling winger who didn't mind the rough stuff. He received one point in the best and fairest points for the first game of the season. He got injured midway through the season and could not play in the finals. John started the season at lock forward. He was a good cover defending lock. He received three points in the best and fairest points in our game against Dapto. I didn't receive any best and fairest points but did receive the "Most Improved" trophy for the year.

We finished the regular season in second place, behind Western Suburbs. We then played them in the major semi-final and prevailed with a very hard fought 10–7 win. I suffered a severe concussion in this game after a heavy tackle by one of their front rowers. I had the following week off work. I did not like taking sickies from work, and that was the last lot of sickies I would take for the next 30 years.

Western Suburbs won the preliminary final, and we met them in the grand final at Shepherds Oval, West Wollongong on the 29th of August 1971. It was a great occasion. Our whole team and families travelled to the game on Claude Harris's brown bus. We had a good crowd supporting us and the atmosphere was electric. I had recovered from the concussion injury and got to play. Mum and Dad came to watch. Dad was a very enthusiastic spectator.

We saved our best for the grand final. We dominated from the start and defended strongly through the entire game. Neil Paget and I scored tries in the first half for us to lead 10–0 at the break. We scored three more tries in the second half and had a comfortable 19–2 win. Conversely Western Suburbs played their worst game of the year in the grand final. Swampy was awarded Best and Fairest Player in the grand final. John Bulters won the Best and Fairest Player award for the 1971 season.

We were euphoric after the game. The bus trip home was joyous, with everyone singing and cheering the whole way. We started the celebrations at Albion Park RSL before we went to a function at Dapto. I was in the back seat of Mick Keys' car for the drive to Dapto. My fellow passenger in the back seat was Ross Greenfield who was very happy and could not stop smiling. Ross had provided that extra touch of class that our team had needed to become genuine premiership contenders.

Tragedy struck the following Friday when Ross was killed in a motor bike accident. He had finished his late-night shift at a local leagues club and was riding his motorbike home. He collided with a truck in a freak accident. His death affected his family and friends enormously; we were all devastated. He was good enough to have had a professional rugby league career, but he had been more focused on his studies and a professional career. His younger brother was also killed in a motor vehicle accident about a year later. I'm not sure his parents ever recovered from those deaths. Swampy's nickname suddenly assumed greater significance because Ross had given it to him.

The standard and professionalism of the YCW competition increased considerably for the 1972 season. Two new teams, Berkeley, and Ingleburn entered the competition. Most of the clubs were able to secure experienced non-playing coaches. Smithy retired after our grand final win in 1971 and we were very fortunate to secure Col "Bubbles" Purcell as our coach. Col was an Illawarra rugby league legend and had extensive playing and coaching experience at high levels. Corrimal secured John Mowbray, an ex-Sydney first grader, as their coach. These coaches all did it for the love of the game.

All teams recruited well, even though it was still a strictly amateur competition. It had earned a reputation for its high standard of rugby league, played for enjoyment, and attracted plenty of new players. Dapto recruited high class players like John Hart and Bill Agnew, and they looked to be the team to beat that year. We recruited a couple of very handy grade players, Bruce Gorton and Mick Baldwin. Swampy also brought along a friend of his, Max "Haze" Hazelton who in turn brought along John Bout. After the season started Peter Waugh brought a school friend of his along to training. His name was Mark O'Neill and he quickly slotted into the fullback role. Michael "Chips" Raftery brought along his school friend, Bert Smith. Bert was a tough, nuggety front rower. These new players added strength to our team and plugged some gaps due to player retirements.

Haze joining the team became very significant for me. He came from a local farming family and was the youngest of six children. He was very likeable, easy going and a very handy footballer. We hit it off as friends straight away in what would become a very close lifelong friendship. We spent many years chasing women together - unsuccessfully 99% of the time. In that regard Mark O'Neill was also a handy recruit. Mark was very smooth with the ladies and always seemed to have a very good looking girl with him. Haze and I marvelled at Mark's style but could never replicate it.

Training became more professional with Bubbles introducing new moves and tactics. He also improved our fitness. We quickly emerged as one of the top teams, together with Dapto and Wollongong. We only lost one game, to Dapto, during the regular season and became the minor premiers. The season included one epic encounter with Dapto which we won 13-12. This game had it all with the Illawarra Mercury writing the next day: "Scores see- sawed and fans saw hard-running forwards. Both teams met one another with bone-shattering tackles in defence and exciting sweeping passing movements among the backs." We were decimated by injury that day. I was fortunate enough to score the winning try after being set up by Neil Paget.

We lost the major semi-final to Dapto. Again, it was a one-point score line 5-4. We bounced back very strongly in the preliminary final to defeat Berkeley 31–5. We all fired in this game as we were determined to play Dapto again in the grand final. Ken Tate reported later that I played a blinder on the wing.

The grand final was a bigger occasion this year. It had received good publicity in the Illawarra Mercury, and most Illawarra clubs were expected to have talent scouts at the game. It was a very tough, hard game. We led 8-7 at half-time but could not sustain our effort in the second half. Dapto ran out winners 18–10 and we knew that we were beaten by a better side. Quite a few of the Outset players, including me, made the representative teams that year. This grand final had an extra special touch for me as each side had several players from my class at school; Steve Long, Tony Day, Bill Agnew and John Hol from Dapto, and Ken McInerney, Tony Bulters and me from Outset.

While we didn't feel the euphoria of winning again, we were all very happy with the year, particularly making the grand final again. We had built up a great squad of players, full of great team men. We had developed an enviable culture in two years, and we were looking forward to the 1973 season.

The YCW competition ceased very suddenly and unexpectedly at the end of the 1972 season. A second division, amateur competition had been formed in the Illawarra region. It was attracting some players from the YCW competition. Some of the founding committee members of the YCW competition, including John Lawler, had decided to step down. A combination of these factors led to the YCW competition ceasing. We were shocked and saddened by the suddenness of the end of the YCW competition.

Strong friendships had formed within the Outset group. A group of us caught up at the Albion Park RSL as often as possible. The Australian tradition of being in a "shout" led to some humorous moments at my expense. We always drank as a group with one person buying a round of drinks for everyone, called having a "shout", until everyone had a turn. Then we would start again. The problem with that for me was that I usually drank less and more slowly than everyone else. You had to be in the shout so I would usually hide a few drinks through the night. The boys caught onto this and if they found a full beer behind a plant, or somewhere else, they would "put shit on me" all night.

We often ended up at the Graham's house in Terry Street, Albion Park, to play cards. Mrs Graham loved it if we came to play, and she did not mind if we arrived at midnight. We sometimes played through the night, but only if it was a weekend night. We played 21, now called blackjack, and acey-deucey. There were some epic nights with considerable financial wins and losses for the participants. They were always great fun.

The Outset group showed their good side on Christmas day each year. We developed a tradition of visiting the various players' families. We did this as a group. We usually went in Swampy's panel van. We started early and generally visited about six homes before we all had to head home for Christmas lunch. The players' parents loved those visits. We did this for a few years.

The cessation of the YCW competition had a silver lining as many of the Outset players decided to play in the Albion Park Oak Flats rugby league teams. The addition of at least ten handy players greatly bolstered the Park teams. A few players, including Mark O'Neill and Ken Tate, became regular first graders. Most, including me, ended up in the third-grade team. This commenced another two years of success on and off the field.

The rivalry that had existed between Outset and Albion Park quickly disappeared and we were soon part of the Albion Park culture. It was tougher and more serious rugby league. Training was compulsory and the coaches had high expectations. I loved being part of a bigger club. If the three grade teams played together it was a huge day. We would play first, then watch second and first grade play, then go to the Albion Park RSL for dinner and plenty of drinks. Rugby league dominated our social lives for those two years.

John got married in 1973 and he decided to stop playing rugby league. Hans was a regular reserve grade player and became a regular first grade player. He was very fast and a prolific try scorer. Fuji and I settled into the third-grade team. I played as a centre that season and Fuji played on the wing. I would often be playing inside of Fuji. His physical skills and my ball skills were a good combination.

Our third-grade team had a very good year and we qualified for the grand final. We were up against Gerringong who we had defeated during the season. We were expected to win. The grand finals were played at Kiama Showground. The day started disastrously for us when there was a major traffic accident between Albion Park and Kiama. Most of the team, including me, were already at the ground but about six of our players didn't get through and were caught in the traffic chaos. They had to turn back and get to Kiama an alternate, longer way. A couple of them missed the kick off so we ran on with a disrupted team. It did not matter in the end.

Gerringong had a legendary aboriginal player, Roy Stewart, in their team. Roy had played many years of first grade, and he was playing third grade as he approached the end of his career. We had contained Roy quite well during the year. Roy started the game at halfback and quickly tackled our halfback very hard, but quite legally. He moved to the other positions in the backline and did the same to his opposing number. When he tackled me, he rattled every bone in my body and then apologised telling me he had to do it because it was a grand final. He also scored four brilliant individual tries in the first twenty minutes of the game and it was all over. Haze and I were our try scorers. We lost the game 27–13.

The next day we had the traditional end of season "Mad Monday". This included going to the Gerringong hotel to catch up with our grand final opponents. Roy Stewart was there and took the time to talk to several of our players about their game, giving them invaluable coaching tips. Roy wasn't interested in any praise for his brilliant game. He was a true sportsman, loved the game and wanted to help others.

1974 turned out to be an unexpectedly interesting rugby league year. I played as a centre in third grade again that year. There were only four teams in the competition, so it was a shortened season. We were the strongest team and became minor premiers. Our reserve grade team also had a strong season. The first-grade team had a poor season and they were out of semi-final contention midway through the season. To keep the reserve grade team as strong as possible for the semi-finals some third-grade players were promoted to first grade to cover injuries towards the end of the season.

I had had a good try scoring season, having scored in every third-grade game, so I was one of the players promoted to first grade. I scored two tries in my first game in first grade. Whilst they were both easy winger tries, they were enough for the selectors to keep me in first grade for about five games.

The physicality of first grade was too much for me. I got tackled so hard a few times that I became quite wary. Then one day I witnessed a blatant, dangerous head high tackle on one of our best first grade players. I went home that day thinking that perhaps rugby league was too rough for me. I made the decision to stop playing at the end of that season. I was very happy several years later when touch football competitions were formed. Touch football suited me as there was no tackling allowed.

We won the grand final in 1974. It was a significant game for me as I played centre and my brother, Hans, played on the wing.

Hans had suffered an injury that year and had come back through third grade. I loved playing with him, as it did not happen very often. Hans was an experienced first grader by then. He was very good at using his experience to help me, and others in the team, to improve our games without telling us what to do. Hans and I both scored tries in the grand final.

This grand final clashed with the wedding of one of our Outset players, John Bout, who was marrying an Oak Flats lady, Sonia Spiewak. Fortunately, Sonia was very understanding, and we were allowed to miss the church service. It was a very happy wedding reception.

When I retired, I had played rugby league for four seasons, played in four grand finals, and won two premierships. Interestingly the two losing grand finals were probably the best games to play in and provided as many lasting memories as the winning ones. The camaraderie from those four years was very strong and I have many lifelong friends from those teams. In hindsight my decision to retire was the right one for medical reasons as well. Years later it emerged that repeated concussions sustained while playing rugby league can have severe medical consequences later in life.

I remained a passionate Albion Park rugby league supporter, but my sporting interests had switched to cricket and table tennis.

CHAPTER 10

WORK AND UNIVERSITY LIFE

— 1971 TO 1976 —

On the 1st of December 1970 I started my first job as a commercial trainee at AIS. I was very excited and a bit nervous as well.

I was assigned to the office at the Hot Strip Mill and worked with about eight other men. This mill was a blue-collar worker area where slabs of steel were converted into strips of steel for sale. Many skilled tradesmen and labourers worked in the mill. I observed hard, manual work for the first time. As a trainee I was "shared around" the office and quickly learnt the various office functions, including stock control and wages. I worked on a ten-day roster which meant that I worked every second weekend. I caught the same train to work that I had previously sold the newspapers at.

The men were all good to me and happy to train me. They got their jobs done but never seemed to be flat out. However, they were always looking for opportunities to do overtime as that provided a nice, and sometimes necessary, boost to their weekly pay. I adopted this culture and was happy to take whatever overtime came along. Some of the men wore shorts and long socks to work.

The office itself was compact with a row of desks against the window side of the office. It was a completely manual office. All work was done with pen and paper. There were no computers and there was not even a photocopier. If you needed a copy of something, you had to use carbon paper to duplicate what you were writing. There were typewriters and adding machines.

I started university (uni) at the University of Wollongong in February 1971. I enrolled in a Bachelor of Commerce degree, majoring in accounting, on a two year part time, two year full time basis. My classes were generally after work. It was a logistical nightmare getting to the classes and then home. After initially catching trains and walking I met people in my uni classes who I could get lifts with. I would sometimes get home after 9pm and catch the 6.10am train to work the next morning.

Mum always had dinner ready for me, irrespective of the time I arrived home. She kept the vegetables warm from dinner and cooked me a piece of meat. These meals were always delicious even though they were much the same as Mum usually cooked for dinner. I guess they tasted better because of the effort and care provided by Mum. I thought Mum was doing this for me because I was going to work and uni, but I realised later that Mum did the same for all the kids from when they started work. After the first year I had dinner at uni so that Mum did not have to worry about my dinner.

I adapted to uni life very quickly. I kept up my studying habits from school. I had a natural affinity with the accounting and economics subjects, probably due to my strength in mathematics.

This wasn't the case for all students, and it became easy to pick the students for whom the "double entry" accounting equation would remain a mystery forever.

Uni life broadened my social world and awareness. The Wollongong campus contained the usual group of professional uni students, typically long-haired men, and braless, heavily pierced women. They were influenced by the hippie generation from the 1960's and they were keen to change the world. Whilst I largely kept to myself and considered uni to be a stepping stone to a professional career, I enjoyed observing these radical students and the freedom of uni life.

Dad's insurance job received a great boost in 1971. Dad went to my school and managed to get a list comprising the names, addresses and telephone numbers of all the boys who left school in my sixth form class of 1970. This became a hot list of prospects for him, and he contacted as many of them as he could to discuss their life insurance needs with them. I still have that list of boys that Dad used. It is now a great memory.

I found this a bit embarrassing at first and it caused plenty of light-hearted humour when I would see someone from that class. However, I quickly discovered that Dad was very genuine with his job and did not "over sell". He tried to do the right thing by his clients and prospective clients. He was happy to build relationships that might lead to a policy down the track, rather than pressure someone to sign up immediately. I think Dad did quite well from that school group and several of the boys became long term clients.

With Dad earning a regular income and four of us contributing board, Mum and Dad's financial position slowly started to improve. Mum and Dad were able to start thinking about some improvements, including fences, around the house.

※

I worked at the hot strip mill for about six months, after which I was transferred to the Central Laboratory department. I noticed a different work culture here with most people happy to cruise along and not work too hard.

The first job I had there was to assist the lady who looked after a big central filing system. She gave me a job to do to reorganise some files. I did it and went back to her the next day to report that I had completed that job and to see what was next. She was quite shocked when I walked into her office and told me that I had six weeks to do that job. She had forgotten to tell me that. I spent most of the next six weeks doing my uni work with her approval.

A few months later I was transferred to the main administration office area, and I stayed there until I went to full time university in 1973. Several hundred people worked in this area, which comprised several buildings. Hans and Renee both worked in this area, and it was great working near my brothers. There was a typing pool, which serviced all the administration offices. This pool comprised around thirty ladies who typed up documents all day. They were supervised by one lady who prioritised and delegated the work. Even for that time the typing pool was almost like watching an old movie. The ladies were always dressed quite properly, were very quiet and happily typed all day. Fuji recalls that he was a frequent user of the typing pool. He had to hand write the sales invoices so they could be typed up by the typists.

There was a photocopier room that serviced all the administration offices. The copies produced were oily and on continuous paper. The photocopiers were manned by trained operators. There was a constant line up at the photocopier room as staff started to get used to this new technology. There was also a high demand for adding machines. There was a limited supply of these on the floor that I worked on. People would get to work early just so they could get an adding machine to use that day.

Over 20,000 wages workers were paid every second Thursday. Most of the administration staff were selected, periodically, to work on the pay day. Hans, Fuji, and I had many turns at pay day duties. There was a large secure payroll office that was used for the pay day. It was heavily manned by security personnel. Staff on duty counted the pays and put them in envelopes, together with the employee's pay slip, for each employee. It was quite a sight seeing all the cash on the tables at the beginning of the day.

The envelope stuffing was completed by lunch time. Then the pays were distributed to a series of secure pay offices throughout the plant to hand out to the employees. The administration staff on pay duty were sent to one of these offices to hand the pays out. This was quite an experience. Many of the wages' workers were European migrants who had not learnt to speak English or write in English properly. Establishing that you were giving the pay envelope to the right person and getting them to sign for it could be both difficult and humorous. It always worked out in the end. I really enjoyed my interactions with these hard working, salt of the earth men.

During 1971 I managed to get my driver's licence at my first attempt despite not having had much practise. Dad had provided some driving lessons to the older boys and that was enough for him. I used a driving school to learn to drive. This was complemented by a few drives with my brothers. I was very inexperienced but somehow managed to get my licence driving a manual car.

I did not drive regularly until about six months later when I got my first car. I purchased a 1966 white Volkswagen Beetle for $1,000. I still remember the number plate, ECC141. I had saved $500 and was able to borrow $500 from the credit union at work. Dad acted as guarantor so I could get the loan.

Having my own car was very liberating. I could go wherever and whenever I wanted to and became independent for the first time. Having a car significantly improved my social life. I was settling into work, Uni, rugby league and a social life that revolved around catching up with my friends at the Albion Park RSL club. Some of the boys were getting girlfriends, which again expanded our social group, but I was very slow in that department. Whilst I was good with people, I was shy and reticent when it came to girls and asking them for dates. I defaulted to having fun with the boys and thoroughly enjoyed those few years.

Fuji had also purchased his first car earlier in 1971, a shiny yellow second hand Toyota Corolla. It was a distinctive car and became almost as well known as Fuji, due to the way Fuji drove it and the regularity of his small dings. At the end of 1971, Fuji, I and two of our friends from the Outset rugby league team decided to go to the Gold Coast in Queensland for a holiday. These two friends were my old school friend, Ken "Swampy" McInerney and Peter

"Suicide" Graham. We all went in Fuji's car for this trip. It was a small two door car, so it was quite crowded, but we didn't care. We were carefree and excited as it was our first boys' holiday together. For Fuji and I it was the first holiday we had ever had.

None of us had much money so we stayed in a tent in one of the caravan parks at Coolangatta. It was good experience for later holidays and learning what to do on the Gold Coast.

Hans had started to play cricket with Albion Park cricket club in the 1970/1971 season. I was a cricket fan and had spent many hours watching the test cricket on the Sercombe's grainy black and white television. Mr Sercombe was an avid cricket fan and didn't miss a ball when the tests were on. I regularly went to watch Hans play and became quite interested in playing. Hans was already making some runs as a batsman, was quite a handy bowler and an outstanding fielder.

After the 1971/1972 season started Hans told me that one of the second-grade teams was looking for players. I went along to training and started playing with the weaker of the two second grade teams. I was very nervous when I started and batted right down the order. I didn't bowl but I was a good fielder. I didn't drop many catches. In that first year I hardly made any runs and only had a few scores over ten. I loved the game even when it was boring. Hans and I, and later Ossie, shared a love of cricket that would last the rest of our lives. I am forever grateful to Hans for introducing me to cricket.

The 1972/1973 season saw the introduction of a third-grade South Coast competition for the first time. Albion Park entered a team, and I was selected in third-grade. I was more confident with my batting and was now in the team as a batsman, batting at number five or six. Gary Reid was the captain of the team. Gary was older than the rest of us and had been a good cricketer in his prime. He was happy to play but wasn't much of an organiser. I soon found myself in an organisational role within the team. This included getting the field ready for home games, making sure we had a full team each week and getting the gear ready. We had one kit of gear for the whole team, so we shared pads, gloves and even boxes. A box covers the private parts and is essential when you bat. There were no helmets.

The team included a couple of my rugby league friends, Paul (Grub) Graham and Ken Tate, and seventeen-year-old twins, Cliff and Maurie Bunker. They were promising young cricketers who could both bat and bowl. We started the season quite well, and I had started to get a few scores in the 20's and 30's. One day Gary took me aside and told me that he didn't really want to be the captain. He asked me if I would like to do it as I was doing everything off the field anyway. I didn't really think much about it and found myself captain of the Albion Park cricket club third grade team at nineteen years of age. I didn't realise it then, but this was the commencement of my organisational "glue" roles in sport and business for the rest of my life.

The team readily accepted my appointment as captain, and we continued to play well. We were in the top few teams and qualified for the semi-finals. We were very fortunate that a player with first grade experience, John (Jumbo) O'Gorman, came back to live in Albion Park just in time to join our team for the semi-finals. Jumbo was a friend of my older brothers and I talked him into joining the team. Jumbo scored 147 not out in the semi-final and 87 in the final. On the back of his batting, some brilliant bowling by the Bunkers and Grub, and generally good pressure cricket we won the final and I had captained the inaugural third grade premiers.

I was fortunate that some of the club's experienced first graders had mentored and guided me through the competition. One of them, Stirling Scard, told me to always bat first. This was invaluable advice in the final. We batted first and only made a low score of around 90. However, it was enough as the pressure got to the opposition, and we dismissed them for less than 50. Jumbo scored big in the second innings and the rest is history.

We wrapped the final up around 3pm on a Saturday. Then I experienced the greatest, drunkest, most joyous night of my life to date. We went straight to the Oaks Hotel and drinks started flowing very freely. The Oaks provided some free drinks, and we all got very merry, very quickly. I was hoisted onto the main bar, as the winning captain, and I'm told that I made quite a lengthy speech from the bar. It seemed that everyone at the pub, including the publican, was happy for us to celebrate our victory.

This turned into a very long afternoon and night. Most of the team went to the Albion Park RSL after the pub. The dress code for men was a tie as the Saturday night dance was on. We were all pretty drunk by then and managed to get into the dance with an assortment of tie substitutes, including socks and shoelaces tied around our necks. The RSL was also happy for us to celebrate.

I went on to play cricket with Albion Park for the next eleven years. I did not win any more premierships. I was awarded the Clubman of the year trophy for the 1980/81 season.

Although I thoroughly enjoyed my four years of rugby league, I found that I enjoyed cricket more. I loved the tactics, the pressure, the camaraderie, and the thrill of getting a good score or taking a great catch. Participating in a close finish in a game of cricket is an exhilarating experience.

Conscription into the armed services was compulsory in Australia from 1964 to 1972. Conscription for compulsory national service for 20-year-old males was made each year by a lottery draw of dates of birth. If your birthday was selected, you were required to serve two years of national service. Conscription was introduced due to Australia entering the Vietnam war. This was very controversial as many Australians were opposed to Australia participating in this war, and many Australian males did not want to go to war.

Conscription was a hot topic in the Lambert household. John and Hans both avoided conscription as their birthdays were not selected. They were both very happy not to be selected. Renee was due to be in the draw in 1972 as he turned 20 that year. He narrowly avoided the draw as conscription ended in December 1972, before that year's draw was made. Consequently, I also avoided the draw as I turned 20 in 1973. Renee and I had been very concerned about being conscripted and we were very relieved when it ended. I'm not sure what I would have done if it had not ended, and I had been called up. I would have been petrified about going into the army.

Several of our friends were called up and completed their two years of national service. This included Steve Dowd, one of our star Outset rugby league players, and John Ryall, who I played cricket with later. The two years of service impacted heavily on their lives, particularly for John who served in the Vietnam war and was deeply affected by that experience. The Vietnam war cast a pall over Australia in the 1960's and 1970's, particularly for those who had also lived through the two great wars.

The second Lambert wedding occurred in March 1973 when John married his long-time girlfriend, Barbara. Barbara was another great addition to the family. She slotted in seamlessly and, as a bonus, was a fantastic cook. She learnt how to cook Mum's favourite Dutch dishes, perhaps better than Mum. This wedding was my first as an adult. It was highlighted by our friend Michael "Chips" Raftery singing "Father and Son" on stage with a group of us supporting him as backing singers. Alcohol fuelled us to foolishly think that we could sing. Chips went on to sing this song at most of our functions and it would become a very important song to me later in life.

I celebrated my 21st birthday on the 26th of May 1974. I had a party that was very typical of that era. It was held at the same venue as Toni's wedding, the Albion Park Rail Progress Hall. Dad wore his best suit, and Mum her best dress. There was a live band, catered hot food from the Chicken Spot and plenty of alcohol. Around 100 people came, which was typical of 21st birthday parties back then.

A drink called Blackberry Nip was very popular at that time. Blackberry Nip was a blackberry flavoured fortified wine. It was usually mixed with lemonade. The syrupy fruity sweetness disguised the alcohol and people who drank it usually got very drunk very quickly. That is what happened at my 21st. I had made sure there was plenty of Blackberry Nip and several of my friends got drunk early in the night. I watched what I was drinking as I knew I had to make a speech. It was a great night.

During 1974 we enjoyed two more Queensland holidays. A group of us drove to Queensland in January 1974 to attend the wedding of John and Christine Bulters. John was one of the founders of the Outset group. On this trip we discovered the various guest houses at Coolangatta. We decided to come back for another holiday in August 1974, at the end of the rugby league season. This group comprised Fuji, Haze, Jumbo, Chips, Mark O'Neill, and me. We flew to the Gold Coast, and I think this was my first flight. We stayed at Pacific Village at Coolangatta, which was "the place" to stay at that time. It was full of young holiday makers looking for a good time.

This was a great holiday. It included Chips winning a talent contest, singing "Father and Son", a fancy-dress party and many alcohol-fuelled nights. Fuji became well known in Pacific Village very quickly. His cheeky humour resulted in us meeting many people very quickly. We even had some success with the girls on this trip. Haze and I met two girls from Melbourne, Leanne and Leearne. They subsequently came to Wollongong for a holiday but by then the holiday romance appeal had fizzled out.

In 1974 the five oldest kids assisted Mum and Dad financially to take their first trip back to the Netherlands since they had left in 1951. Mum and Dad really enjoyed that trip back home.

I had been on a few dates and accompanied girls to weddings and other functions. Towards the end of 1974 I got my first girlfriend. One of the rugby league players, Ken Tate's, girlfriend Debbie had started bringing her younger sister along to the games, and to the RSL club after the games. Her name was Sue Nicol and we started talking a bit, and then a bit more. After being prompted by Ken I mustered up the courage to ask her out on a date and she accepted. She was completing her Higher School Certificate, so we caught up mainly on the weekends. We went out together for several months and it was great to be like everyone else and have a partner for weddings, parties, and other functions. Sue was lovely, great with people, attractive and a very intelligent conversationalist. However, after several months I found that I was missing my old lifestyle which revolved around sports and my mates. I guess I wasn't ready for a serious girlfriend yet and we went our separate ways.

We had developed a tradition of having New Year's Eve parties at the Keys' farm, a few kilometres from Albion Park. They were held near a creek. They were great nights with plenty of drinking, dancing, swimming, and games. The numbers increased each year but there was never any trouble. We always slept there, in the open air, and cleaned up the next day. At the 1974 New Year's Eve party I sprained my right ankle quite badly.

I had sprained this ankle many times, but this time felt worse. When I got up the next day, I could hardly walk on it. I went to my local doctor a couple of days later. He told me it was a bad sprain and he strapped it up. My recovery was very slow but eventually I was running again. I found out many years later that I had torn the main ligament in the ankle, and it should have been surgically repaired. Instead, the ankle repaired itself but, unbeknownst to me, into the wrong position. I had ongoing problems with this ankle for the next 30 years until I had an ankle fusion in 2006.

My work and uni were both progressing well. I had gone to uni full time in 1973 and 1974 and worked at AIS during the uni holidays. I had a casual lawn mowing job, and I saved enough money from work to support myself through uni. I continued to improve academically during the time I went to uni full time as I had more time to study. I was consistently in the top few students. The lecturers started to take notice of me and were encouraging me to consider an academic career. They also thought that I should continue studying and complete an Honours degree.

I got excited by this prospect as I liked the uni life, both academically and socially. However, I felt that I was obliged to AIS as they had supported me through uni and I had thought that I would have a long term corporate career there.

I completed my Bachelor of Commerce at the end of 1974. The Professor of the University of Wollongong Accountancy Department then approached me and offered me a part time role as an Accountancy Tutor so I could complete my Honours Degree, which would take two years part time. He had discussed this role with my lecturers. They thought that I would be a good tutor as I related well to people, and I knew the content of the accounting subjects. By then I had resumed my job at AIS and was a Pricing Officer in the Budget Control Department. I found myself in a bit of a dilemma and was very uncertain about what to do.

I decided to be transparent and discuss my situation with my boss in the Budget Control Department. I asked him for a meeting and had only started to explain my situation when he looked directly at me and said, "Get out of here while you can." He left me in no doubt that he thought I had far better prospects by leaving AIS. I was initially shocked by his advice, but it caused me to have an objective look around at the workplace I was in. It was an uninspiring culture where most people just got their jobs done. Their jobs were a means to an end.

On the other hand, I had seen a real vibrancy at uni. Most of the lecturers were young and enthusiastic. It was a much livelier culture. This was my "sliding doors moment". I resigned from AIS and left in February 1975. I accepted the Tutor role and started the next week in time for the commencement of the uni year. I commenced the Honours Degree at the same time.

I was given several classes of first year accounting students to tutor. My only training was to meet with the lecturer, who would set the assignments for the tutorials and provide me with lecture notes, so I knew what he was lecturing each week. I received no training in how to tutor. It was just assumed that if you knew the subject content you would know how to teach it. I talked to more experienced tutors and picked up any tips I could. I decided to be transparent with my students. I told them I was a young, 21 year old tutor and that some of them would be more experienced at practical accounting than I was. There were several mature age students in my classes who appreciated me acknowledging them and they assisted me a bit through that first year. They already knew all the accounting content that the first year school graduates were struggling with.

I slipped into the tutor role quite seamlessly and enjoyed the interaction with students. I made time available for students who needed assistance and became one of the more popular tutors. There were only a few students doing Honours. We were working directly with the Professor, and I found it hard going. The subjects were very theoretical, rather than practical, and the Professor had very high expectations. I was also 21 and starting to want to get out and enjoy life more. I no longer had the same zest for studying that had got me to this point.

A very significant event occurred in Australia on the 11th of November 1975 with the dismissal of the Whitlam Labor Government. This caused a constitutional crisis which the academics at Wollongong University fiercely discussed and debated. A group of them were so outraged that they organised a full-page advertisement in the Illawarra Mercury, which they asked all the academics at the uni to sign. I did not sign as I felt I did not know enough about what had happened.

My enthusiasm for tutoring got me through those two years. At the end of 1976 I graduated with a Bachelor of Commerce (Honours Class II, Division 1).

In February of 1976 I was still playing cricket every Saturday. My friend, Haze, had been complaining that we (that is me and some of the other cricket players), were too tired after cricket each Saturday and we no longer raged on all night like we used to. We challenged him to play one game of cricket, and then we would go out that night and see who could last the longest. He accepted the challenge and was confident that he could handle a game of cricket, and still go out. These were famous last words.

We played cricket and we decided to stay local and go to the Oaks Hotel that night. Our plan was to get Haze drunk as quickly as possible and then we could all sleep at Mum and Dad's place, which was only 5 minutes' walk away. Mum and Dad were in the Netherlands at that time. The plan worked a bit too well as I managed to get almost as drunk as Haze. We were having a great time and at some stage Fuji connected our group with a few girls who had come from Kiama for a night out. Fuji was very good at making new friends very quickly.

I found myself sitting next to a very attractive young lady and the rest is history. That young lady was Martina (Tina) Kelleher. Despite my inebriated state I must have made enough sense to deserve a date. Being a gentleman, I did offer to drive Tina home. I thought I was ok to drive but she told me later that I was swerving a bit going around the Minnamurra bends. Whilst the drink driving laws were more liberal then, I was still disappointed with myself as I had planned not to drive that night. As a group we were generally quite careful that someone should stay sober to drive everyone home. Tina invited me to a barbecue at her parents' home the following weekend, and we started going out.

There was an interesting ending to that night. We lost Haze at some point during the night and thought that he must have gone home. The next morning, we were having breakfast when Haze walked in. He was bleary eyed and scruffy. He said he had fallen asleep walking from the Oaks Hotel to Mum and Dad's place and he had lost his wallet. He wasn't sure where he had slept. We searched the paths he could have taken from the Oaks Hotel. One path went past a big blackberry bush. We saw a perfectly formed shape of a human body lying down in this blackberry bush. Then we found Haze's wallet in the bush next to this body shape. It was clear that he had slept in the blackberry bush all night. We presumed that he fell backwards and then didn't move, as he didn't have any cuts from the bushes. He did not play cricket again and stopped whingeing about us playing cricket.

The 1975 and 1976 years were notable for the number of weddings and engagement parties we attended. It was usual at that time to marry your first serious girlfriend. The typical ages for weddings were between 22 and 25 for males and between 20 and 23 for females. Most of my friends from the Outset and Albion Park rugby league days were approaching these age groups and the weddings were coming along very frequently.

Every wedding that I attended was very special and they all had some individual, memorable aspects. One wedding that comes to mind is when Swampy married Helen Bowden in February 1975. Helen was a cousin of the Graham boys, who were in the Outset team. It was a huge, traditional wedding. They had to have the wedding at the Kiama Pavilion, at the showground, as it was the only venue in Kiama that was big enough to accommodate the 270 guests. It was a special wedding for me as I was the best man.

It was a very wet day, and the male toilets became flooded before the reception started. The female toilets were big enough to accommodate all the guests. The organisers solved the problem by dividing the female toilets into two halves by using portable partitions. As frivolities increased at the wedding one of the partitions was partially moved, and before long all the partitions had disappeared. Women and men were using the same toilets. No one took credit for the disappearance of the partitions, but it seems highly likely that some of the Outset boys were ring leaders.

This is when Fuji came into his element. He recalls that he and a few of the other guys started escorting ladies to the toilets. It was so wet that they had to carry some of the ladies through the water. Fuji then "stood guard" at the ladies' cubicles so they could have some privacy. The toilet situation quickly became a talking point at the wedding. All the guests embraced it, with no one getting annoyed with the unisex toilets. It seemed to bring everyone together and helped to make it a very memorable wedding.

By 1975 table tennis had become a more serious sport for me. I was playing in all the RSL club championships. Ocka and I won a couple of doubles titles and my best result in singles was runner up. Rod Raftery was one of the best players at the RSL. He, Ocka, and I decided to enter an RSL team in the local Illawarra competition. We played in the Division 2 competition for about five years. We did not win a title, but we had plenty of good times. A highlight of these years was that Rod's mother cooked a roast meal for us before most of the away games. We met at Rod's place to go in one car. His mother then naturally included us in the evening meal. Her meals were delicious.

One of the Outset guys, Chips, had bought a ski boat. We soon developed the routine of having a water ski on Lake Illawarra very early on Saturday mornings. We found that it was a good hangover cure. I was slow to develop as a skier but eventually became adept on one ski. They were big days for me as I skied in the mornings and played cricket in the afternoons.

In mid-1976 I left home and never went back. Fuji and I decided to rent a flat together. We found a small, old two-bedroom flat in Pleasant Avenue, North Wollongong. Our flat was on top of the garages for a block of flats, so we were totally separate from the other flats. It was only two minutes' walk from North Wollongong beach.

This flat soon became the meeting point for our friends and the scene of many parties and good times. The most memorable party occurred when we organised a barbecue and around forty people turned up. It started to rain very heavily and there was no outdoor sheltered area. We decided that we had no choice but to move the barbecue indoors. It was a gas barbecue so we thought it would be ok as there was no fire. We carried it into the lounge room and cooked the barbecue there. We managed to feed everyone. The next day we discovered that we had blackened the lounge room wall and made quite a mess. We painted the wall, cleaned up the mess and the landlord never found out.

We lived in the flat for around 18 months until I got married. Fuji was a good cook, and we were quite good with the domestic duties. We had a flushing indoor toilet for the first time. We did not have a telephone but still managed to stay in touch with family and friends. I was always working, studying, spending time with Tina or playing sport. Fuji on the other hand was working and socialising. If he came home late, after a night of drinking, he would regularly wake me up, sit on my bed and give me a report on the night's activities. I did not mind getting woken up and went straight back to sleep after our little chats.

Haze and I had been planning an overseas trip together. This was to be the obligatory trip to work in England and travel around Europe during work breaks. Many young people were doing this, including my brother John, and his wife Barbara. They had a great couple of years in Europe and spent valuable time with our relatives in the Netherlands. Towards the end of 1976 I was getting serious with Tina so I let Haze know that I would not be going overseas on our planned "trip of a lifetime". It is fair to say that he was disappointed. He continued with his plans and went to London in May 1977. I was very pleased that he quickly made plenty of new friends and had a great time away.

The little kids were growing up. Dianne had left school in 1973. She worked at the Illawarra Mutual Building Society for one year until she turned 17. She then started nursing at Wollongong Hospital as a live-in nurse five days a week. Terry had a lawn mowing job in his last couple of years at school. He also worked at Oranges' chicken farm. He left school at the end of 1975 after completing fourth form. He completed a full time pre apprenticeship course, and he then got a job as an apprentice Carpenter & Joiner.

Adrian was very active with part time jobs while he was at school. He had lawn mowing jobs and delivered brochures, for the Albion Park Rail Golden Circle grocery shop, from year 6 to year 9. When he was in year 10, he got a job at the Shell garage, only five minutes' walk from home, as a petrol pump attendant. He kept this job for three years, working weekends and school holidays. Adrian was also a keen chess player and was the year 7 chess champion in 1973. Steve delivered the brochures with Adrian. He also mowed lawns from the age of 12 until he finished high school. He had several regulars in Kaylaur Crescent and picked up a few more through word of mouth.

By the time they left school all nine Lambert kids had done a variety of jobs. Mostly each kid got the job by themselves. No one ever got any pocket money. These school jobs established a solid foundation for all the siblings, who went on to have a very good work ethic for the rest of their lives.

Dianne had started dating a guy named Joe Wilson in 1975, at the age of 17. Joe was very sporty and fit in well with all the Lambert boys. Dianne and Joe did not waste any time. They got married in September 1976. It was another great family wedding with the reception held at the Whitehall reception centre in Wollongong.

CHAPTER 11

AN EYE-OPENING TRIP

— 1977 TO 1984 —

1977 was a huge year as I managed to fit three major life events into one year. I changed jobs, bought a house and got married.

Whilst I was enjoying my tutoring role, I didn't think I had enough accounting experience to be a career academic. I had a few discussions with Bob Jego, one of the Outset rugby league footballers, who was a chartered accountant. Bob heavily influenced me to consider a career in chartered accounting as I would get experience in the "real world" in the areas of auditing, taxation, and accounting services.

Bob connected me with Coghlan and Allen, one of Wollongong's oldest and most respected chartered accounting firms. They created a position for me as they were keen to employ an accounting graduate. It was relatively new at that time for chartered accountants to qualify through a university degree.

I followed my gut instinct that this was the right move for me and accepted the position. The Professor was quite shocked by my decision as he thought an academic career was the pinnacle. I did continue my tutoring role part time for the next seven years. In hindsight my decision was absolutely the right one as my years in chartered accounting provided the foundation for my future interesting, enjoyable, and successful corporate career.

It was a huge decision for me both in relation to my choice of career and financially. I was receiving an annual salary of around $11,000 at the university and the starting salary at Coghlan and Allen was around $8,000. I received no recognition, salary wise, for having completed the Honours degree. The reduction in salary was particularly significant as I was getting serious with Tina, and we were starting to think about a house purchase.

I commenced work with Coghlan and Allen on the 1st of February 1977. It was a very traditional accounting firm. One of the founders, Mr Coghlan, was around 90 years old and still coming into the office regularly. The other founder, Mr Allen, was always resplendently dressed and was a statesman leader. The office manager, Miss Quinn, smoked at her desk all day.

I started in the audit department. This involved both auditing and accounting services as we often had to complete the financial statements for the client. It was all manual work as computers were still a few years away. The fact that I had taught accounting was an advantage and I became quick and accurate at compiling financial statements.

I loved the work and was soon managing some big audit clients. One of these was a company called South Coast Equipment (SCE). Paul Newman was the owner and managing director. He was a very astute businessman. Even though I was the auditor he took a liking to me and took me under his wing. He sensed quite quickly that I needed real work and life experience to complement my academic skills. He perhaps thought that I was too naïve.

In my first year on the SCE audit, I observed that they were way ahead of their time with human resources policies. They were a transport company, with many trucks in their fleet. There was a broken-down truck in the corner of the yard. The staff all knew that if they were assigned that truck for work the next day that meant your services were no longer required. No dismissal procedures were necessary.

I got off to a good start in that first-year audit when I found an incorrect miscellaneous debit that had appeared on one of the company's bank statements. It was a significant amount. The bank accepted the error and refunded the money. Paul was impressed.

On another occasion Paul called me to tell me that the Taxation Office was coming to SCE to do an audit and asked me to be there on the day of the audit. I observed a master at work when two young, very keen, tax office representatives arrived at the start of the day to do the audit. Paul promptly suggested that they should understand the business if they are going to do an audit and he bustled them into his car to show them the company's operations. Paul included a long lunch in the tour and arrived back with them just before the close of business. I was still there when they arrived back. The two representatives thanked Paul for a great day and left. To the best of my knowledge that was the end of that audit.

I worked on the SCE audit from 1977 to 1984 and during that time the use of computers gradually became more common in businesses. SCE was ahead of its time and purchased an enterprise system. I became involved in the installation of this system and was fortunate to gain great experience from this. I learnt a great deal about business from Paul.

By 1980 Coghlan and Allen had merged with Touche Ross, an international accounting firm. A new audit partner was appointed from the Sydney office to head up the Wollongong office audit practice. Paul did not want to be allocated the new audit partner, together with the audit processes that were required by the Sydney office. He also thought that I was good enough to manage the audit without a partner. He called me into his office one day and requested that I get the new audit partner removed from the SCE audit. In other words, I had to sack my boss from the job.

I managed to achieve the desired outcome by initially discussing Paul's request with the other long term Wollongong office partner. Then we both discussed the client request with the new audit partner. To his credit he agreed to let me run the job. He realised that he had to "earn his stripes" in Wollongong. He did just that and became a respected audit partner in the Wollongong area.

Paul told me later that, whilst his request was genuine, he didn't expect me to do it. Just like the brothers did at the end of fourth form, he was testing me and preparing me for my business world journey. Paul remained very sharp and today, at 90 years of age, continues to go to the office a few days a week.

February 1977 continued to be a very big month as Tina and I got engaged. My proposal was very basic, by today's standards. I don't mean to make it sound unromantic, but it wasn't a big deal in those days. We had been out in Wollongong, and I drove to Wollongong lighthouse, a well-known "parking" spot. I just came out with it and asked Tina if she would marry me. I was quite nervous. I'm pretty sure we were both sitting in the car at the time. She said yes. I didn't have a ring as I knew that Tina would want to select that herself. I then did the right thing and formally asked her father, Martin, for permission to marry his daughter. His response was something like, "Yeh, Yeh Charlie about time." We decided to get married relatively quickly and set a date of the 3rd of September 1977. Tina and her mother, Joan, did the wedding planning.

All my friends from rugby league, cricket and work were moving on with their lives also. There were frequent weddings to attend, kids were coming along, and others travelled overseas for long periods. I was still playing cricket and table tennis.

To make my life even busier I enrolled to do the Professional Year (PY) of study with the Institute of Chartered Accountants. Passing the PY was a requirement to become a chartered accountant. I commenced the PY in the middle of 1977. It was a challenging course. We had to submit assignments regularly and I was back to long hours of studying.

We got married on the 3rd of September 1977. Tina's parents generously paid for the whole wedding. Her father, Martin, had received an inheritance a couple of years earlier so they were able to host a big wedding. It was a very big wedding with over 200 guests. It was made more humorous, and a bit challenging, when we discovered that the master of ceremonies, Tina's uncle Phil, had drunk a bit too much before the reception began. He was quite nervous stepping into the shoes of his father, Selby, who had always been the master of ceremonies at family functions. Selby had passed away in the year before the wedding.

As soon as Phil started going off script, including asking a random person to come up and make a speech, my brother and best man, Fuji, stepped in and took over to guide Phil through the rest of the night. It all ended well. After a great reception we emerged from the surf club to find my car covered in toilet paper, branches of trees and various other decorations. There were rocks in the hubcaps and shaving cream sprayed across the windows. I cleared the debris off enough to be able to drive to the motel. We had a low-key honeymoon on the Central Coast, NSW. I had to study on the honeymoon as I had PY assignments to complete.

There was an unexpected upside to my salary reduction. I qualified for a low interest housing loan through a scheme whereby the interest rates were partially subsidised by the government. One of the loan conditions was that we had to select a new house and land package from several developments that were underway. We signed a contract to purchase a house that was to be constructed at 52 Laurel Street, Albion Park Rail. The purchase price was $29,000. We had savings of around $5,000. We borrowed $20,500 through the low interest loan, and an additional $4,000 through a personal loan from the National Australia Bank. We were stretched financially with these loans.

We moved into the new home in November 1977. It was only about one kilometre from our Kaylaur Crescent house, so I was back very close to home. It was a very basic three-bedroom, one bathroom cream brick home. There was no garage, no driveway or paths and no built-in wardrobes. The yard was untouched. Our furniture was all second hand. We had a small black and white television. We did not have a telephone.

The great news is that we did not have a dunny can toilet. Septic tanks were in use at that time to store the household toilet and water waste. The septic tanks were pumped out once a month. That old familiar smell sometimes re-emerged when someone's septic tank overflowed and leaked effluent before the pump out date. Fortunately, it was only a few years before sewerage was connected in Albion Park Rail. It was a great joy to smash the septic tank into the ground and cover it forever.

We spent the next year settling into the house and transforming the yard into lawns and gardens. Tina's parents, Joan and Martin, were a tremendous help during that period. One day I arrived home from work to find that several loads of topsoil had been delivered. They had bought the topsoil and Martin had already started spreading it. They, and Tina's sister Patsy, were always at our place helping. My brothers also assisted when they could. Malcolm, Toni's husband, made the balustrade for the front patio. Tina completed decorating the interior of the house very quickly. It looked great. We had a telephone connected in the middle of 1978.

Tina obtained a job as a medical receptionist for a General Practitioner in Wollongong. I passed the PY in June 1978 and qualified as a Chartered Accountant. I had been studying for twenty-one consecutive years. I was very happy to stop and focus on family and work.

In early 1978 Fuji resigned from his long-term job at AIS. He had decided to join the travel rush. He went to Europe and joined our friends, Haze, and John "Jumbo" O'Gorman, who were already there. He had a fantastic trip, which included several months on a kibbutz in Israel. He returned to Australia in the middle of 1980 to attend Hans's wedding.

John started a kitchen business, Lambert Kitchens, with his wife, Barbara, in 1978. They formed a very effective partnership. John was a very good tradesmen and loved making kitchens. Barbara was a very good administrator. She did the bookkeeping and looked after all the non-operational areas. The business grew gradually, mainly through word of mouth. They moved into their own factory in Doyle Avenue, Unanderra about ten years later.

John is still running Lambert Kitchens today, at the age of 73. It has become something of an institution in the Wollongong area.

When he was about 15 Adrian was playing rugby league for Albion Park. One of his team mates, Brett Matthews, called him Ossie one day. Brett said that he ran like an ostrich, with his long legs and long stride. He has been called Ossie ever since. Ossie completed year 12 in 1978. He started his first job as an accounts clerk at Shellharbour Council in January 1979.

Hans was involved in a serious car accident in 1979. He had been to an event in Sydney with one of his work colleagues. He was a passenger for the drive home and the car inexplicably left the road and hit a telegraph pole in Engadine. The driver was badly injured. Hans was not badly injured but still spent a few days in hospital.

There was an upside for Hans. He had met a lovely young lady, Diane Wood, at a party a few weeks before the accident. They had been out together a few times. She came to visit Hans in hospital and their romance blossomed from there.

In mid-1978 two unexpected events occurred simultaneously which resulted in Tina and I going on the trip of a lifetime and spending six months overseas. Firstly, Tina's parents won a trip to Europe in a competition. They gave this trip to us to use for a belated honeymoon. Secondly, Touche Ross asked me if I would like to participate in a work exchange program with one of their USA offices. The program involved exchanging staff between offices in both countries for their respective peak audit periods. This was the first time the Wollongong office participated in the program. The partners were keen for me to go as that office's first PY graduate.

I accepted the offer, and I was allocated to the Touche Ross, Kansas City, office. Kansas City is in the mid-western state of Missouri. It is a small city, by comparison with the United States capital cities. It was decided that this would be a good fit for me as I was coming from one of Australia's smaller cities.

We combined both trips. We rented the house out and departed in November 1978. We flew straight to the Netherlands and, in a whirlwind couple of weeks, we met many of my relatives. The highlight of the trip was meeting my Oma, Dad's mother, and my only surviving grandparent. I had envisaged meeting a stern old lady, but it was the complete opposite. She was extremely emotional, very happy to meet us and very friendly. Through interpreters she explained how she had always thought of us so far away in Australia. It was apparent how much she had missed Mum and Dad and our family. She had a photo of our family on the wall behind her chair.

Through this meeting with Oma and all the other relatives I realised that Mum and Dad's decision to live in Australia had significantly impacted the entire family in the Netherlands. They had missed our family and were thrilled that the Lambert siblings were gradually starting to visit the Netherlands. It was quite an experience meeting so many cousins with similar looks and mannerisms to us. When we visited Jan Van Ammers, my uncle's home, I remember the shock I felt when the door was opened and there stood one of my cousins who looked just like my younger brothers.

We visited Mum and Dad's home towns, including the church where they were married. It was very enlightening to see how different the Netherlands was to Australia. Everything, including the size of the houses, the climate, or the use of bicycles as a standard means of transport, was virtually opposite to life in Australia. It made me more aware of how massive the move to Australia was for Mum and Dad.

One experience reminded me of one of Mum's standard meals. We had lunch at my aunt's home in Bemmel. There were four of us and she brought out a huge dish of mashed potato, with sauce, as a side. That was the meal. The Dutch do love their potatoes.

I did not realise it before I went but I needed that trip to the Netherlands. I was very grateful that I was able to meet Oma and so many of my aunts, uncles, and cousins. It was a more emotional trip than I had envisaged. It was almost forty years later before I went back to the Netherlands.

We completed a quick, two week, Kon Tiki tour of Europe. Then we spent a week in London before it was time to fly to the USA so I could start work.

The trip from London to Kansas City was unforgettable. We arrived at Heathrow airport to discover that our flight had been delayed due to severe weather conditions at Chicago airport, which was our first stop. After a delay of several hours and two flights being merged into one, we departed and arrived at a bitterly cold Chicago at about 2am. I had to find a way to call Philip, our contact in Kansas City, and let him know the new arrival time. Philip had been posted to Kansas City from his office in Malaysia and had arrived a few weeks earlier. It had been arranged that Philip would pick us up from the airport and take us to our accommodation. I had no US dollars, and all the airport shops were closed as it was 2am. I asked the airline if they would let me make a call and they were kind enough to provide a telephone. I called Philip and he said he would be there at the revised arrival time of around 4am.

We boarded the flight to Kansas City for an approximate three hour flight. We were both very tired after a very arduous day. The plane was almost empty. After taking off we started talking to an African American man who was seated a couple of rows behind us. He moved forward and we talked for most of the trip. He could tell how nervous we were, and he settled us down with plenty of information about Kansas City and the USA generally. He was a very calming influence.

When we arrived in Kansas City I stood up and shook his hand to thank him for the conversation and being such a great help. He took my hand, but he reversed the acknowledgement. He looked me in the eye and said, "I want to thank you, this is the longest conversation I have ever had with a white guy!". This was a defining moment for me. I could tell that he was serious and very appreciative that we were so friendly and non-racist. This conversation was a timely warning for me that I would experience racism over the next few months.

We arrived at Kansas City at 4am and a cheery Philip was there to greet us. He was not concerned that it was four o'clock in the morning. We were beyond shattered by then and just had to find a bed. Philip had a car, and all went well until we exited the airport. He suddenly said something like, "Sorry but I took a wrong turn. I will pull over and do a u-turn." He was getting flustered. He pulled over onto the shoulder of the road. He did not realise that this would be soft due to recent snowfalls. He pulled over and then very slowly the car just tipped onto its side as the ground underneath gave way. Could any more happen in one day? I did not know whether to laugh or cry.

The three of us climbed out of the car through the doors on the top side. Philip was very flustered and did not know what to do. We were in the middle of nowhere, with no mobile phones, with a car on its side and with a guy we had just met. Then before we had time to do anything a big utility, something like a Holden Rodeo, stopped. Two young friendly guys jumped out and said, "We will get you out of there in no time." They applied a tow rope and pulled the car back onto the road in about ten minutes. Our relief was palpable. The rest of the trip went smoothly, and we arrived in our unit at around 6am. We were shattered with exhaustion.

I started work at Touche Ross, Kansas City office, on the following Monday. I knew that I would be working very long hours and that I would be doing audit "grunt" work. I was thrilled to be in the USA and the approaching workload did not concern me. We had organised that Tina would spend most of the three month work period at a family friend's place in Albuquerque, New Mexico. It would be too lonely for her in a unit in a Kansas City winter while I worked 15 hour days.

I settled into work and found myself to be a novelty as no one there had ever met an Australian person before. The audit work was like the work I had done in Australia, and my managers were good to work for. They told me that I would need a car to drive to the audit jobs. They organised a brand new Chevette for me. I picked it up on a Friday afternoon and navigated a tricky drive home across Kansas City at peak hour. I was very cautious as I was driving on the right-hand side for the first time.

It snowed very heavily over that weekend. I had been given some hints by a few of my co-workers about driving in snow and ice. One of the most important things was to never stop going up a hill even if you come to a red light. They said there was a code of conduct between drivers whereby drivers in the most vulnerable positions are given the right of way.

It had stopped snowing by Monday morning when I had to go to work, but the roads were still very slick. I was driving up a small hill in the middle lane, when I noticed the car next to me start to slide. It ran into the car in front of it which then collided with the car in front of me. I remembered the advice and quickly slipped into the next lane and overtook the car in front of me, which had now stopped because of the accident. I returned to the middle lane and looked in my rear vision mirror. I saw that it was now a five-car pile-up. I was the only car in the group of six to emerge unscathed. I arrived at work with a sense of triumph and relief.

I was in Kansas City for the winter months, and it was the coldest winter they had had for many years. The temperature was regularly below zero with an even colder wind chill factor. I was snowed in one weekend. The only way to get to the shops was to walk on the paths that were regularly cleared. Tina also experienced a very cold winter in Albuquerque. The cold weather was part of the adventure and we loved it.

My work period went very quickly, and I learnt some valuable lessons, both work and life, from this job. One of the managers I worked with had told me that he wanted to have the highest charge out rate in the firm over this audit season. This would require beating a legendary partner who managed on four hours sleep a night. I had dinner at this manager's place one night and I spoke to his wife about his goal. She told me that she expected him to go hard and then collapse at the end of the audit season. This was based on the previous year when he had health problems after the audit season and had to have his spleen removed. I remember thinking to myself that I was never going to take work that seriously.

My last job was the audit of a large car dealer, and I was there for a few weeks. At the end of that job one of the ladies in the office asked me if I had to learn to speak English before I came to the USA. My flippant response was something like, "Yes, and haven't I done a great job learning it." I did not tell her that we spoke English in Australia. There was also a lady in that office named Danita. As you will see both Tina and I liked that name.

During my time in Kansas City, I found that American people knew very little about Australia, and the rest of the world. They were very focused on their own country and were extremely patriotic. I was the first Australian most of them had met and they loved talking to me. I also saw the darker side of the USA as racism was very evident. African Americans were still commonly referred to as negroes or niggers. Some of the white people I worked with spoke disdainfully of African Americans in their everyday conversation. I was struck by this as I had not experienced anything like this in Australia.

Tina and I saw each other every few weeks, as it was a relatively short flight from Kansas City to Albuquerque. I finished work in March 1979. Joan and Patsy flew to the USA to join us on a brief holiday. I thought I was familiar with driving in the USA by then. I hired a car so we could visit the various tourist spots on the West Coast. Our first stop was San Francisco. I decided to drive through the city one day to have a good look around. I had no destination in mind. I drove into one suburb, and we decided to stop and get something to eat. We were getting out of the car when an African American man came over to me and said, "You are not supposed to be here." We had driven into an area of town that was not safe for white people. I thanked him and then got out of there very quickly. I did not make that mistake again. I checked every trip in advance after that experience. The rest of the holiday went smoothly.

We returned to Australia in April 1979. Tina and I both resumed our jobs. This was short lived for Tina as she became pregnant within a couple of months. We were both very happy to be starting a family. This first pregnancy did not agree with Tina. She was very sick for virtually the entire nine months. She had severe morning sickness in the early months and had to stop work. Sometimes I would come from work to find that she had been retching in the bathroom all day.

To top off the difficult pregnancy Tina also had a long, arduous labour. After about 24 hours of labour, the doctor decided to do an emergency caesarean. A very healthy Danita Maree was born on the 18th of March 1980. Tina was a very confident mother right from the start. Danita was a very good first baby and we settled into our new life relatively seamlessly. The biggest adjustment, as with all new parents, was sleep deprivation. We were supposed to take turns for the night feeds, but Tina ended up doing more than me. When it was my turn, I found that it was best to get up, go to the lounge room, turn on our little black and white television and then feed Danita.

We were very fortunate to have besotted grandparents in Martin and Joan, and a very besotted aunt in Patsy. Danita was the first grandchild and niece for them, and they were all in. Patsy stayed at our place as often as she could and, like Tina, she was a natural with babies. Joan was always available to babysit. My parents were very happy to have another grandchild, but they were not active grandparents. When Tina became pregnant Mum had told me that she could not babysit anymore as she was simply worn out.

Life was changing for us as my older siblings, as well as most of our friends, were starting families. Everyone's lives became centred around their children. Nights out became less frequent. Our social world changed to visiting each other's homes for dinners or barbecue's.

Hans and Diane were married in July 1980. Hans was a very happy groom that day. He had waited longer than some of his siblings, and friends, to find the right bride. You could tell that he thought that Diane was worth the wait. Diane came from a great family unit who readily accepted Hans into their family. And Diane was a very welcome addition to the Lambert family.

Fuji had returned home from overseas for the wedding. He had intended to return overseas after the wedding. However, John asked him to come and work at Lambert Kitchens, so he stayed. Fuji had met a young lady, Rita Viselli, in 1976. They reconnected in 1980 and started going out together. They have been together ever since.

By this time Terry also had a steady girlfriend. Her name was Rae Vogel. She was a local, beach loving girl from Warilla. They met when Rae was 16 years old and are still together today. Terry was playing rugby league for Albion Park by then. He was a handy player; he was very nippy, gutsy and was a very good tackler. He mainly played second and third grade, but also had a few games in first grade. He was just too small for first grade.

At the end of 1980 the last Lambert left high school. Steve had been selected as School Captain at the beginning of 1980. He finished that year as the dux of year 12. He was the only sibling to be either a school captain or a dux. Steve then chose a different path. He moved to Sydney to become a Christian Brother. He enrolled at Mount Saint Mary Teachers' College and commenced his training to become a Christian Brother in 1981.

When Steve left school Mum and Dad had had children in school for 27 years. Steve left home as soon as he finished school.

Tina became pregnant again in early 1981. Fortunately, she had a much better pregnancy this time and Bradley (Brad) Martin was born on the 29th of November 1981. Brad was a very good baby and we settled into having two children seamlessly. Joan and Patsy continued to be very hands on and greatly assisted Tina with two children under two. Tina was now a full-time mother and I focused on my corporate career.

Brad was born a day after Dad's birthday, and on the same day as Dad's father. Dad always had a soft spot for Brad, and they were close. Perhaps Dad understood Brad from an early age. Dad kept a photo of Brad and him, which was taken on Brad's first birthday, next to his lounge chair until he moved into aged care.

I progressed to a manager position at work. I was doing more accounting and tax work, as well as auditing. Our office purchased a computer and one of the partners, Lin Baker, spent many hours getting it operational. He had to write the programs. I was getting computer experience both through our office and clients. It quickly became apparent that computers were the way of the future.

Whilst auditing is generally, and correctly, perceived as boring, I had plenty of good times and memorable experiences during my seven years doing audit work. One of my audit clients was Dapto Dogs. During each audit we would visit a greyhound racing meeting to observe cash receipts procedures. I had been asked by the client to watch a certain barman as they suspected he was taking cash from the till. After observing the gate receipts, I went to the bar and ordered a beer. I had hardly taken a sip when I saw that barman serve a customer and pocket the money. He did it once more and I reported my observations to the client. I don't think the barman finished his shift.

On another occasion I was driving past one of my clients on a Friday afternoon, so I decided to call in and do a surprise cash count. This was one of our normal audit procedures. When I walked into the office to count the petty cash the accountant looked up and said, "you have caught me". He had been taking the petty cash float, which was around two hundred dollars, home every Friday to have a punt. He would return it on the following Monday. I'm not sure how he returned the money if he didn't win on the weekend. I think he resigned before any action was taken.

In addition to South Coast Equipment, I worked on the audits of the Wollongong Hospital and the Illawarra Mercury, Wollongong's daily newspaper. Working with diverse clients like these provided me with invaluable business knowledge and experience. This experience was to serve me well in my future corporate career.

I was still playing cricket in summer and table tennis throughout the whole year. In the late 1970's touch football competitions were starting to emerge. Touch football suited me perfectly as it was effectively rugby league without the physical side of tackling or being tackled. The competitions increased in popularity and seriousness very quickly. I loved it from the start.

By 1981 we had formed a team. It was called Lambert Kitchens as it was sponsored by John's business. The team comprised most of my brothers as well as several players from the former Outset rugby league team. It was great to be back playing with this tight group of mates. I knew some of the journalists at the Illawarra Mercury from my audit work there. I was chatting to one of the journalists one day. I told him that I was playing touch footy with five of my brothers. He asked me if there were any more brothers. I told him there was one more, Steve, who was not in the team. We discussed that we would recruit Steve for one game so he could do a story about the seven Lambert brothers playing together.

A touch football team only has seven players, so we were the entire run-on team. The seven of us were photographed and the journalist took some notes. We were expecting a small article in the paper in the next couple of days.

Two days later, on the 24th of December 1981 we all received a nice surprise when the Illawarra Mercury article appeared in prime position on the back page. It was headed, "Seven Brothers Keep in Touch" and occupied over half of the back page. This article is a great memory for all of us. We were very grateful to our other players for allowing the seven of us to run on. For the record we lost the game 4–2.

Terry and Ossie went on to play touch football for many years with Ossie still playing today. They both played in representative teams. Terry was the best of the Lambert brothers at touch football.

Fuji and Rita were married in February 1984. Rita was the only daughter in a traditional Italian family, so it was a very special, memorable, and large wedding. Rita also brought another great, large family unit into our lives. She had become an integral part of our family by then.

Fuji had become a lighter drinker by then. He had progressively reduced his alcohol consumption since his "party" days. He recalls that whilst he enjoyed drinking when he was younger, he always knew that he did not want to be like the regulars that he saw at the RSL club night after night.

CHAPTER 12
THE BIG MOVE
— 1984 TO 1990 —

Tina's sister, Patsy, had moved to the Gold Coast in 1982. She was soon followed by their mother, Joan, who took the opportunity to leave an unhappy marriage after many years of putting up with it.

Tina and I had a huge decision to make. Tina was very close to Joan and Patsy. She naturally wanted to live where they did, particularly after the big decision that Joan had made. We had to decide whether I would stay at Touche Ross and continue my chartered accounting career or move to the Gold Coast where I could pursue a corporate career. I had a discussion with my boss at Touche Ross, Lin Baker. Lin told me that I would probably be the next partner appointed in the Wollongong office but that would not happen until I turned 33, which was almost three years away. That was the minimum partner age requirement at Touche Ross, and there were no exceptions.

Lin also told me that I would already have been offered a partnership if the firm had remained as Coghlan and Allen. He was very generous with his advice and steered me in the direction of placing family first. We made the decision to move to Queensland as soon as I could find suitable employment.

Cheryl, Tina's cousin, and her family had also moved to the Gold Coast a couple of years earlier. Cheryl and her husband, John, operated a newsagency at Mermaid Beach. Cheryl offered to check the positions vacant section of the local paper, the Gold Coast Bulletin, daily and mail me any prospective job opportunities.

I answered an advertisement for a "Mining Accountant – Gold Coast based" job. This led to a breathtaking corporate journey over the next six years. I had no experience in mining accounting, but I thought that all accounting is pretty much the same and I would give this one a go. After I applied for the position, I received a telephone call from Grahame Brown & Co, the accounting firm who were handing the job applications on behalf of their client. After an initial telephone discussion, they suggested I meet with their client.

They organised for me to meet the client for an interview at the Wentworth Hotel in Sydney on a rainy Saturday morning in early March 1984. The client was scheduled to be in Sydney for business that week and he was happy to stay until Saturday to meet me. The Wentworth is a beautiful, old hotel with interiors reminiscent of the great hotels in the old English movies. It was a daunting location for an interview. I wore my best suit. I was nervous as I didn't know much about the job, the client, or the Gold Coast more generally. I was waiting patiently when a very casually dressed, friendly guy named Les Ward introduced himself and started chatting. Over the next hour Les told me about his business interests, which were much broader than the mining company.

He was an entrepreneur with businesses in the mining, property, and hospitality industries. While he was primarily looking for an accountant for the gold mining exploration company, he said that there was probably more work that I could do across his various other companies. This proved to be an understatement. Les was a very interesting, enthusiastic, and engaging person. After about an hour of talking about the businesses he asked me if I would like to take the job. He didn't ask me any normal interview questions. He must have trusted his gut feeling to offer me the job. I said yes on the spot, and we organised that I was to start on the Tuesday after Easter and would meet him at the office that day. There was nothing in writing. We just shook hands and agreed.

Once again, I found myself in the right place at the right time and secured a great job relatively easily. This would prove to be the only paid job I ever applied for.

This started a frenetic six weeks of activity which included the sale of the house.

There were a few times that I caught myself reflecting that I was leaving everything I had grown up with, including my own family. Tina knew it was a massive, and quite adventurous, decision for someone like me. I was very embedded into my family, sporting and work lives and I had thoroughly enjoyed this life until then. Tina asked me more than once if I was sure I was happy to go. She did not want me to leave Wollongong and regret that decision later in life. Surprisingly I did not find it a difficult decision to make. I must have been ready for a new chapter in my life.

I spoke to Mum and Dad, and they were very happy for us to go. Mum realised that families usually follow the wife's family. They were excited for us, and happy that they would still see us reasonably regularly. There were various going away parties which were both happy and sad at the same time. They reinforced the big decision that we had made. One of the toughest ones for me was the Albion Park Cricket Club farewell. This club had been an integral part of my life for the past 12 years.

My two biggest audit clients, the Illawarra Mercury and South Coast Equipment, hosted farewell lunches for me. The South Coast Equipment one was very special. Paul Newman, and the office staff, took me to a long lunch, with plenty of French champagne, at the Charcoal Tavern, a legendary Wollongong restaurant. He also gave Tina and I a Wedgewood dinner set. This was a very unexpected, luxury gift. It was also a continuation of Paul educating me on the finer points of life. I had no idea what a Wedgewood dinner set was before then. That dinner set would remain fully intact and be passed on to my daughter, Danita, many years later.

Tina flew to the Gold Coast, with the kids, about two weeks before me. She went to find a rental house and get things settled on the Coast. I was tasked with finishing everything back home. After an exhaustive month I set off to drive to the Gold Coast on Good Friday with a packed car and two dogs. I slept in the car for one night and arrived on the Gold Coast late on Saturday the 22nd of April 1984.

I arrived to find that Brad was in hospital with severe gastro. I did not know as I did not contact Tina while I was driving to the Gold Coast. He recovered quite quickly. Tina had found a great house to rent at 7 Pearl Key, Broadbeach Waters. It was a big house on a canal with a separate living area downstairs. In typical Tina style she had the house organised within a few days. Joan moved in with us and was an enormous help in those first few months.

This house started a lifetime affinity with the Broadbeach area for me. I now live about one kilometre from that first home.

We quickly settled into the Gold Coast lifestyle. I worked and Tina looked after everything else. She started researching the property market for a house we could purchase. The prices were very favourable by comparison with the Wollongong market. We had a good deposit through the profit we made selling the Albion Park Rail house.

After a few months she found a 4-bedroom, 2-bathroom house on a large block at 15 Dunkeith Avenue, Benowa. This was a real step up from our first house. We purchased it for $86,500. It was only about three kilometres from my office. Benowa was considered an outer suburb at that time. It was a very peaceful, quiet place to live. By sheer coincidence one of the guys that I worked with, Phil Cunningham, lived across the road, a few houses down. The Cunningham kids, Lisa and Jason, became very regular visitors. Jason played with the kids for hours while Lisa loved to chat with Tina. Lisa became our first babysitter on the Gold Coast.

I found a local touch football team to play in and Tina made new friends through other mothers she met at the kids' kindy. We also had a good social network with Tina's family. The Gold Coast lifestyle was very different to the Wollongong lifestyle. It was very relaxed, healthy and outdoors focused. We went to the beach every weekend. Our kids were thriving, and we didn't miss Wollongong's cold, windy winters.

Patsy had met a local guy, Scott Widdicombe. Scott was an entrepreneurial plumber. They became partners and started a family in 1983, with the arrival of their first son, David.

After settling into the Dunkeith Avenue house we received a nice surprise when Tina became pregnant again. Tina had had a copper 7 contraceptive device removed and replacing it was delayed for six weeks due to an infection. We struck the jackpot in that limited time frame. Chantal Lee was certainly meant to come along and was born on the 6th of August 1985. It was a reasonably quick, but slightly complicated birth and the doctor advised Tina not to have any more children. Danita and Brad quickly became doting older siblings.

Chantal brought great joy to our family. Somewhat surprisingly to me she brought great joy to my workplace as well. She was the first baby born to a staff member since I had started there. Tina brought her into the office quite often and everyone gushed over the baby. It helped that Chantal was a very placid, happy kid who was generally either smiling or asleep. She was quite plump, which added to the cuteness.

After Chantal was born Brad quickly became a "typical middle of three" child. I'm not sure how accurate it is but the perception then was that the middle of three is likely to be the naughtiest child. In Brad's case this was exacerbated by Danita being a very well-behaved eldest child and Chantal being the cute, adored youngest child. Also, Brad was the only boy, so he was always going to be the most mischievous of the three kids.

Haze, my close friend from the Outset football days, got married in September 1985. He had met a lady named Sue Albrecht two years earlier. The story of how they met is a good one. He went to a beach in Mackay to go fishing. He saw two topless ladies fishing. That caught his attention so, being Haze, he went up to them and asked, "are you getting any?". The ladies had quickly covered up while Haze was walking towards them. Those ladies were Sue and her sister. Haze and Sue have been together ever since.

Sue and Haze went on to have three children, Stuart, Tim and Jessica. They are like family to my family. A visit to the Hazelton farm was, and still is, a must for my kids on every trip to Wollongong.

Toni and Malcolm had a very eventful few years in the early 1980's. They had purchased their own property in Industrial Road, Oak Flats. It was an industrial property, so they were able to have a work factory and a house on it. Malcolm built the factory himself, with assistance from John and Hans. They moved their home and the Antiques Bathrooms business to this site in 1980. They expanded the business into the production of balustrades and other cement products, as well as the bathroom renovations. They also welcomed their third child, Mark, in 1981. He was born almost twelve years after their second child, Melissa.

Unfortunately, the business did not maintain the additional revenue levels required to fund the expansion. They sold the property and closed the Antiques Bathrooms business in the middle of-1983. Their marriage started to fall apart after this. They separated in July 1985.

Dianne's marriage also ended in 1986. Dianne did it very tough financially. She had four children living with her and she rented an old duplex in Botany. She then started studying to obtain a nursing diploma at Sydney University.

One of the benefits of my job was that it required considerable travel, mainly to Sydney. I regularly saw my family in Wollongong, and I tried to visit Dianne on every trip to Sydney. If we could organise it, I would include Dianne in my work dinner at the Wentworth Hotel. I always stayed there on my trips to Sydney. She enjoyed these meals, and always took her time choosing what to eat. She told me later that the real benefit for her was the adult conversation as she was either studying or looking after kids all the time.

Dianne pushed through those tough years and so did her four wonderful children, Pauline, Graeme, Belinda, and Christine. The children all pitched in at home and grew up quickly. They were a very tight knit, happy family. Belinda became like another daughter to me during this time.

Dad turned 65 in November 1986. He retired from his insurance salesman job. He had stuck with this job for 17 years. While he did enjoy his job, and the interaction with people that came with it, it was also quite stressful for Dad. It was always a commission-based job, so he had to keep selling to make money. He had also started to have some health issues by then. We understand that Mum and Dad owned their home by then and had some modest savings. They planned to live off the age pension and looked forward to a quiet, comfortable retirement.

The Lambert family was rapidly expanding. By the end of 1986 John and Barbara had three children, Hans and Diane had three children, and Terry and Rae had one child. Five siblings had started families, and there were already 17 grandchildren for Mum and Dad.

My work travel also had a significant downside as it meant I was away from home more than I wanted to be. Tina continued to carry the full load at home. She found a great Catholic primary school, St Kevin's, at Benowa. It was only a few kilometres from our home. We enrolled the kids there and Tina soon found herself heavily involved in the school community. Danita settled into school very well. She was always well behaved and did very well with her schoolwork. She made friends at school very easily.

Brad's first day at school was eventful. At the first little lunch break he, and another kid, decided not to go back into class. They found that they liked playing on the bars, so they stayed there while all the other kids went back to their classrooms. The teachers soon found them, and their playground adventure was short-lived. We did not know at the time, but this was a sign of things to come with Brad. Brad also made friends at school very easily.

Tina maintained a keen interest in the local housing market. She was very keen to build our own home and was looking for a suitable block of land to buy. My salary had increased, and we could finance a larger loan. Towards the end of 1986 she found the block she liked. It was located at 77 Cabana Boulevarde, Benowa Waters, which was only about two kilometres from our current home. It was a waterfront block with a northerly aspect, situated on Lake Capabella. We bought it for $42,000.

We sold our Dunkeith Avenue home, making a small gain and started planning our dream home. We signed a contract with Home Makers, a prominent Gold Coast building company, to construct the house. I reviewed the contract with our solicitor, Mike Webb, and met with the builder to discuss a few changes that we would like made to the contract. He agreed to the changes and at the end of the meeting he told me that I was the first purchaser to thoroughly review the contract and request changes. He really liked that as he wanted his purchasers to be satisfied.

In early 1987 we rented a house at 12 Eady Avenue, Broadbeach Waters, while our new home was being built. Again, this house is very close to where I live today. A few months after we moved into this house, I was washing our car one day. I decided to give the inside of the car a thorough clean as well. I smelt something when I started cleaning under the front seats. I reached under the driver's seat and pulled out a mushy, smelly pile of sandwiches. I called Tina to have a look. She knew immediately that they were Danita's school sandwiches.

We called Danita, who was seven years old, and she quickly admitted that she had been storing the sandwiches there because she could not eat them at school. She then told us that we had better come inside. She took us into our bedroom and asked me to reach up to the top of our wardrobe behind the clothes. I found another pile of rotting sandwiches there. Danita had decided to hide them as she thought she would get into trouble for not eating her lunch. She also could not throw them out at school as that was not allowed.

Danita recalls she could not eat them because, "they were hot and sweaty and terribly undesirable by the time the lunch break came". Danita did not get into trouble and Tina changed her lunch diet.

The house was completed around August 1987. We were both very happy with it. It was a large house with four bedrooms, a study and two large living areas. It had a large outdoor entertaining area which overlooked the lake. We had also built an upstairs granny flat for Joan. She contributed to the cost of the granny flat. Joan was a perfect mother-in-law to have living in the granny flat. She lived her life independently but was still generally available for baby-sitting duties.

As is generally the case when building a new home, we went over budget. We also planned to purchase new furniture and install a pool as soon as possible. To fund the extras, I decided to sell some of the employee shares I had in City Resources. I obtained the required approvals and sold the shares in July 1987. I think this was at least $30,000 worth of shares. This was very fortunate timing as the stock market crashed three months later and the share prices never recovered to the levels I sold for. I would never have sold the shares if we did not build that house.

The next few years were very happy in that home. The kids loved it. The neighbourhood was very safe, and the kids went exploring around the lake or visited other kids' houses. It wasn't as free as when we were kids, but it was much freer than it is today. Video machines and video cameras had been invented and were becoming common additions to households. I bought a VHS video camera on a business trip to Hong Kong. Tina put it to very good use over the subsequent years. Electronic games were also being introduced for children. Everyone with kids, including us, had a Mario Bros Nintendo game. The kids played that for hours.

Television was still the main form of entertainment in households. We were generally home on Saturday nights, and we developed a ritual based around two long running Australian television shows. We started with a barbecue dinner, which had to finish by 6.30pm. 'Young Talent Time' came on then. This was a show with talented school children singing and dancing. The kids loved it and didn't move while it was on. This was followed by 'Hey Hey It's Saturday'. It was a very funny, light entertainment show which could get very risqué. Tina and I, and most of Australia's population, loved it.

Danita and Chantal both did jazz and tap dancing after school. They played the violin and Danita also learnt the organ. Brad played various sports. He was happy to have a go at everything. I thought the sport he was best at was rugby league. He was a very good, around the legs, tackler. He also learnt the guitar for a while.

Chantal developed a daily routine with Joan. Every day she would sneak upstairs after dinner. Joan would make her a cup of tea and a slice of toast with peanut butter on it. She claimed to be still hungry. They did this for several years.

We entertained frequently in this house. Having a barbecue with 20 or 30 people was not unusual. Tina also liked to host smaller dinner parties. She was a fantastic cook and there was never a shortage of food. When we entertained Tina liked to encourage the kids to showcase their musical and dancing skills. I'm not sure the kids liked this as much as Tina did. Chantal was a little performer and her rendition of the song "Perfect" became a favourite for guests. She would only perform, however, if Danita did it with her.

I continued with my sporting interests. I played touch football and indoor cricket competitively and had a regular social game of tennis.

Throughout primary school Brad was mischievous, and his report cards consistently reminded us of that. He was also very caring, friendly, and popular. Brad was always the type of kid who would talk to the kid that was on his own. He had a natural way with people from an early age. He had a great sense of humour and loved to make people laugh. Brad was significantly better at school if he liked the teacher and the teacher understood and liked him.

When we lived at the Cabana Boulevarde house, we had dinner every night around the small table which adjoined the kitchen bench. On many occasions Brad disrupted the dinner conversation by making us all laugh. He was a master at it, and it usually ended with all of us unable to stop laughing, with tears rolling down our cheeks. When Brad did this, he usually got away with not having to eat all his vegetables. Perhaps he had that in mind as he was not the greatest eater.

By the end of the 1980's Fuji and Rita had started a family. Ossie had met a lovely young lady, Jodie Colbran, and they were getting serious. Ossie had seen Jodie at touch football at Milton years before they met; she came from Ulladulla and had moved to Albion Park for work opportunities. She lived with friends of Ossie's. Ossie and Jodie met through these friends and have been together ever since.

Toni started going to a Catholic Solo group. She met a guy named Vince O'Dwyer at a Catholic Solo night in mid-1987. Vince's wife had passed away after a battle with cancer. He had decided to try these nights as well. Toni and Vince hit it off and were married by a civil celebrant on the 1st of May 1988. Toni was not content with a civil ceremony. She was successful in having her first marriage annulled by the Catholic Church. She and Vince were then married again in the Catholic church in November 1988.

It was unusual for the Catholic church to grant annulments. Being married twice in the same Catholic church, as Toni was, was very rare. Toni and Vince were a "Brady Bunch". They had three kids each. They had some challenges along the way but before long they became a very happy, merged family.

Terry married Rae, the love of his life, in October 1987. It was another great family wedding with the reception held at Kiama Surf Club. Rae was a stunning bride and another great addition to our family. It was a memorable wedding for me. I was the master of ceremonies. I had flown in the day before the wedding and Terry gave me the run sheet for the wedding. He assumed that I would brief the respective speakers, but I assumed that he had already done that. This was a rookie error for a master of ceremonies.

I called up the first speaker and discovered that he did not know he was going to be called up. I had a quick break, briefed the rest of the speakers and it ended well. Some of the speakers told me they were happy they did not have to worry about preparing the speeches beforehand. The more impromptu speeches were great.

CHAPTER 13

THE CITY RESOURCES YEARS

— 1984 TO 1990 —

I reported for work at around 8.30am on the Tuesday after Easter 1984, as agreed with Les. I walked into the office at 42 Bundall Road, Bundall. It was a big, open plan office with no reception area. I walked over to where there were several offices along the wall and saw a good looking, blonde-haired man in one of the offices. He was sitting at his desk, with a burning cigarette in the ashtray. He looked up and said, "Who the f..k are you?" I was a little taken aback but then he smiled, and I realised he must have known I was coming.

His name was Phil Cunningham. He explained he looked after the Pizza Hut's business. The Ward group operated four Pizza Huts on the Gold Coast. Phil also said that I was way too early for Les, as he never came in before lunchtime. Phil suggested I find a desk and set myself up. By then another girl had arrived in the office. Her name was Lex Golding. She worked for the mining company, so she helped me settle in. Lex was dressed in her gym gear. Phil was also casually dressed so I thought the Gold Coast was quickly looking like the paradise it had the reputation for.

As predicted by Phil, Les arrived in the office around 1pm and took me straight to lunch. This was the first of many long lunches at the Southport Yacht club. Les went through his businesses in more detail. He told me that I should talk to Ken Tierney, from Grahame Browne & Co, as they had told Les that he needed an in-house accountant. Prior to my appointment Les had left the accounting work in their hands. During this lunch Les told me he was expanding my job across some of his other businesses. I knew I was on a very steep learning curve as Les talked about corporate structures and financing arrangements that I was unfamiliar with.

Ken Tierney sent a guy named Bruno Bamonte down to see me during that first week. Bruno had done the accounting work for the group that year. He was familiar with all the companies and the status of their accounting systems and operations. Bruno was very helpful. I found out that the Ward group's operations were growing very quickly, and the accounting systems were very basic. I had a lot of work to do. This was good old fashioned accounting work writing up manual general ledgers and other accounting records for every company.

The Ward group had diverse business investments and operations. These included a gold mining company, United Gold Pty Ltd, which had various exploration tenements as well as a mining lease for a small gold mine at Ravenswood in North Queensland. The group had several property investments. Another company housed the four operating pizza huts which were run independently by Phil, Les's brother-in-law. Pizza Hut was a mature, successful business at that time.

There was only a small office structure in place when I started. Everyone was located together in one large office. United

Gold was headed up by Laurie Johnson, a geologist, with Lex in an administrative role. The only external communication was via telephone, mail, or telex. Everyone gathered around the telex machine every morning to see what the gold price would be when the daily telex came in. Fax machines were introduced a couple of years later. They were a big step forward by providing instant written communication between third parties. Fax machines quickly became extinct when the internet was invented.

The pizza huts had a few permanent staff and there were several consultants who seemed to "come and go". These included two experienced real estate consultants, Barry Ryan, and Paul Ryland, who were constantly looking for property deals for Les.

There was a Gemini motor vehicle, which was the office car. I was given this vehicle to drive to and from work. This was a big help as it left Tina with a car all the time.

At the end of the first week there were a few drinks in the office and Phil's family came in. I met his wife, Gwen, and kids, Lisa, and Jason who would become neighbours a few months later. The Lambert's and Phil's family have been firm friends since then.

Even though Les "did not know what I was going to do," I quickly convinced him that I would need help to get everything up to date. I employed another accountant within the first six weeks. He was the first of at least 20 accountants employed across the group over the next three years. Bruno also agreed to join us about a year later in what would become a long term working and social relationship. Many years on in 2022 Bruno and I still meet to play trivia together each week.

The first accountant I employed only lasted about six weeks. The workload was too much for him. He took the petty cash float home one weekend. He left me a note saying that he could not handle the job and that he took the petty cash as his final payment. Fortunately, I had more success with subsequent recruitments.

Within the first few weeks I flew to Townsville to visit the gold mining operation at Ravenswood. It was a two-hour drive from Townsville to the mine site. Joe Hill, the mine manager, drove me there and briefed me on the status of the mining operations. I discovered that the accounting records were not up to date. This had caused problems with creditors who were chasing payments. This company became a priority for me. We were able to bring the records up to date, resolve all issues and move forward within a few months.

I became very sick on this trip. I developed a very heavy cold and became very run down. The move to Queensland, and starting work at such a brisk pace, had caught up with me. I remember lying in my hotel room in Townsville thinking to myself, "what have I done?". I was well and truly out of my comfort zone. This was a long way from the secure, predictable chartered accounting career I had envisaged for myself. These thoughts disappeared very quickly as I realised the opportunities that lay ahead with the Ward group. However, I could not have predicted just how wild the ride would become over the next six years.

Les was one of the mining entrepreneurs who emerged in the 1980's. He was an extraordinary project finder and deal maker. He had a chartered accountancy background. He had used this background to develop an unusually high level of business acumen. His main interest was mining, particularly gold mining. He was very keen to find good exploration areas for gold mining and bundle them into corporate structures that would enable their value to be realised. I quickly moved my focus to this area as Les wanted to float a gold mining company before the end of 1984. Floating a company is when you list its shares on a public stock exchange and raise capital from new shareholders. By then I had met most of the key advisors including our corporate lawyer in Sydney. I phoned the lawyer and told her that I didn't know much about floating companies. She was very helpful, gave me a crash course in floating companies, and I never looked back.

The corporate environment in Australia in the 1980's was very buoyant. It benefited significantly from the floating of the Australian dollar in 1983 by Prime Minister, Bob Hawke and Treasurer, Paul Keating. Australia quickly became more globalised. Robert Holmes à Court had emerged as Australia's first corporate raider. Many corporate entrepreneurs followed, including Alan Bond, Kerry Packer and Christopher Skase. The corporate world was alive with activity as the entrepreneurs sought out undervalued corporate targets or assets that they could include in a float. Merchant banks and corporate advisory firms emerged to assist companies with their plans. One of these merchant banks was Tricontinental. They were to become the major lender for City Resources, the first company floated by the Ward group. This corporate environment suited Les perfectly.

I found myself in a whirlwind of activity. I had early success in the financing side. Les had previously handled the financing, including managing the various bank relationships. I had met the group's local ANZ bank manager. One day Les sent me off to speak with this bank manager about a small loan that we required. I came back with a loan approval for $100,000 more than Les had requested. That was a turning point, and I gradually assumed more responsibility in this area. My initial mining accounting role had quickly turned into a Financial Controller role across the Ward group of companies.

By the end of 1984 we had taken over a listed company shell, City and Suburban Properties Limited. We floated it on the Sydney Stock Exchange through the injection of United Gold's gold mining projects and exploration properties. This company became City Resources Limited. Through a subsequent major joint venture with Esso, its mining operations became focused in Papua New Guinea (PNG).

The corporate group had grown dramatically through 1984. Staff in United Gold grew exponentially, and the group soon occupied the entire top floor of our office building. At the end of 1984 Les did his version of a performance review with me. He firstly asked me what salary I was on? I told him what it was and that it had been set by Grahame Brown & Co when I started. Les told me I was going very well and gave me a significant salary increase. He told me that he planned to keep growing the group and he had just one piece of advice for me, "Keep replacing yourself with someone better than you".

He reiterated that I would need to keep doing that if I wanted to keep pace with him on the journey ahead and remain as his "right hand man."

That advice was put to the test a few months later when we opened a Sydney office for City Resources. We were appointing a Company Secretary and we had found a very experienced, suitable candidate. He was appointed at a starting salary considerably more than mine. I had replaced myself, in that part of my role, with someone better than me. That one piece of advice enabled me to better understand the benefits of good delegation, and significantly aided my future corporate career.

One of the young ladies who worked in the Sydney office, Liz Specker, decided to move to the Gold Coast. She became the ideal Executive Assistant for both Les and I. She also went on to marry one of the auditors, Kevin Rodgers. Tina and I attended the weddings of both Liz and Lex about five years later.

I made several trips to Papua New Guinea during the early City Resources years. These trips included project inspections, meetings with staff, and dealing with financial and accounting matters. I had several memorable experiences on these trips. One day a group of us were catching several helicopters to visit an exploration site deep in the jungle. I was about to board a helicopter when my shirt was pulled from behind. It was our exploration geologist and he told me that the pilot of this helicopter had "too many accidents". He directed me to another helicopter. Fortunately, there were no helicopter accidents during my time with City Resources.

On another occasion I attended a dinner that was hosted by Esso, our joint venture partner. We were staying at a hotel in Lae. The dinner was held at the Esso staff compound situated about ten kilometres from Lae. There were a group of us at the dinner and I volunteered to drive home as I did not drink much at the dinner. The same exploration geologist sat in the passenger seat of the car that I was driving. We were about halfway back to Lae when he told me not to slow down or stop the car under any circumstances. A few minutes later I could see a group of people on the road ahead, starting to signal for me to slow down. I took his advice and kept driving at the same speed. They stayed on the road until they could see I was not going to slow down. They then jumped aside, and I drove straight through. The geologist told me that we would have been robbed, or worse, if I had stopped. I should note that there were also many great times with the locals in Papua New Guinea.

After one trip I had returned home, and Tina was washing my clothes from the trip. She found a leech, which I had unwittingly transported from the jungles of Papua New Guinea to the Gold Coast.

In 1986 the Board of City Resources decided to consider floating a company on the Hong Kong stock exchange. I was involved in the planning and analysis of this float. A group of us went to Hong Kong for the final negotiations and preparations for the float of City Resources (Asia) Limited. We were there for around ten days. It was nonstop meetings, negotiations, and dinners. By the last day we had reached agreement with the brokers, underwriters, and corporate advisors to proceed with the float.

It was both a successful and very exhausting trip, so it was decided to upgrade our flights home to first class. I was very excited as I had never flown first class before. We boarded the plane, settled into our seats and I thought I would have a brief nap before dinner and drinks arrived. I reclined my seat, closed my eyes and was woken up by the air hostess eight hours later telling me to prepare for landing. I had slept the entire flight and missed the first class experience. I can report, however, that it was easy to sleep in first class.

City Resources continued to grow significantly through 1985 and 1986. It had developed a significant portfolio of exploration projects, mainly through the Esso joint venture. Several of these projects were advancing in maturity and value as promising drilling results were achieved. Exploration projects had also been secured in Fiji and Vanuatu. We had commissioned the construction of a large vessel to service the projects in the Pacific islands. I was now travelling to Fiji and Vanuatu as well.

City Resources also expanded corporately. The float of City Resources (Asia) Limited was finalised. This was followed by the successful float of City Resources (Canada) Limited. These companies were run independently with their own boards, projects and funds but were linked to City Resources through shareholdings.

By 1986 we had formed a Pizza Hut touch football team. A group of people from work played, including Bruno Bamonte. We recruited a young solicitor, Mike Webb, who worked at Short, Punch & Greatorix, our legal firm. Mike is still my solicitor today. Kevin Rodgers, from our audit firm, provided some much-needed try scoring ability. Brian Kidd, who was Lex Golding's boyfriend, and Jason Cunningham, at 15 years old, rounded out the team. Kevin, Bruno, Brian and I would go on to play an annual game of golf together for the next thirty years. Kevin reminded me recently that I still hold the try scoring record for the team, with six tries in one game.

Ossie was a bit miffed when I told him I had scored six tries in one game as he had just scored five tries in one game in his competition. He went on to surpass me with seven tries in one game. Then his sons, Jacob, and Nicholas, went on to surpass Ossie's record. He got miffed again. Ossie and his three sons are all very good, high level, touch players.

We also formed a Pizza Hut indoor cricket team. Once again it comprised a group of people from work, plus Mike Webb, Brian Kidd, and Jason Cunningham. We won the competition in our first year.

I unintentionally created some entertainment, at my expense, after one game. I was fielding close to the batsman and was hit in the genitals by a ball travelling at full speed off the bat. I managed to get home, albeit very sore. As luck would have it, Tina was hosting a Tupperware party that night and there were about a dozen ladies there when I walked in very gingerly. Tina was busy so I went to the medical cabinet and found a tube of Deep Heat cream. I was desperate for some pain relief, so I went into the bedroom and rubbed the Deep Heat into my genital area where I had been hit. I did not read the instructions and did not know that Deep Heat should not be applied to that area. My pain level quickly rose as the deep heat took effect. I had to go into the lounge room and tell Tina what had happened in front of all the ladies. While there was some sympathy the room erupted into laughter, with Tina leading the way. I did recover ok.

The Ward private group was also growing rapidly. By 1986 we had purchased the Magic Mountain amusement park at Nobby

Beach, Gold Coast. This was an opportune purchase, made for the long-term property development potential of the site. It was an operating amusement park when we purchased it, so it became another asset we had to manage. It was quite run down and its days as an amusement park were numbered. We operated it for a couple of years until it became too difficult to break even. It was great for our kids as they had multiple visits to the park and never tired of the various attractions. Magic Mountain was a Gold Coast icon, and it was quite sad when we had to close it down

The group also secured an interest in the Castaway Island resort in Fiji. This was an idyllic resort that was also run down and needed an upgrade. I travelled to Fiji several times and was able to incorporate a couple of family holidays into my trips. The kids loved it, particularly sampling the wonderful Fijian culture.

Around 1986 we floated another company. We had purchased a company shell called Mangrovite Industries Limited (Mangrovite) and relisted it on the Sydney Stock Exchange. I became a Director of this company. The intention was that Mangrovite would focus on property investment and development. This company made some astute, opportunistic property purchases including several parcels of land situated on the islands at the north end of the Gold Coast. We had considerable interaction with the local and State governments in relation to these properties. I met the legendary Queensland premier, Joh Bjelke-Petersen, several times. He was a larger-than-life character and lived up to his reputation.

I found myself in the position of spokesperson for Mangrovite. This included appearing in a front page story for the local paper, the Gold Coast Bulletin. I was not comfortable being a media spokesperson and extricated myself from this role as quickly as I could. Mangrovite remained a relatively small, listed company and did not expand like City Resources had.

With the continuing growth I travelled regularly and sometimes was required to travel at short notice. On one occasion I, and a couple of work colleagues, had to get to an important meeting in Sydney. The only way to get there on time was to catch a flight from Brisbane. We did not have time to drive to Brisbane. One of Les's sons was a helicopter pilot, and he had a helicopter available. He flew us to Brisbane and dropped us off right near the plane that we had to catch. I felt like I was in a movie that day.

By 1987 we had refurbished the entire 42 Bundall Road office building. It was an upmarket refurbishment in line with the corporate environment in the 1980's. City Resources and the Ward private group occupied almost all the building. My office was massive and contained a Boardroom table. The offices were a hive of activity as City Resources and the other companies were continuing to expand. The economy was buoyant.

Tina's cousin, Cheryl Webster, had joined the staff of City Resources as a "Girl Friday", as in someone who does all the general office tasks. Cheryl had worked in jewellery all her life and had no experience in office work. She took to it, like a duck to water, and soon became an invaluable, popular staff member. She did anything for anyone and became like a mother hen in the office. Cheryl's husband, John, had taken up the cleaning contracts for all the offices. He also assisted with general office matters.

Cheryl decided to organise Friday drinks every week. This initially started as City Resources, but soon expanded to include the other companies as well. These Friday drinks are now some of my greatest memories of those times. We already had a very good culture but these drinks, and various other social activities, enhanced the culture further. Cheryl and John were at the core of this great culture. Tina and the kids came down for the Friday drinks, as did other families. This really helped when you were spending so much time at work.

Tina and I flew down to Wollongong for Terry and Rae's wedding, on the 17th of October 1987. Despite being away Les managed to track me down over that weekend and told me the stock market was anticipating a significant fall in share prices the following Monday. He asked me to stay in Sydney on Monday and not return to the Gold Coast after the wedding as initially planned.

Tina flew home, with all our clothes, on Monday morning and I went to Sydney to City Resources' office. I expected to be flying home that night. As soon as the stock market opened there were spectacular falls in share prices exactly as Les had warned. We were witnessing what became known as Black Monday in the 1987 stock market crash. All share prices were affected. Overall, the Australian share market fell by more than forty per cent in October.

The prices of speculative mining companies, such as City Resources, fell much more than forty per cent. By the end of that week the shares of City Resources had fallen by over eighty per cent. They never recovered. I was the only finance executive in Sydney and made appointments to see our various banks, advisers, and solicitors. The dramatic fall in share prices caused immediate issues for loans that had been secured by shares, and further issues relating to confidence in the market. I was 34 years old and in the middle of a corporate crisis.

We got through the week. Les attended to high level issues from the Gold Coast. I stayed in Sydney to go to the necessary meetings and meet with staff. Things stabilised by the end of the week and we survived without any loan defaults. I had to buy extra clothes throughout the week and finally got home on Friday night.

The stock market crash affected all our businesses, except for the Pizza Hut operations. There was an air of doom and gloom after the buoyant years of the early and mid 1980's. The banks immediately became very conservative and sought loan repayments. New loans were virtually impossible to obtain. We had to dramatically revise all our corporate plans.

I also became aware that several staff members were directly affected by the stock market crash. They had taken out margin loans to finance share purchases and were being called upon to either repay or top up their loans. I did not have any margin loans and was not directly affected. It was sad to witness some of these dramatic events caused by the stock market crash.

After a period of consolidation, the Board of City Resources acted. They realised that they needed a "big brother" to provide the funds required to bring their various exploration assets to production. A deal was struck for Barrack Mines, a successful Western Australia gold mining company, to take over City Resources, subject to shareholder and regulatory approvals. I remember that we worked through the night for two consecutive nights to prepare for and then execute all the documents for this transaction. The boardroom table was covered with documents that required signatures.

With the sale of City Resources, and a worsening economic climate, the private group also began to wind down. Staff numbers in the Bundall Rd offices decreased. The halcyon days of the 1980's were well and truly over. One of the victims of the 1987 stock market crash was Tricontinental, our major financier, which collapsed in the 1990's.

The 1980's are looked upon as a period of corporate excess and unsustainable hype. There were many boom-and-bust scenarios. I am pleased that I lived and worked through it and came through relatively unscathed financially. It was hard work, exhilarating, stressful and challenging. There were many exciting times for Tina and I and the family. There were many valuable lessons that I took into my future career. The main corporate lesson was that all companies should have solid core businesses that provide the desired return to shareholders. Companies that rely on the "blue sky" future value of assets or worse still, on inflated asset values, should be regarded as highly speculative and treated with caution.

The Outset rugby league team in 1972. Standing (L-R) Me, John Keys, John Bout, Ken McInerney, John Lambert, Peter Waugh, Max Hazelton, Bruce Gorton, Bernie Livermore, Tony Bulters, Michael Raftery, Col Purcell, Bert Smith. Front row (L-R) – Bill Bulters, Neil Paget, Ken Tate, Mick Keys, Mark O'Neill, Mick Baldwin

Family photo at John and Barbara's wedding in March 1973. This is the earliest photo I could find with our entire family of eleven in it. Back (L-R) Toni, Fuji, Me, Mum, John, Barbara, Dad, Dianne, Hans. Middle (L-R) Steve, Ossie, Terry. Front – (L-R) Melissa, Tracey (Toni's children)

Mine and Fuji's first holiday, to Queensland, in 1971. (L-R) Peter (Suicide) Graham, Me, Swampy. Front - Fuji

My first car, the Volkswagen Beetle, with me, Max (Haze) Hazelton and Steve, in 1974

The Outset players at John and Barbara's wedding in March 1973. Barbara is "the rose among the thorns" here. Back (L-R) Geoff King, Bob Jego, Steve Dowd, Swampy, Neil Paget, John, Barbara, Me, Chips, Suicide, Bernie Livermore, Paul (Grub) Graham. Front (L-R) John Bulters, Fuji, Mick Keys, Ken Tate, Hans

The bridal party at our wedding in September 1977. (L-R) Joanne McDonald, Hans, Patsy, Me, Tina, Fuji, Anne Miller, John

Photo of the Kaylaur Crescent house in 1974 with John's flashy Holden car in the driveway. I am on the porch with Steve, Terry and Adrian.

Tina and I at our engagement party, February 1976. (L-R) Martin (Tina's father), Joan (Tina's mother), Tina, Me, Mum

Mum handing out the Xmas presents in December 1981

Dad with Brad on Dad's 61st birthday and Brad's first birthday in November 1982. Dad kept this photograph next to his chair until they left the Kaylaur Crescent home.

Seven brothers keep in touch. Headline of an article in the Illawarra Mercury on 24 December 1981, accompanied by this photograph. Front to back – John, Fuji, Steve, Terry, Hans, Ossie, Me

The family home that we built at 77 Cabana Boulevarde, Benowa in 1987. Brad, Joan and Danita are in the foreground

Fuji and Rita's wedding in February 1984. There are too many to name. It was a big wedding!

Family photo at Mum and Dad's 40th wedding anniversary in February 1986. (L-R) Steve, Ossie, Terry, Dianne, Me, Fuji, Hans, John, Toni, Mum, Dad

A portrait of my family in 1988. (L-R) Danita, Me, Chantal, Tina, Brad

My Oma, Dad's mother, with Tina and I on our trip to the Netherlands in 1978. This is the only photo I ever had with a grandparent.

A great, relaxed photo of Mum and Dad circa 1989

Me sitting at my desk at work in 1988 in the heady corporate years. I had a very large office with a private garden.

The four oldest boys playing cards, euchre, in June 1989, with the obligatory plate of chips. (L-R) John, Me, Fuji, Hans

Mum and Dad with Tina and my kids in March 1990. This photo highlights how Tina liked to dress the kids!. (L-R) Brad, Dad, Danita, Tina, Chantal, Mum

The seven Lambert brothers having fun at Terry's buck show in October 1987. This photo epitomises how well we all get along. (L-R) Fuji, Steve, John, Me, Ossie, Terry, Hans

All the runners after the 1993 race in their Lambert t-shirts. (L-R) Joe Cachia, Bob Jego, John, Vince, Danita, Me, Steve Whelan, Ossie, Hans. In Front – Chantal, Brad

Mum and Dad's 50th wedding anniversary celebration in February 1996. Mum and Dad with all their grandchildren

Mum and Dad and their children at the 50th wedding anniversary celebration. The siblings are in age order from the eldest down. (L-R) Toni, John, Hans, Fuji, Me, Dianne, Terry, Ossie, Steve

Before the 1991 Gold Coast Half Marathon, the first race we did together. (L-R) Ross Patterson (friend), John, Ossie, Me, Vince

Hans doing the Music Man at the 50th wedding anniversary celebration.

Brad's 18th birthday celebration in November 1999. (L-R) Me, Danita, Chantal, Tina, Brad

CHAPTER 14

SINGLE PARENTHOOD AND FAMILY MARATHONS

— THE 1990'S —

My role with the City Resources group ended in the early 1990's as the various businesses were sold or wound up. The economic environment was worsening with Australia going into a recession at the end of 1990.

Chantal started school in 1991. Tina had been out of the workforce for eleven years. She had become interested in opening a children's clothing store. She researched this industry and came across a brand called Coco Kidz. She went to Sydney to meet the owners who were operating a store at Darling Harbour and were keen to expand with other business partners. Their stock was a combination of their own Coco Kidz brand and some imported brands. Tina liked the stock range and thought it would sell well on the Gold Coast.

We decided on a 50/50 partnership arrangement with the owners to open a Coco Kidz shop at Pacific Fair Shopping Centre in Broadbeach, Gold Coast. This was a bold move as Pacific Fair was, and still is, the pre-eminent shopping centre on the Gold Coast. Rents were very expensive, so we rented a very small shop. The shop opened on the 5th of November 1990. The timing was perfect to capture the Christmas period trade and the shop was a success from the start. Tina looked after the operational side of the business. She was a natural retailer, with a particular skill at presenting the store to optimise the prospects of selling. I looked after the accounting and financial side of the business.

With Tina working and me having more time available, I was able to help more on the home front. This was a big shock initially. When Tina went to Sydney for a weekend of Coco Kidz training, I discovered that I did not know how to use either the dishwasher or the washing machine. I had to call Tina for instructions.

I decided to look for business consulting work as I did not have time for a full-time job. I used my corporate contacts and found some small consulting jobs before a larger one came in. This was to assist one of the Gold Coast's listed companies, Gordon Pacific, wind down and enter a scheme of arrangement. They had been a successful property development company but had been severely affected by the economic downturn in the early 1990's. The "Girl Friday" at Gordon Pacific was a very friendly, energetic lady named Mandi Read. I managed to recruit Mandi, about five years later, to a company I worked with. We have been firm friends ever since.

Around this time our next door neighbour, Liz Speirs, started dating a very friendly, energetic American guy, Bill Clift. We met Bill through Liz, who became Liz Clift, and they have both been in my life ever since. Bill taught Brad how to sail in the little lake behind our houses. Bill and I have had many deep and meaningful conversations. He has been a special friend.

In early 1990 one of my work colleagues, Robert Knight, told me that he ran in the Gold Coast Half Marathon the previous year and was about to start training for the 1990 race. He encouraged me to give it a go. I did and started training with Robert and one of his friends. I completed my first half marathon, 21 kilometres, in July 1990 with a time of around 1 hour 53 minutes. The last four kilometres were excruciating. Robert ran with me and brought me home. I was equally thrilled and exhausted at the end of the race. I decided that I would prepare much better if I ran another one.

After that race I talked to my brother, Hans, about the half marathon. Hans regularly jogged for fitness and had done some running in the Wollongong area. Hans then started talking to my other brothers in Wollongong. A few of them, as well as Toni's husband Vince, decided to start planning to run in the 1991 Gold Coast Half Marathon. This started a tradition which lasted until 2011.

The Lamberts again showed that they just "get on with it". Around February 1991 they started training for the 1991 Gold Coast Half Marathon. I also trained from February. I planned my training and ran more long distance training runs than I had the previous year.

There was a welcome interruption to everyone's training on the 22nd of June 1991, when Ossie and Jodie got married. It was another beautiful family wedding, with the reception held at Albion Park Bowling Club. Jodie had already firmly entrenched herself into the family, but it was still great that it was official.

Ossie went on his honeymoon, then came to the Gold Coast to run his first half marathon.

The race was held in July 1991. John, Hans, Steve, and Vince joined Ossie on the Gold Coast for the race. They all stayed at our place at Cabana Boulevarde. It was a great weekend of bonding, carbohydrate loading and card games. There was plenty of nervous energy expended before the race as it would be everyone's, except mine, first half marathon.

The day came and we all rose early as the race started at 6am. Tina and the kids got up as well and came as the support crew. It was a very cold day, which was good for marathon running, but not so great for Tina and the kids. The race went well for most of us. Hans finished first out of our group with a time of one hour, 45 minutes, with Vince second in one hour, 47 minutes. I finished in one hour 51 minutes, a slight improvement on the previous year. Everyone except John finished in their targeted time range.

John had run the race at his own pace, and even had time to stop for an orange when he saw Tina and the kids at the halfway point. After I finished the race, I was completely exhausted and could not have walked another 100 metres. I saw Hans and he asked me if I knew how far back John was. Hans still looked comparatively fresh. He then told me that he was going to jog back, look for John and run back with him. He did that and found John about five kilometres from the finish line. John was exhausted and was alternating between walking and jogging slowly. Sure enough, Hans guided him home and John finished in two hours 51 minutes. This was still a commendable time and he beat plenty of runners' home. He found out later that some medication he was taking contributed to his slower time. After the race John said that he wasn't sure if he would have finished the race if Hans did not come and get him. This action epitomised Hans's character.

Through the preparation for, and the running of this first half marathon we learnt that nothing had changed regarding sport with the Lambert brothers. Hans was the best prepared, most professional, and fastest runner out of the brothers. He was very tough mentally and I don't think he realised how good he was at distance running.

Everyone loved that first half marathon, both for the race itself and for the opportunity to have a brotherly catch up on the Gold Coast. We all found that running was a bit addictive, which is weird because it was also painful and boring. Everyone was keen to do it again in 1992 and by then a few more friends from Wollongong joined the group. Steve Whelan, Tracey's husband, also ran.

A few weeks before the 1992 race I hurt my left knee playing touch football. I went to my local doctor. She was not worried about the knee but noticed that my right ankle looked swollen and not right. She sent me off for x-rays which revealed that the main ligament in my ankle had torn many years before, and never properly healed. It had caused my ankle to shift out of position, and it had grown an outer casing to protect the injury. She was surprised that I could walk - let alone run! She referred me to an ankle specialist who recommended an operation called a calcaneal osteotomy. The specialist also told me that I could run the 1992 race, if I still wanted to, as I would not damage the ankle any further. I decided to run.

We all ran the 1992 race and improved our times. I had trained harder for this one. I found a good training partner, my work colleague Michael Gordon, and we were aiming to do a five minute per kilometre pace. Our target time was 1 hour 45 minutes. I ran with Michael for about 17 kilometres when I started to fade. He ran on and I struggled home but missed my target time, finishing in 1 hour, 46 minutes, 5 seconds. This was to become a significant time as Ossie tried to beat it for the following 10 years.

This was the last race I ran. I had the operation a few weeks later and it was a failure. My ankle did not shift back to its correct position as the surgeon had planned. Not only was the operation a failure it left my ankle worse than it was prior to the operation. I could not run after the operation so my days of running, touch football and tennis were over. After a while I could walk without a limp, but not long distances, and I could still manage a game of golf. I changed my exercise regime to swimming and gym work. Whilst I did miss the various sporting activities, I knew that I was responsible for my wonky ankle and I decided to focus on what I could do, rather than what I couldn't do.

A significant birth occurred in the family in 1992. Terry and Rae's second child, Byron, was born on the 9th of February 1992 when Rae was 26 weeks pregnant. He weighed 740 grams and was in hospital for 14 weeks before they were able to bring him home. Terry recalls that he placed his wedding ring over Byron's arm, and it slid up to his shoulder. Byron is now a happy, healthy 30-year-old man.

The Coco Kidz store was going well so we decided to open a second store in Brisbane. We settled on a good location in the Myer Centre, just near the Queen Street mall entrance. This time we owned the store one hundred per cent and agreed on a royalty fee arrangement with the Coco Kidz owners. Tina became much busier as she went to Brisbane at least three days a week to work in that store. That store was also profitable but not as successful as the Pacific Fair store. I maintained accurate, manual accounting records for each store. All sales were recorded.

We operated both stores successfully until late 1992. We were then approached by a business broker to inform us they had a buyer interested in purchasing the Pacific Fair store. We discussed this approach with our partners. We all agreed that if we could get a good price we would sell. We did just that. We sold the store for a goodwill figure more than $100,000, plus stock. It was a very profitable store for us and our partners.

We then decided to sell the Brisbane store as well. We sold it to one of the staff members. We did not make a goodwill profit on this sale. We felt that this store needed more local, hands-on management. Overall, we had done very well from our Coco Kidz stores. Tina was ready for a well-earned break.

The 1993 Gold Coast Marathon race came along in July that year. We hosted everyone at our place again. I was still heavily involved even though I could no longer participate. I felt quite wistful on the morning of the race. However, I also found that I thoroughly enjoyed being a spectator. That year we decided to have special Lambert themed T-Shirts made for everyone. The Lambert names given were:

"John – Lighter Lambert.
Hans – Legendary Lambert.
Me – Local Lambert.
Ossie – Lounge Lizard Lambert.

Vince, Brother-in-law – Lucky Lambert.

Bob Jego, Friend – Lured Lambert.

Joe Cachia, Friend – Latched on Lambert.

Danita – Lively Lambert.

Brad – Laughing Lambert.

Chantal – Littlest Lambert."

To be fair to Ossie he probably got the Lounge Lizard description because we had run out of adjectives starting with L. He has always been very active, and never a lounge lizard. I am very pleased in hindsight that we called Hans "Legendary Lambert" because that summed him up perfectly.

The Sunday Telegraph newspaper photographed us in our t-shirts and ran quite a large article featuring us on the day of the race. My children, Danita, Brad, and Chantal competed in the shorter distance power walks that year. In 1993 the Lambert Trophy was instigated. This was organised by Hans and Ossie. The trophy was awarded to the most outstanding performance each year. It was voted upon by everyone participating, including me. The inaugural winner was John. He completed the 1993 race in one hour, 58 minutes and improved his time from 1991 by almost one hour. Hans and Ossie became multiple winners of the trophy.

In 1994 Hans, Vince and Joe Cachia ran the marathon. Unbelievably Joe and Vince tied in a time of 3:36:43. They were competitive until the last stride, jostling each other as they rounded the final turn. They were jointly awarded the Lambert Trophy that year.

Hans, Ossie, and Steve Whelan all went on to race more than ten half marathons. They all received the coveted "Gold Coast Half Marathon 10 Year Club T-Shirt".

In 2002 Ossie ran the half marathon in a time of one hour, 46 minutes, 15 seconds. This was to be his fastest time and he missed out on beating my best time by 10 seconds. He got miffed again. Ossie was kind enough to do some research on the half marathons for this book. He discovered that 1:46:15 was his clock time and 1:46:03 was his net time. He then called me proudly claiming victory as he had beaten my best time by two seconds. I then did my research and found that my time was a clock time only as net times were not recorded in 1992. I think an objective assessment would still grant me victory. And yes, the Lamberts are a bit competitive!

Tina continued to monitor the housing market. In 1993 she suggested we sell the Cabana Boulevarde house and find an acreage block to build on. She was very keen to build another house and we both thought an acreage block would be great for the kids. We had mixed feelings about leaving Cabana Boulevarde as it was a great house in a great location.

Tina found a great block of land in Handel Avenue, Worongary. It was about one acre, in a gated estate, and had sweeping views of the Gold Coast. We sold Cabana Boulevarde, rented a house in Sorrento for six months, and built a large, sprawling house on the block. Patsy's husband, Scott Widdicombe, was a builder by then and he built the house. He won a building award for the house. We moved into the house in 1994.

The kids loved the open space and soon found other kids to play with in the estate. Danita and Brad did not have to change schools as we now lived closer to their high school, St Michael's College. Chantal stayed at St Kevin's, Benowa until the end of 1994.

Brad was starting to display some behaviours which we later identified as mental health concerns. After he started high school

Tina and I noticed signs of difficulty at school. He was getting into trouble with teachers, mainly for being inattentive and disruptive in classes. He was also becoming naughtier at home and outside of school. Brad complained of "voices in his head" a few times. He also complained of stomach pains.

Tina took Brad to the doctor several times. They checked for allergies. Mental health issues were not raised by the doctors in those early visits. We did not obtain any clarity that Brad had a mental health illness until a couple of years later. Despite his naughtiness Brad was a very popular, active kid. He mixed with people very well and made friends easily.

I had picked up a consulting role with a Japanese company, called Maruko. Maruko was the developer of the Rivage Royale residential high rise building in Southport. It was a very luxurious development and had cost more than $100m to construct. My first task was to manually reconstruct the construction costs to be able to determine an accurate cost to allocate to each unit. It took me six months to complete this task. I then stayed on as the part-time accountant until the building was sold out several years later.

I travelled to Tokyo on one occasion for various Maruko meetings. Just visiting Tokyo was great, and I also had a few memorable experiences while I was there. On the first night I was there we worked until very late, around eight o'clock. Then a few of the guys from the office took me to dinner. We had dinner and then went to a bar. They all drank very freely. At the end of work the next day I told the guys I was happy to look after myself so they could go home to their families. I planned to have a quick dinner, check out a bit of Tokyo and get to bed early. They then told me that they go out, like the previous night, after work every night. Their culture was to work hard and play hard. One of them had a two-hour train trip to and from work each day.

On the last day I was there we went to lunch at a local restaurant. There was no alcohol consumed. At the end of lunch, a karaoke machine appeared. As the guest of honour, I was expected to do the first song. There I was nervously singing an Elvis Presley song in the middle of the day, with a group of serious, sober Japanese work colleagues. I'm pleased that my performance was not recorded.

On another occasion a group of the senior Maruko executives were in Australia to check on the progress of the Rivage Royale sales. A meeting was scheduled on their last day to discuss all aspects of the project. I attended part of the meeting, presented the financial report, and answered questions, through an interpreter. They smiled and thanked me at the end of my report. When the meeting had finished the executives left, and I spoke with the Japanese lady who oversaw the Australian operations. She spoke English very well. I said to her something like, "Well that seemed to go well, they looked very happy". Her response was "They have got the shits Gerry". The executives were not happy with the progress of the project, but their culture was still to be polite and friendly.

Our very competent bookkeeper at Maruko was a lady named Dianne Edwards. I recruited Dianne to a company I worked with several years later. We have been firm friends ever since. A couple of years ago I attended her wedding to her long-term partner, John Gundry.

Whilst Scott Widdicombe was building our house, we discussed forming a property development company together. We sourced a Singaporean investor and formed a company called Pacific Villas. We each injected $100,000 in capital into the company. Our first project was a three storey walk up, unit project in Peninsula Drive, Surfers Paradise. This was a significant project and we required additional equity funds for the project. The Singaporean investor sourced the additional funding, and we completed the project. It was moderately successful. It was completed on time and on budget, but the sales lingered. Eventually we sold out, but we did not make the profit that we had forecast.

We did some further house and land projects, including six houses on land owned by the Robina Bowls club. The property market was sluggish. The property development business was struggling to make money. It was stressful. I had a full workload with Maruko, Pacific Villas, and several smaller consulting jobs.

There were ongoing disputes with the Singaporean partner. After a couple of years, I sold my interest back to Scott and decided to focus on business consulting.

A wonderful thing happened in our family in July 1994. It started with our usual family gathering for the Gold Coast marathon. By this time Steve had decided not to become a Christian Brother and was a catholic schoolteacher at Innisfail, North Queensland. Steve came for the weekend, although he was not competing in the race that year. He bought a male friend with him for the weekend. This male friend was clearly gay. I thought nothing of that, but

Tina did. She told me that she thought Steve was trying to tell us something. I was still none the wiser.

Unbeknown to us Steve had written a letter to Mum and Dad earlier in 1994 to let them know that he was gay. Dianne also knew and they all kept it confidential until July 1994. Steve spoke to Mum after that marathon weekend and said it was time for everyone in the family to know that he was gay. He had thought that we all should have known by now, but he decided to make sure. Steve indicated that both Mum and Dad were one hundred per cent supportive. Mum was very happy for Steve that he could now come out and get on with his life. Dad was also totally supportive, and in typical Lambert fashion always had something funny to say about it.

By sheer coincidence I was in Wollongong later that week and all the siblings, except Steve, were at a gathering at John and Barbara's place. By that time Steve had spoken to most, but not all the siblings. Steve then called and asked to speak to all the siblings individually. We were all in the room so we could hear one side of each conversation. All the conversations were supportive and quite serious until it came to Fuji's turn. He grabbed the phone and said to Steve, "Well we have tried two brothers-in-law and they didn't work out, so can you please find us a good one". Fuji was referring to the fact that Toni and Dianne were both divorced by then.

Fuji's words were spot on as they were both humorous and reflected total acceptance. The rest of the conversations were great, and Steve was very happy that everyone knew at last. The support and acceptance were unanimous. And Steve did exactly what Fuji asked him to do. He met his life partner, Justin Cooper, in 2001 and they are still together.

After Steve came out it became obvious to us that he was gay. I had never considered that he could be gay prior to that, which is perhaps a reflection of my naivety. Steve had received female attention all his life and, interestingly, he still received female attention after he came out. In hindsight it may be regrettable that Steve did not come out to his family until he was 31 years of age. He had his reasons for that, the main one being that it could have jeopardised his career as a catholic schoolteacher. He became increasingly open when he knew it would not affect his employment.

He has had a wonderful life with his family and friends since that time. While he has experienced his share of bigotry and homophobia, he has let us know that there has never been anything other than full support from his family. Steve and Justin became officially engaged on the day that same sex marriage was legislated in Australia on the 9th of December 2017.

Around the middle of 1994 Tina got a call from her father, Martin, to let her know that he might have cancer. He had retired from his job several years earlier but had never stopped working. He had started selling loads of rocks from the Dunmore farms. He loaded the rocks by hand onto his utility by himself. It was very hard, manual work. I was in Wollongong the weekend after Tina got this phone call. I took Brad down as he was to be the godfather for Ossie and Jodie's first child, Jacob, that weekend. Martin was in hospital, so I went to see him with Brad.

I walked into the ward and Martin saw me from a distance. He yelled out, "Over here Charlie, I'm riddled." Martin called everyone Charlie. This was the start of a very difficult six months for

Tina and Patsy. It became clear quickly that Martin had terminal cancer, and Tina decided to spend as much time as possible with him. She came home every four weeks, for a couple of weeks. I looked after the home front, as best I could. To top it off our dog, Cindy, had a litter of six pups and our cat, Lucy, had a litter of kittens. Fortunately, Tina was home for both births.

This was a very stressful period, with Martin's illness, Tina being away, looking after the kids and doing all the domestic stuff. One night after all the kids were in bed I went outside and sat on the floor of the back verandah. I wanted some quiet time, and I sat there looking at our fantastic view. I had been sitting for about five minutes when Cindy emerged from her kennel, a few metres away. She came and sat across my lap. She put her head down and went to sleep. A magical thing then happened. The six pups came out of the kennel one by one and followed Cindy. They all lay in a perfect row across my legs, from my waist to my ankles. They all stayed perfectly still and went to sleep. I felt like they could sense my tension and were reassuring me. I also stayed perfectly still and left them there for about fifteen minutes. This was a very powerful experience for me, witnessing this level of intelligence and empathy in dogs.

Martin passed away on the 22nd of December 1994 at 69 years of age. There was an unexpected consequence from this stressful period when our marriage broke up in early 1995. I won't go into any private details of this other than to say the end outcome was a good one for all of us. Tina and I settled the financial matters quickly and amicably. There were no child support payments determined by formulas and income levels; we determined and agreed these figures ourselves. We liaised very well in all matters regarding the kids. There were no strict custody arrangements. The kids could basically stay where they wanted to.

Chantal changed schools at the beginning of 1995. She went to King's Christian College, Reedy Creek, as it was much closer to our house at Worongary. She was nine years old, and it was daunting for her to start a new school without knowing anyone in her class. The timing also wasn't great as the marriage break up had occurred during those Christmas holidays. On her first day she was eating alone at the lunch break when a girl came up to her and asked her to join her group. That girl's name was Nicole Ambrose, now Nicole Anderson, and they have been best friends ever since.

1995 was a tough year for me as I adapted to a single life. Whilst I had not contemplated life as a single parent, I adapted to it reasonably quickly. I did have some stressful and emotional times, but I am a person of routine and that helped me. I developed new routines around work, kids and domestic duties and just got on with it. Danita was a huge help when she was at my place. She was already a good cook and very responsible for her age. I rented a couple of houses before I was able to buy a property again. Brad lived with me most of the time and the girls generally spent every weekend at my place. Cindy, the dog, also lived with me and Brad.

The second house I rented was in Tarbert Close, Carrara. We had a wonderful neighbour, named Clarrie, next door. If it looked like it was raining and I had washing on the line, she would get it off the line and have it neatly folded for me in the garage. All the kid's friends loved that house. I wasn't the strictest parent and generally had some junk food on hand, which the kids all loved.

Danita's best friend, Linda, and her sisters, Natalie, and Bianca were frequent visitors. Chantal and Bianca became best friends as well. I could have four or five extras sleeping over on weekends.

When it was time to leave that house and go to a unit, I gave Cindy to Clarrie and her husband. They adored that dog and she lived very happily with them for the next ten years until she passed away.

After our marriage break up Brad lived with me most of the time. In hindsight I realised that this was very important for me. I had never lived on my own and I don't think I would have enjoyed living on my own at that point in my life.

Brad was 13 years old then, in his first year at high school, and one night when it was just the two of us at home, I thought that we should have the father and son talk about the "birds and bees". I was cooking a BBQ and I suggested to Brad that we should have a talk about sex. Brad said, "can we wait until after dinner?". After dinner we were both doing the dishes and I asked Brad if this was a good time. He said yes and then said, "what would you like to know Dad?".

I learnt a fair bit. He said he already knew all about sex and that about one third of the kids in his grade at school were already sexually active. (I didn't ask for more details of this!). I never get to tell Brad anything about sex. This is one of my all-time favourite Brad memories.

When he was 15 years old, I took him to Wollongong for a family visit. We visited Haze's farm which Brad loved. During this visit Haze's wife, Sue, took me aside and suggested that I get Brad checked for Attention Deficit Disorder (ADD) or Attention Deficit Hyperactivity Disorder (ADHD). Sue had experience with mental health issues and thought she saw signs of ADD in Brad.

I had heard of ADD and ADHD but didn't know much about them. There was no internet then to google. When I returned home from that trip I phoned my sister, Toni, as I knew that one of her kids had been diagnosed with ADHD at a young age. Toni told me that she been waiting for this call. Like Sue she had thought that Brad had some form of mental health illness. Toni knew all about ADD and ADHD and was very helpful.

Things accelerated after the conversations with Sue and Toni. I made an appointment to see a paediatrician. On the first visit he made a preliminary diagnosis of ADHD. He then organised further testing and he confirmed the ADHD diagnosis a couple of visits later. As we left at the end of that first visit, he said to me, "Whatever Brad has got I'm pretty sure he has got it through you". He had not met Tina yet as she was unable to attend this appointment.

I never did find out why the paediatrician said that. I did not have to as I called Toni again. I told her what he had said, and she told me that she was very confident that we had got it from Dad's side of the family. Toni had been researching mental health illness for years. My layman's understanding of Brad's ADHD, from the explanation provided by the paediatrician, was that it came from a chemical imbalance in his brain. This chemical imbalance resulted in him having lower than normal levels of the chemical, Serotonin, in his brain.

It became clear that Brad's mental health illness was genetically inherited. It is highly likely that I had carried it and given it to Brad. Whilst I probably had some of the chemical imbalance it never manifested itself into any mental health issues with me. I probably had a minor chemical imbalance, although plenty of people who know me will say that I display some signs of Obsessive Compulsive Disorder (OCD).

For Brad however the chemical imbalance was significant and required treatment. Brad was very open to understanding his ADHD and he was very happy that it was going to be treated. He was prescribed Ritalin, which was the main medication used to treat ADHD. This medication initially worked well for Brad. He became more attentive, and less naughty, at school.

A few significant things happened in 1997. I bought a unit in the Eliza building, Eady Avenue, Broadbeach. The property market was very subdued and the developer of this block of units was having trouble selling them. I inspected a big, three-bedroom unit, on the ground floor that would suit me perfectly. I did not have enough money for the deposit, so I negotiated a rent to purchase contract to buy the unit. I rented the unit for six months, with the condition that the rent I paid during this time would be deducted from the purchase price of the unit. The rent I was paying would effectively act as my deposit for the purchase of the unit. I purchased the unit, under this arrangement, in November 1997.

I loved this area from the start. The kids also loved the unit and the location. They could walk to Broadbeach and Pacific Fair. Once again, this unit became a gathering place for all the kids' friends. I maintained the Saturday night barbecue routine.

I had adapted to a single life by then. I went on a few dates but was not interested in a relationship. I had a busy life with my children, my consulting work, domestic duties, and my broader circle of family and friends.

About one year after his ADHD diagnosis, I took Brad to the paediatrician for one of his regular appointments. Brad asked me if he could talk to the paediatrician alone. This was the first time he had requested that. After about thirty minutes the paediatrician called me in and said that Brad would like to tell me something.

Brad told me that he had been getting up every night, in the middle of the night, to go and search for a dead body in the vacant lot next to our block of units. He was 16 years old then. He said that "voices in his head" were telling him to search for the dead body. He could only get to sleep after he satisfied himself that there was no dead body. He also revealed another habit he had acquired was that he had to keep reading a book until a paragraph finished at the bottom of a page.

The paediatrician changed Brad's diagnosis to OCD. Most importantly he changed his medication, I think to Zoloft. Brad improved significantly both with the knowledge of his diagnosis and with the right medication. Brad knew that he could now talk about the "voices in his head". He told me years later, "no one knows what it is like living inside my head". I was very pleased that Brad now had a clearer diagnosis and good medical support. Brad was very happy with his paediatrician.

Around this time, I became aware that Brad had been drinking for a while. I had my first experience with Brad's drinking when he was fifteen and a half years old. It was my birthday, and I had some full-strength beers in my fridge. This was unusual as I generally drink light beer. I asked Brad if we should have our first beer together on my birthday, thinking that it would be his first alcoholic drink. He said sure and got two beers. He drank three beers before I had finished the first one. He was not at all affected by the three beers.

I was to find out later in life that alcohol and drugs, particularly marijuana, are quite prevalent for young people with mental health issues. They are forms of self-medication and they were with Brad.

In early 1997 I received a call from Barry Cronin, a solicitor who I had worked with on the Gordon Pacific Scheme of Arrangement. Barry told me that John Potter, who was an emerging property developer on the Gold Coast, was in the final stages of listing his Citie Centre property group. Barry and John were going to be directors of the new listed company. They were looking for someone with finance and governance experience to set up the systems and processes for the listed company, and who could also become the third director. This call commenced an involvement with John and Villa World that lasted until June 2019.

I met with John. It was another one of those interviews which turned into a good chat, rather than an interview. We initially agreed on a part time consulting role, with my focus to be on preparing the business to operate as a listed company. We listed in June 1997 as Citie Centre Limited. I was much better prepared for this role due to my experience with the City Resources group in the 1980's. It was a small staff group of around fifteen employees. There was a great culture, and everyone was enthusiastic about growing the business as a listed company.

John was an experienced property developer with a keen, astute eye for acquisitions. John felt that you could make money by buying the right property at the right time and I saw him do this many times in the following years. The company was successful, and I became very busy very quickly. One day John walked past my office and saw that I was immersed in paperwork. He poked his head in the door and said, "I don't know what you are doing but you are doing a great job". It was the right comment at the right time for me and reflected John's intuitive people skills. After I had been there about six months there was great excitement in the office that a young lady was coming back to work, after having gone on an extended European holiday.

Her name was Shannon Hill. She was John's Executive Assistant and did most of the office administration work. Shannon was very vibrant, intelligent, and hard working. It quickly became obvious why everyone wanted her back. Shannon also became my Executive Assistant and we worked closely together for the next eight years.

I became the Financial Controller, and a full-time employee, in early 1998. We all worked hard as the company grew. We also had plenty of good times. Every Friday, if we were in the office, we all went to lunch at Costa D'Oro Italian restaurant in Surfers Paradise. John regularly invited our builder, other contractors, and consultants to these lunches. Many issues were discussed at these lunches, resulting in potential problems being resolved before they escalated. John was ahead of his time in forming a team of staff and consultants who worked together amicably and effectively.

Whilst Citie Centre was successful it was a very small, listed company. John was starting to consider growth options. He had become more comfortable in the listed environment, and we had a good, established network of brokers, analysts, advisors, solicitors, and accountants. We decided to make a play for another Gold Coast based building company, Berela Constructions Limited. It had been a long-term luxury home builder and its founders were starting to consider exit strategies. Our discussions with one of the founding directors were initially very amicable and we decided to make a takeover bid. It quickly turned into a hostile takeover bid as several of their other directors opposed the takeover. They wanted to keep running Berela independently. Our local newspaper, the Gold Coast Bulletin, picked up the story and I was frequently in the paper as Citie Centre's spokesman.

It became a very intense, hard-fought battle as both company's solicitors sought an advantage. Eventually we made the takeover bid. I spent many hours calling Berela shareholders, seeking their support for the takeover. I had to follow strict instructions from our solicitors in how to conduct these telephone calls. I went into the office every Saturday for a few weeks to call shareholders who we could not contact during work hours. One day I called a shareholder and it turned out to be one of my bigger audit clients from my Touche Ross days. We got his vote.

Whilst we had secured enough votes for the takeover there still had to be an Extraordinary General Meeting (EGM) of Berela to ratify the takeover. On the night before the EGM the Chairman of Berela called John Potter to suggest we meet and present a united team at the meeting. We did and the takeover was then completed amicably. This was a relatively small takeover, but it was still very interesting and exciting to be involved in. It was good preparation for a more significant one that would occur in 2000. It eventuated that the Berela takeover was not successful financially as it had some significant legacy building issues which we had to fund over the next few years.

One day John asked me if I would like to go to an auction with him. He said he had been researching a caravan park at Nobby Beach, opposite the old Magic Mountain site. He was confident that we could obtain approval for a residential development on the site. It was being sold as an existing caravan park and we were the only developer at the auction. John had done the numbers and knew that it was worth considerably more as a development site than for its existing use. The bidding started slowly with all the caravan park buyers bidding low figures. The auctioneer indicated that the reserve price had not been reached. John then made one bid of $2.7m. which was around $500,000 more than the previous highest bid. The room was stunned as everyone turned around to see who had bid as we were sitting in the back row. That was the final bid, and we purchased the property there and then. As we walked out John turned to me and said, "Now that's better than sex Gerry". He loved the thrill of a great purchase. We developed the Chamonix residential townhouses and villas on the site.

We continued to seek corporate opportunities. Villa World Limited was the Gold Coast's most successful property company to that time. They were a property developer and a builder. They had developed a model of "spec building" homes on their own land estates. Tony Bawden was one of the Villa World founders. John had used Tony as a mentor and sounding board during the Citie

Centre years. During one of their lunches in late 1999 Tony and John started to discuss Villa World.

After I had been at Citie Centre for about six months one of the guys who worked there had noticed that I favoured my back occasionally. I had a long-term back issue with ongoing minor pain, probably due to my wonky ankle. He referred me to a chiropractor named Lara Beutel. Lara stopped the pain in a few visits. I went to her for back maintenance from then until about one year ago. She severely injured both of her wrists, while attending to a patient, and had to retire from practising as a chiropractor. I probably referred about 50 people to Lara over the years, including most of my family. She was a gifted healer and an even better person. Our friendship has continued.

The 1998 and 1999 years were happy, eventful, and interesting as my kids maximised the use of the Broadbeach unit as a meeting place for their friends. The unit had become very popular as the launching pad for their nights out in Broadbeach. As part of this circle of friends Brad knew a guy named Davor Maksimovic.

Danita met Davor's brother, Sasha, through Brad and Davor knowing each other. They met at Fortunes nightclub in the casino. They met in April 1999 and started dating in June 1999. Sasha lived in Toowoomba as he was studying there, to become an accountant. Their romance blossomed and they have been together ever since.

Sasha was, and still is, a very interesting person. His family is Serbian. They were one of many families who fled Serbia when the Bosnian War broke out in 1992. Sasha's family spent one year in Russia before they emigrated to Australia. Sasha and Davor went to a Russian school for one year, without knowing how to speak Russian. Then when they arrived in Australia they went straight into Palm Beach Currumbin high school, without knowing how to speak English. They both got through school without repeating a year.

Sasha was still adapting to the English language, or more particularly the Aussie slang, when we first met him. He must have heard the saying, "he's as happy as a pig in mud". He liked that saying but said it slightly differently, "he's happy like a pig in the mud". It was very funny, and he still uses that version, deliberately, today. Sasha's family embraced Danita very quickly. Not long after they started dating, I was invited to a barbecue at their home. It was wonderful and the extended Serbian family were all there. I was offered a glass of Rakija, the traditional Serbian alcoholic drink. I thought it would be impolite not to drink it, so I did. It was extremely potent. It was the first of many family gatherings hosted by Sasha's parents, Zoran and Mira, but it was the last glass of Rakija I ever had.

Sasha was a trendy, sharp European looking guy. Brad promptly nicknamed him Guido, after the comedy character, Guido Hatzis. They listened to the real Guido together many times.

Brad always had jobs while he was at school. He worked at various supermarkets and usually got the jobs himself. He had saved up some money by the time he started learning to drive. He begged me to let him buy a bright green V8 Holden Torana that one of his mates, Matty Snow, was selling. He loved cars and knew a bit about them. I agreed on the proviso that if he did anything wrong while driving it, then I would sell the car. He absolutely loved that car. It drove my neighbours mad as it was very loud.

Brad left school just after he started year 12. He was 17 years old, and school had got to be too much for him. He had his green Torana and wanted to get a job. He got various jobs ranging from more supermarket jobs to landscaping. By the age of 17 he was drinking regularly and was also smoking marijuana. I say this with the benefit of hindsight as I was largely oblivious to his marijuana habit. One of his mates once left some in our letter box for him. I threw it out because I thought it was rubbish. I did not know what it was.

He did not have the Torana for very long. He lost his licence for six months after driving under the influence of alcohol. We did sell the Torana. Whilst Brad wanted to keep it, he reluctantly accepted that it was better for him to have a less powerful, less conspicuous car when he got his licence back.

Brad turned 18 in November 1999. We had a party at my unit. It was attended by the Gold Coast family members and all the kid's friends. Steve came down from Brisbane. One of our relatives from Wollongong, Scott Baxter, flew up for the night. Scott loved Brad and wasn't going to miss that party. It was a great night. Scott, who is one year older than me, kept drinking with the younger crowd. He was happy by the end of the night. He was on the back balcony when he somehow managed to fall backwards over the balcony. People went to check on him. He was lying backwards in a tree which had cushioned his fall. We got him out of the tree, and he carried on. I looked at that disfigured tree for the next three years until it finally grew back into the right shape.

Through the 1990's Mum and Dad had enjoyed a quiet, happy retirement. They were reasonably comfortable financially. Dad became a very active gardener. They had dinner at Shellharbour Workers club once a week. Dad had given up smoking when he was 70.

By 1999 they were struggling to look after the house and the yard. Toni's son, Mark, had been mowing the lawns every Saturday morning since 1992. He started when he was 11 years old. If it was raining, he would help Mum inside the house. Mum, Dad, and Mark grew very close through those years. Toni recalls that Mark would happily talk to Mum and Dad for hours.

Mark stopped mowing the lawns when he left school. The Wollongong based siblings then organised a roster to help Mum and Dad. Two of the siblings went to Mum and Dad's place every Saturday morning and did all the household chores. John organised to have their yard maintained. He did this until they moved into aged care.

CHAPTER 15

NEW BEGINNINGS AND THE VILLA WORLD FAMILY

— THE 2000'S —

There was both much excitement and trepidation about the turn of the century occurring on 31 December 1999. The excitement was around bringing in a new century, coupled with an optimism that it would mean great times ahead. In Australia there was added excitement as Sydney was to host the Olympic Games that year. They would later become known as "the best games ever".

The trepidation was due to what became known as the "Y2K Bug". There had been much fear generated that computer systems would crash all around the world because of the digit change from 1999 to 2000. Computer experts were kept very busy in late 1999 preparing for the changeover. The fear was unfounded as most systems kept operating seamlessly through the night of 31 December 1999.

The turn of the century was also significant for me as my children were becoming adults, and I could start planning more time for myself. Danita and Brad had left school and were studying or working. Chantal was 14 years old, and already quite independent. She was very happy to catch the bus to school from my place. This turned out to be quite fortuitous as she met her first boyfriend and later husband, Patrik, on the school bus. Danita and Chantal had voluntarily taken over the cooking duties at my unit, which suited me perfectly.

Tony Bawden and John Potter's discussions about Villa World became more serious. Tony, and his co-founder Greg Phillips, were keen to step back from the business. They had built a very successful company, with Villa World recognised as one of the leading listed property companies in Queensland at that time. They had relinquished their executive roles several years earlier. The Board was keen to find a CEO who would have a significant shareholding in Villa World. They were impressed with John's property knowledge and the quality of developments that Citie Centre had completed. Consequently, a merger between Villa World and Citie Centre was agreed by the parties, subject to approval by both companies' shareholders. Through the merger John became an Executive Director and the CEO. He also became the largest shareholder of Villa World post the merger. I became an Executive Director and the Chief Financial Officer (CFO). The merged company continued to be named Villa World.

The merger was approved and came into effect on 1 July 2000. Ironically this was the same date that the 10% Goods and Services Tax (GST) became effective in Australia. The introduction in Australia of the GST caused an immediate downturn in the property market. Villa World's operations were significantly affected by this downturn. The Citie Centre staff moved into the Villa World office on 1 July 2000. At that time there was only one computer in the Villa World office that could be used to send or receive emails.

The Citie Centre staff found themselves in an unusual position. We were the smaller company in the merger. We had about twelve staff who moved into Villa World's office. Villa World had over sixty staff, with around thirty based in the head office. John and I came from the smaller company, but we were moving into the two most senior management positions. The same applied for a couple of the other senior Citie Centre executives, who were moving into the most senior roles in their area.

We realised that the key to successfully merging the staff into one cohesive team was developing the right culture. There was some low-hanging fruit that we took advantage of. The company had developed a silo organisational structure, where the various departments worked largely independently of each other, and reported separately to the CEO. At that time this was not an unusual structure. The culture was still quite good and there were some outstanding employees. It was a good platform from which to build a more modern culture.

We organised a management meeting in the first week and discussed that we thought an integrated, harmonious structure would be desirable for the merged company. That first management meeting was a significant step forward. Everyone was in favour of breaking down the silos and sharing information between the departments. The enthusiasm was palpable.

During the first week John sent a memo to all head office staff inviting them to office drinks on the Friday afternoon. He also included in the memo that he would like everyone to know all the staff by name by then. He gave notice that he would be randomly asking people to go around the group and name all the staff. This was clearly going to be a harder task for the Citie Centre staff as they had many more new names to learn than the Villa World staff. Shannon sent an office plan, with staff names on their desks, to staff to assist them to learn all the names.

The Friday drinks came. Almost everyone was there. After a little while John made a short speech welcoming everyone to the merged company. He then asked for a volunteer to have a go at naming everyone. One of the accounts payable ladies volunteered straight away. She started and got a few names right. Then when she got to a person who she didn't know she just said any name, like Tom, Dick, or Harry, and kept going. At the end she just acted like she got it all right. She was quite a character, and it was hilarious.

More people then volunteered. A few, including John, got all the names, that is first names, right. Then at the end Shannon said she would have a go. She stood up and proceeded to perfectly name everyone by both first and last name. She did not refer to any notes. No one else even thought about learning the surnames. This was a culture clincher, and that group merged seamlessly over the next few months. This wasn't the last time that Shannon would show us the way culturally.

The first year at Villa World provided some significant challenges for me. Following the GST induced downturn we needed to prioritise the company's financing arrangements and relationships. I was also responsible for the investor relations area, which involved meeting with the company's existing brokers and analysts and establishing new relationships. I was also planning to be more of a 'General Manager CFO' than a 'financial CFO'.

I remembered my lesson regarding delegation from Les Ward. I had worked with Caroline Barton, the Financial Controller and Company Secretary, through the merger process and I knew she was good. We had a discussion and agreed that she would take responsibility for all aspects of the accounting and auditing areas. She loved the technical stuff and I had delegated a significant part of my role.

As a result of the GST induced downturn, we had to make some tough decisions to cut costs, including making some staff redundant. While only a relatively small number of staff were affected it was still a very difficult process. We did this quickly and decisively so that everyone else could get on with their jobs and we could start building the desired culture.

During the first six months we had an important meeting organised with our corporate bankers, ANZ. The meeting had the dual purpose of ANZ meeting the new senior management team, and our team presenting a full project and financial update to ANZ. The meeting was to be attended by ANZ's Head of Property in Australia, so it was an important one. We organised our presentation with John Potter to do most of the talking.

On the morning of the meeting John called to inform me he was sick and would not be able to attend. We only had a couple of hours to reorganise. Our Senior Development Manager, Sales Manager, and I jumped in to do the respective parts of the presentation. The meeting went very well. ANZ's Head of Property thanked us at the end and said that it was somewhat fortunate John had gotten sick as it gave them the opportunity to get to know the other management team members. They already knew John very well. While the project and financial updates were important the quality of the management team was more important to ANZ. I learnt some important lessons from this day.

Villa World had an accounting program that had been produced internally for the company's sole use. This was quite normal then as off the shelf accounting packages for large companies were relatively new. We prioritised the replacement of this program due to the reliance on the staff member who had written the program and risks with the program itself. This became a significant project for Caroline and I. It became as much about people management as planning the technical aspects of the project. There were frequent differences of opinion between our IT manager, the consulting project manager, and the various software companies. The whole process took about twelve months. We successfully replaced the inhouse program with a tailored software package produced by a very reputable software company based in Brisbane. Pleasingly the accounting program that we selected was still being used in Villa World in 2019, almost twenty years later.

I discovered that the IT world can be very stressful. I'm not sure this has changed much to the present day as companies now tackle the challenges of the digital world.

The company's operations were going well, despite the property downturn. Everyone was always busy. We introduced executive coaching to assist senior executives both individually, and as a management team. We always had Friday drinks and plenty of celebrations for things like birthdays and project milestones. A hard working, enjoyable work culture was developing.

I had a very enlightening executive coaching session after we had settled into our new roles at Villa World. The coach knew me quite well both through our coaching sessions and because I was coordinating the various coaching programs. At the beginning of the session, she talked about the distinction between the entrepreneurial style of employee versus the technical style of employee. You could have someone like a sales manager, who is one hundred per cent entrepreneurial and someone like an engineer or an accountant, who is one hundred per cent technical. Staff can sit anywhere between zero and one hundred per cent on this scale.

She told me I was right in the middle of the scale between entrepreneurial and technical. In fact, she said I was the most "in the middle" person that she had ever coached. We discussed this was a good thing but that I should be more aware that I am "in the middle". She then told me she thought I was like this due to my family upbringing. I was the middle sibling and I had always been an organiser or a coordinator. This was the first time I had thought about the link between my personal life and my work life.

My brother, Steve, lived in Brisbane in the year 2000 and we caught up quite often. One day he came down to my place and said he had something important to discuss with me. He told me that he had agreed to become a sperm donor for two lesbians, Kerry Cody, and Marina Thacker, who he knew in Brisbane. They already had one child and were keen to add to their family. They had asked Steve both because they really liked him and thought he would be happy to help two women add to their family.

Steve explained that he had donated the sperm and Kerry was pregnant. The three of them worked out a non-legal agreement that focussed on the rights of the child to be born and they spent time together getting their heads into the right space. They agreed that everyone would maintain confidentiality about the identity of Steve as the sperm donor. The agreement further provided that Steve was allowed to tell one person about the arrangement, providing that person kept it strictly confidential.

The idea of maintaining confidentiality was to keep the focus on the child's parents rather than people speculating about who the donor may be. For a non-traditional family this made it easy for people to focus on the parents. Steve being able to tell one person was included as it had been recognised that the sperm donor would need someone to be able to talk to through the process.

Steve chose me as the person that he could tell. This was because I was the sibling who lived closest to him, and Steve felt that I could handle this information. I was honoured to have been entrusted with such an important secret and very happy for him that he was going to become a father.

The baby girl, named Nejmere Margot Clare Thacker Cody, was born on the 4th of January 2001. Steve was very happy. Steve met Nejmere as a very young baby and visited whenever he wanted to. When Nejmere was old enough they introduced Steve to her as their friend. Nejmere knew him as Steve. Kerry and Marina explained to Nejmere from an early age that she had a donor dad, and what that meant.

When Nejmere was five-and-a-half she asked who her donor dad was and Kerry and Marina explained that it was Steve.

Nejmere had asked well before Kerry and Marina expected her to. She then called Steve and asked him, "Are you my donor dad?". Steve said yes.

Steve had met a guy named Justin Cooper in 2001. They were introduced by a mutual friend. They started going out and are still together today.

Kerry, Marina, and Steve had previously agreed that when this became public, all three families would be told quickly as they all came from large families. Steve recalls that he called Mum first. He told Mum she had another grandchild. Mum thought that Steve had a love child. When Steve told her it was a child through sperm donation Mum found her assumption about having an unknown love child very funny and had a good laugh. She was laughing at herself for thinking it was a love child. Mum was thrilled and could not wait to meet Nejmere.

Steve then travelled to Wollongong with a party of six people, Nejmere, Justin, Kerry, Marina, and Kaspar Cody George Thacker, Nejmere's brother. It was an amazing time, and everyone remembers this trip fondly, especially the first time Nejmere and her Oma first met. Mum slowly came around the corridor in the aged care village with her walking frame. Nejmere saw her and ran up for a big hug. Everyone cried. Nejmere and Steve have a good relationship and are in regular contact.

There was a significant upside for the broader Lambert family from Steve's decision to become a sperm donor. He was required to undertake very detailed medical testing prior to the sperm donation. He discovered that he had Factor V Leiden, a blood clotting disorder. Also, he carried the Cystic Fibrosis mutated gene. He did not have Cystic Fibrosis but carried the gene, that if matched with another carrier, could result in a child being born with Cystic Fibrosis.

This was vital medical information that Steve was now able to pass onto the entire family. All the siblings, and most of their children, were tested for both medical conditions. For some members of the family, it has proven to be very important medical information. I discovered that I had Factor V Leiden. I have the moderate version of it. The only impact on me to date has been that I must jab myself with Clexane, an anticoagulant, when I go on long haul flights.

In December 2000 a very close friend of Brad's, Rafer Hart, celebrated his 18th birthday. He had a party at one of the hotels in Surfers Paradise. Our whole family was invited. I took a female friend to this party. She drove and we took Chantal and her friend, Nicole, with us. This is the same Nicole who befriended Chantal on her first day at her new school. Chantal and Nicole were both 15 years old.

I was just settling into the party when Danita came to tell me that I should check on Chantal. She said that Brad may have given her a glass of champagne. It was around 9pm. I found Chantal and she said that she wasn't feeling very well. I then noticed that Nicole wasn't looking that great either. It turns out that they had been drinking since we got there. Brad and his mates must have thought it was time. They were both drunk, so we had to leave the party and get them home. We only had to drive fifteen minutes home but even that was too far. One of them vomited in the back seat.

We got them home, got them into bed and cleaned the car. Chantal told me the next day that was the first time she had drunk alcohol. Her and Nicole didn't even know they were going to have a drink. She thought they only had a couple of champagnes each but that was enough.

Danita was settled in her relationship with Sasha and her job as Practice Manager for Surfers Health, a General Practice in Surfers Paradise. She turned 21 in March 2001. Shortly after, she and Sasha decided to move in together. They bought a townhouse at Carrara. Zoran and Davor helped them renovate it. This was the start of a very productive real estate journey for them.

In January 2002 my brother John organized a trip to Parkes. He, Hans, Ossie, and I went for a weekend there. It was a very nostalgic and emotional trip. I had never been back to Parkes after we left in 1960. Ossie had never been to Parkes.

On arrival in Parkes John drove us through the town. I noticed that it was a combination of new developments and many buildings seemingly the same as when we were there. He drove us to Pearce Street so we could have a look at the house that we lived in, at number 26. He drove past the house slowly to show us. I asked him to stop, and said I was going to knock on the front door and see if there was any chance of us having a look at the house. I remember John saying, "you can't do that" and I said I hadn't come all this way not to give it a try.

I knocked on the front door to be met by a very lovely lady, Pat Harbridge, who invited us all in after I told her who we were. This was a typical country welcome. John immediately noticed some things that were unchanged from when we left 40 years ago. The distinctive desk Dad built into the lounge room and the original kitchen were still there. I then asked Pat if the old garage was still in the backyard. She was immediately apologetic as she explained that the garage was still there. Further they had not touched it since they had moved in. She then led me out to the backyard, and I saw the garage that I spent the first year of my life living in. I went inside and discovered that the dividing wall that Dad had put in, to divide the garage into two rooms, was still there. It was a very eerie and emotional feeling. After I told Pat about us living in the garage whilst Dad built the house, she said that she would probably have to leave the garage there forever now. I then went to get John, Hans and Ossie and we all spent some time in the garage.

We then went to the workshop, in Close Street, that housed the original building business run by Dad and Mr Holman. We also traced the walk that we made from the Pearce Street house to the Holy Family Primary School, as it was now named. It was around two kilometres.

We visited my godparents, Gerald and Ria Holman, the next day. This was much more emotional than I had anticipated. They were very happy to see us and asked lots of questions about Mum, Dad and all the kids and grandkids. They were especially interested in me, as their godchild, and I felt very comfortable with them. Little did we know that Ria would pass away not long after this visit.

On the last day we visited the office of the local newspaper, the Parkes Champion-Post. We were keen to search the old newspapers to see if we could find any references to Dad's soccer days in Parkes. Whilst our search was unsuccessful the manager of the Champion-Post started chatting to us and was curious about why we were in Parkes. He took some notes, organised some photos and we were the front-page story in the Champion-Post on the 11th of January 2002.

John and I visited Parkes again a couple of years later. This time Steve and Dianne came with us. It was another great visit. One highlight occurred when Dianne went into a local real estate office, to find out about the price of houses in Parkes. I went in with her. We waited at the counter and a very old man very slowly came to the counter. He asked what we were doing there. We explained and as soon as we mentioned that our name was Lambert he said, "Your Dad built that house at 26 Pearce Street." He remembered Dad and we had a great chat with him.

Around the middle of 2002 Chantal started going out with Patrik (Pat) Goransson, the school friend she had met on the school bus. Their romance got off to a rocky start as Brad was not enthusiastic about his little sister having a boyfriend. He was an overprotective big brother. We managed to settle Brad down and he and Pat became great friends. Chantal and Pat went from school sweethearts to boyfriend and girlfriend.

Towards the end of 2002 I attended a charity lunch at Melba's, a famous restaurant in Surfers Paradise. I found myself sitting opposite a very striking lady, named Dianne (Di) Harland. I had met her before as we had some friends in common. This was the first time we had a good chat. She was in a relationship, which enabled me to use the line, "If you were single, I would ask you out".

Di won the best dressed award that day. She had a beauty business in Southport, and we discussed that my daughters might be handy photographic models for the business.

We stayed in touch, mainly discussing Di's business. Di's relationship ended in early 2003 and we started going out together just before my 50th birthday in May 2003. We went out for a few months. My domestic situation was still busy with kids, and friends, there all the time. It wasn't the type of relationship that Di envisaged. Di was very astute regarding people. She thought I was too soft on Brad and not as aware as I should have been about his drinking and drug taking. She decided to move on. We had formed a solid friendship, which we would maintain.

Around this time another one of the siblings' marriages ended when John and Barbara separated after 30 years of marriage.

In early 2003 John Potter informed me that we should start succession planning for his CEO role at Villa World. He was happy to remain as a major shareholder but did not want to remain in the CEO role. Villa World was going very well.

We discussed possible candidates. I mentioned a guy called Brent Hailey. John and I both knew Brent through a joint venture that Villa World had with BMD, a national land development and civil engineering construction firm. Brent was the CEO of BMD. Even though we didn't think that Brent would be interested, John suggested that I meet with him and let him know about the impending opportunity. I did that and after the usual processes were completed Brent was appointed as CEO about six months later. One day John discussed Brent's appointment with me and said something like, "If we put Brent on it may cost you your job one day". He meant that Brent was likely to be a more corporate CEO than he had been. John had been a property focused CEO and left most of the corporate stuff to me. I responded to John that if that happened, that would be a good thing as it would mean I have replaced myself with someone better than me. Les Ward's delegation advice came back to me again.

John's words turned out to be prophetic.

Brent came on board and Villa World continued to grow. John was still involved through a property committee, and as a sounding board for Brent. By this time Villa World had developed a culture that could best be described as "enviable". We introduced bonus schemes and had very low levels of staff turnover. Shannon recently told me that it felt like we were one big, happy family. A key aspect of this culture was the trust that senior management placed in staff to do their jobs. It was a culture of empowerment and enjoyment, rather than control and micro-management.

I had moved into more of a General Manager than a CFO role and had been referred to as "the glue" at Villa World. There were still plenty of challenges and stressful times, commensurate with Villa World being both a property and a listed company.

John had been introduced to a significant Chinese property developer who had several large projects underway in Shanghai, China. This developer was impressed with the finishes in the Villa World houses. The connection led to Villa World taking an interest in a small project in Shanghai, China. I travelled to Shanghai about five times in the 2003 year to attend to matters regarding this project.

Towards the end of 2003 Mum was ageing. She had been diagnosed with Parkinson's disease when she was 78, and it was getting worse. She got sick and spent nine weeks in Kiama Hospital. She then moved into aged care. Ossie was able to get her into the low care section of the Warrigal Care home in Albion Park Rail. Mum knew this home and was very happy to go there.

Dad wanted to keep living at home. He only lasted one week on his own. He joined Mum and they had adjoining rooms. We, the nine siblings, organised that we would meet at the Kaylaur Crescent house on one Sunday in December 2003. The plan was to clean up the house and decide what to do with any stuff that Mum and Dad had left there.

As it turned out there was an important Villa World meeting regarding our project in China on the Saturday before the designated Sunday. This meeting had to be attended by one Australian director. Unfortunately, I drew the short straw and I had to go to China. I flew to China on the Friday, attended the meeting on the Saturday, flew back to Sydney on the Saturday night, and arrived at Kaylaur Crescent on the Sunday morning in time for the siblings meeting.

This was an emotional, very special meeting. It was just the 9 of us. Whilst we caught up with each other reasonably often for a large family, it had been many years since we had all been at our childhood home together. We had a meaningful, amicable discussion about the next stages of Mum and Dad's lives, including their wills. We then chatted about how we would allocate Mum and Dad's stuff. John said he would take anything left over and keep it at his factory. He still has a few of those boxes.

I have a clear memory of how pleasant that day was. We enjoyed being with each other. We knew what we were there for and after our discussion we just got on with it. There were no disagreements, and no harsh words were spoken. That day reinforced our closeness as siblings, and how much we loved each other. I can't recall ever having a serious disagreement or fallout with any of my siblings and I am very grateful for that.

I was very fortunate as I secured the chess set that we had played with our whole lives. Dad had hand made this chess set in Holland in 1942. I brought the chess set home, had it restored and gifted it to Brad. Brad loved it but left it with me for safekeeping. I use this chess set today to play with my grandkids. I also got the photo of Dad and Brad that Dad had always kept on the shelf next to his lounge chair.

I snared some old medical receipts that Mum had kept. One of those receipts was for an x-ray of my right ankle in November 1966. The cost of the x-ray was eight dollars. I learnt that I was having trouble with my right ankle from 13 years of age.

Villa World achieved record profit levels in 2004 and 2005. It expanded into aged care, on a small scale. By the 2005 financial year the company's balance sheet had approximately doubled in size from the 2000 year when the merger occurred. By this time Caroline Barton had replaced me as the CFO and I was in a General Manager, Corporate role. It became clear by mid-2005 that my role was coming to a natural end. John's prophecy from 2003 had come true. I accepted a redundancy, and we agreed on a termination date, being the 31st of December 2005. We also agreed on some ongoing consulting work in Villa World's aged care area. It was a very amicable departure, but still emotional as Villa World had become like family to me.

The team organised a farewell lunch for me and Shannon Hill, who I worked with very closely, wrote a poem and read it aloud at the lunch:

"After a year abroad in 97 back to Citie Centre I trotted
But into my tight-knit working family a new person had been slotted
With his floppy hair and goofy grin, I instantly felt at ease
If only I had the foresight to know how bloody hard, he'd be to please
He was quick to learn that, to work for JP (who has an incredible eagle eye)
It was impossible for anyone to think, that under the radar you could fly
So when Gerry came back from the barbers one day with a dramatic spiky cut to his mane
John got to indulge in his favourite pastime; it was called the "let's hang shit on the new guy" game

So like many before him, as the recipient of jokes he had to do some time
Lucky for us he took it with a grain of salt… and probably some strong tequila and lime
Now I'm not saying we drove him to drink, after all, consumption was a must
He took his flak, but he gave it back, never biting the dust
A highly intelligent individual with a wealth of knowledge under his belt
And, thanks to his personal trainer, under his belt is looking quite svelte
University Lecturer, Chartered Accountant, CFO, General Manager
Yes, he's had a colourful working career
But honestly, it's a bit hard to take a man seriously when his middle name is Maria!

Gerry, Gerald, Gezza, G-Spot, G-meister, G-man by all these names we affectionately know him

I guess that's a sign of how much we adore him, and that's why we're here today, to show him

The culture and value you have contributed simply cannot be measured

And I think I speak for everyone when I say you are truly treasured

Sure, we've had our moments, there have been disagreements, there's been dummy spitting, tantrums, and tears... (and let's not get started on me)

But at the end of the day, I have thoroughly enjoyed working alongside you throughout the last 8 years

Good luck Gerry with whatever challenges, excitement, and opportunity the future may hold

There is so much to come and so much to look forward to, after all you are 52 years young, not old

Oh goodness me how will we cope without you Gerry, you've been our mother duck

But I guess you'll just give us that cheeky smile, shrug your shoulders and say, "who gives a ..."

Dad's health deteriorated towards the end of 2005. His body had worn out. He had been moved to the high care section. I saw him for the last time on his 84th birthday on the 28th of November 2005. He was semi-conscious, but still managed to say, "Gerald you have to take me home". He had not called me Gerald for many years.

I'm told that the local Catholic priest came through the ward every Tuesday to see if any residents wanted to take the last rites. Dad, perhaps a little impolitely, declined that request every week. However, one week Dad did not wait for the priest to ask.

He told him that he would like the last rites. Dad died peacefully in his sleep two days later, on the 15th of December 2005.

Dad was ready to go. He had enjoyed his retirement years up to the time when he went into the aged care home. He did not like the lack of freedom there. He told me once that he would just like to cook his own bacon and eggs again. Every time I came to visit Dad when he was in the low care section, he requested that I get KFC for him. Dad lived through World War II, moved his family to another country, raised nine good children and struggled financially for most of his life. I felt like his 84 years were the equivalent of 100 normal years. He had earned a good rest.

I took a few months off after I left Villa World. I did not want to take another full time job. I decided to have a go at running my own business. I set up two companies, Lambert Corporate Consulting Pty Ltd and Lambert Corporate Coaching Pty Ltd. I already had my first consulting client in Villa World and planned to look for further general business consulting and mentoring work.

I had really enjoyed the people side of the business in both of my previous corporate roles. I was approached by an executive coaching company to take up a master franchise for their company. I became quite busy setting this business up and engaged two coaches as franchisees. The coaching business opened more doors for me as I was responsible for obtaining the coaching clients. It also enhanced my knowledge of the people side of a wide variety of businesses. I enjoyed the operational side of this business. Unfortunately, it was very difficult to get the coaching revenue to the levels required for everyone, including me, to reach their desired income levels.

I had gone into a business that required a disproportionate amount of time and effort for the return obtained. I persevered but always had to maintain a level of business consulting income along the way.

Danita and Sasha were married, in a traditional Serbian church wedding, on the 4th of March 2006. Danita was a stunning bride. The reception was held at the Gold Coast International hotel in Surfers Paradise. It was a fantastic wedding, and it was memorable for many reasons. It rained all day, and it was torrential at the end of the service. There were only a few photos possible outside the church. It seamlessly blended a very large Australian family with a very large extended Serbian family. Fuji was in his element going around to meet every Serbian guest throughout the night. The music comprised a normal DJ for a set, followed by a traditional Serbian band for a set.

Brad was resplendent in a very bright lime green suit. Tina had the suit tailored for the wedding and Brad chose his favourite green colour. He promised to be on his best behaviour, which he was. When Sasha made his speech he said, "I would like to thank Brad for not spending all of Ged's money," implying that he was glad that I had enough money left for the wedding. Right on cue Brad stood up and bowed to the crowd. It was one of those moments in time, which is now a great memory.

The wedding was attended by most of my siblings and partners and most of Danita's cousins, on both sides of the family.

I'm pretty sure Brad took on the responsibility of making sure his cousins had a great night out in Surfers Paradise after the wedding reception finished. I was told later that Daniel, Jessica and Ryan, cousins on the Lambert side, particularly enjoyed the night.

Di and I had stayed in touch, and we got together again in early 2007. I could say it happened because the timing was now better, but what really happened was that Di had a few too many drinks one night and stayed at my place. She never left. This was the start of a ten-year partnership that enriched my life. Di taught me more about life than anyone I had met before. She taught me how to set boundaries and establish a better relationship with Brad. She became a great friend to my daughters and to Brad. Tina and Di also became great friends.

The first time that Di met my family was at a family wedding in May 2007. It was Toni's daughter, Melissa's wedding. Di was her usual vibrant, striking self and formed a quick rapport with the Lamberts. During the night one of my brothers pulled me aside and said something like, "We have just had a chat so I'm just letting you know that if you break up with this one you will have to go." Di had made an impression. This was the last family wedding that Mum attended.

At the end of 2007 I bought a large house in Surf Street, Mermaid Waters. It was big enough to house us, Di's business, Chantal for a short period, and two poodles, Lily, and Maddie. I was back to residential living. This proved to be a great house for the grandkids over the next decade. Life was great and very busy.

Di's father, Athol, mother, June, and brother, Harvey, were regular visitors and quickly became like family to me. Athol caught the bus to our place every day so he could take the dogs for a walk. June worked with Di and came to our garage office every day. Harvey could fix anything and it seemed like we needed him at least once a week as there was always something to fix in an older house!

In the middle of 2007 the Global Financial Crisis (GFC) hit. The GFC resulted in economic downturns all over the world. While Australia technically didn't go into a recession, the economy was severely affected. Share prices plunged. The house I had just bought fell in value by around twenty-five per cent over the next couple of years.

The most significant aspect of the GFC for me was a severe loss in business confidence. The business world was shell shocked. My coaching business suffered. Companies were cutting costs, and this included spending money on an optional item like executive coaching. Fortunately, I had developed a solid base of clients who realised the benefits provided by the coaching programs. I maintained enough business to get through the next couple of years.

During 2007 Mum started to age more noticeably. She had been moved to the high care section of the home. Steve visited Mum on a weekend in November 2007. When Steve arrived the nursing staff told him that Mum had taken a turn for the worse and was not likely to survive the weekend. This was unexpected.

Steve contacted all the siblings. He called me on that Saturday morning. I was able to book a flight for that evening and arrived at Mum's bedside around midnight. All the siblings were there. Mum was drifting in and out of consciousness. They had all spoken to Mum, so I went to the bedside. Mum looked like she was unconscious. I sat next to her and quietly said something like, "Mum it's Ged here, just letting you know that I'm here with everyone else". She opened her eyes, looked straight at me, and said, "What are you doing here, am I going to die tonight?" I was taken aback by Mum waking up and blurted out, "Yes, that's why I'm here". Mum had asked my siblings the same question before I arrived and had received much the same answer. This was probably not the most appropriate response, but we do tend to say it as it is in the Lambert family. Mum did not pass that night and we all went home a few hours later. Toni told me many years later that she remembers Mum was ready to die at that stage of her life; she had stopped eating.

Mum passed away very peacefully six weeks later, on the 4th of January 2008. Di and I saw her again two weeks before she passed. At Mum's 80th birthday celebration, 4 years earlier, there were many great speeches, but John nailed it the best when he got up and told Mum she was a saint. That was the perfect word for Mum. She had an extremely hard life. Like Dad she lived through World War II, moved her family to another country, raised nine good children and struggled financially for most of her life. Mum did all of this and still maintained her amiable personality all her life. She was tough, resilient, and quietly intelligent. I am extremely grateful to have had her as my mother.

Three weeks after Mum's death Danita gave birth to a beautiful baby girl, Evie Maree, on the 29th of January 2008. The circle of life was complete for me with Evie replacing my mother.

Becoming a grandparent was very exciting and it really is as good as they say. Sasha and Danita, and the whole family, were ecstatic. I was about to find out how wonderful and devoted Serbian grandparents were. Zoran and Mira were happy to babysit Evie every Saturday night. Tina, and her husband, Rob, were also very active grandparents. Evie's arrival brought a lot of joy to a lot of people at the right time.

Evie was a good baby, after being a bit unsettled for the first few months. It wasn't long before her individual characteristics emerged. As soon as she started learning to talk Evie learnt English and Serbian simultaneously.

Brad left home, for the last time, when he was 22 years old. He continued to work in a variety of jobs. He did an Information Technology (IT) course and got a good job with an IT company at Varsity Lakes. He was very interested in computers. The emergence of the internet and social media were great for Brad. He embraced the digital world. Brad loved it when Terry O'Connell, our "computer guy", came to attend to my computer. He would talk to Terry about computers for hours. Terry is still my computer guru and a close friend today. He also plays (that is, stars!) in our trivia team.

Brad got himself a little dog after he left home. He was a very friendly little Pomeranian. Brad called him Ernie Dingo. He loved that dog and took him everywhere. He could not take him when he went into a rental house with a few of his mates, so he gave Ernie to Danita and Sasha. He became their much-loved family dog for the next 13 years, until he passed away in 2018.

During the years after he left home Brad loved family dinners. He enjoyed them equally whether they were at one of our homes or at a restaurant. He would take his time eating the meal and enjoying the conversation. The last family meal I recall having with Brad was at a restaurant in Broadbeach. I recall him saying, "no rush Gedro" as he was slowly finishing his meal.

In 2008 Brad secured a great job at Technigro, a vegetation management company. He moved into a responsible position quickly, driving some of their most sophisticated machinery. Technigro really valued Brad as an employee.

Brad met a girl, Jacqui, and they were happy together. He lived at Matty Snow's, one of his best mates, house. He was financially independent and was getting more responsible with his money. While Brad always had mental health issues, 2008 was a good year for him, as he had a girlfriend and was settled at work.

Things started to go downhill for Brad in mid-2009 when he hurt his ankle at work. He had an extended period off work. He and Jacqui broke up and we knew from his friends that he was drinking heavily again. Things escalated quickly and he had an incident, whereby he perpetrated some property damage, on the 22nd of September. He was injured in this incident, which required police intervention. He spent a night in hospital and was released despite my request that he be admitted as he was suffering severe mental health issues. Whilst the medical staff were sympathetic to my request, they explained that they were only treating Brad for his physical injuries and we would have to go back to his own doctors for the mental health issues.

Brad sadly and unexpectedly passed away, by taking his own life, on the 3rd of October 2009. The autopsy disclosed that he had taken a fatal overdose of his prescription medication, Seroquel. Even though he had been having a tough time we did not know that he was suicidal. His doctors also did not know as he saw them in the week before he passed away.

I talk more about Brad's life and death in Chapter 17.

In 2009 I joined a Gold Coast fundraising committee for the Act for Kids charity. We did some good work on this committee. It opened my eyes as to the number of people who work selflessly for charities. One of these was a lady named Simone Bennett-Smith, who I met through this committee. She was an actress, an MC, and the face of the Suncorp TV advertisements at that time. Simone was a classically trained dancer. She had worked in London for five years with artists like Cher and Simply Red. She often hosted lunches or corporate events. I learnt that whenever the opportunity was appropriate at these events Simone would raise money for Act for Kids. Despite her glitzy showbiz background Simone was, and still is, a good person who has always tried to help other people. In later years I would meet more good people like Simone through my role with yourtown.

I then met Simone's husband, Adam. He became a client of my coaching business, and we have worked together, on and off, since then. Simone and Adam have been very close friends ever since.

Chantal and Pat's relationship had its ups and downs and they had broken up after initially going out for a few years. They got back together after the tragic death of Pat's brother, Niklas, in a motorcycle accident in 2007. By the end of 2009 they had settled into a serious relationship and moved in together. Chantal left home for the last time. Danita was the only one of my kids who left home and didn't come back. Whilst it was sad when Chantal left home, as it was the end of that part of my life, it provided me with the opportunity to focus on my relatively new partnership with Di.

The 2000's was a decade of great change. The use of the internet became widespread and affordable. This was followed by the emergence of social media companies. Facebook was founded and it changed the way people, particularly young people, communicated. All my grandkids were born as "digital natives" and will not experience life without digital technology.

A significant cultural change during this decade was the emergence of coffee shops. If you wanted a cappuccino in the 1970's and 1980's you generally went to an Italian restaurant so you could have the cappuccino with your meal, but in the 2000's coffee shops sprung up everywhere. They became a social phenomenon. It became "the thing" to meet for a coffee. By 2022 it would be commonplace to transact business in a coffee shop.

I had a client in the coffee industry and when he was planning to start his business in the late 1990's, he approached his bank for a loan. The banker pointed to all the office workers walking on a busy footpath and said something like, "Look at all these people going to work. They are never going to drink coffee out of a paper cup". How wrong was he?

CHAPTER 16

REACHING THE PINNACLE

THE 2010'S

If I had thought the 2010's was going to be an easy decade as I transitioned to retirement, I would have been very mistaken. It was a decade of ups and downs, fortunately with the ups outweighing the downs. I also had another career reinvention working on Boards and with Boards.

By 2010 it was apparent that the executive coaching business was not going to achieve the revenue levels required for the coaches and myself to make the desired income targets. My master franchise term was due to expire in March 2011. I negotiated with the franchisor and the coaches to cease the various agreements before the expiry date so we could all get on with other business opportunities. It was an amicable termination; all parties were cognisant of the changed business environment after the GFC.

The coaching business proved to be a costly financial exercise. I had to write off the master franchise fees I had paid. I had spent almost five years working very hard to make the business viable. During that time, I did not derive much income from the business. The opportunity cost of income that I could have earned was considerable. Further the value of my self-managed superannuation fund had halved following the GFC. I was starting my last planned decade of work in a much worse financial position than I had envisaged.

Despite this I derived some valuable non-financial benefits from the coaching business. I broadened my business network and enhanced my knowledge of the people and culture areas of business. These benefits significantly assisted the development of my business consulting career.

Through 2010 a few things happened that set me on the way to a mostly enjoyable, but at times stressful, decade of work, and a reasonable recovery of my financial position. Firstly, I received a telephone call from Wayne McCrea. I knew Wayne from my City Resources days. He was another mining entrepreneur and he had floated a mining company, CuDeco Limited, several years earlier. He was the Chairman and was looking for a non-executive director who could chair the Audit and Risk committee. Cudeco had discovered a copper deposit, named Rocklands, situated near Cloncurry, Queensland. Mine development planning was underway. I accepted this director role.

I also had a call from a guy named Brad Dunne, the owner and Managing Director of a shop fitting company called Projects Queensland (PQ). He had been referred to me by a mutual business contact. I met Brad and a scheduled one hour meeting turned into a four hour discussion about both the business and our personal lives. I started work with PQ as a business consultant. I set up an advisory board, which I chaired. I stayed in this role for the next decade, making some great friends, including Brad, along the way.

Around the same time, I had a few catch ups with a guy named Anthony Griffiths. I knew Anthony from the coaching business. He was running a company called Aizer Building Solutions (Aizer). We decided to set up an advisory board for this business, which I also chaired. Aizer grew quite quickly, and I stayed in this role for the next six years. I started to network more and picked up various consulting jobs, including another short term board advisory role. My board, advisory board and consulting roles progressed nicely, and I was earning a reasonable income.

Towards the end of 2010 I saw an advertisement for a director role with the charity, BoysTown. I was interested in finding out about this role as I had been thinking about how I could contribute to youth mental health causes following Brad's death. I knew that BoysTown worked with disadvantaged and troubled youth but did not know much more than that.

I called and spoke to a lady named Carolyn Penklis, from Directors Australia, the company handling the recruitment. Little did I know that this call would directly lead to two of my most significant roles for the next decade. Carolyn and I had a good discussion. They were looking for two directors, one with finance and accounting expertise. They were a Catholic, De la Salle, organisation, so my background with the Catholic church was an advantage. Carolyn encouraged me to apply. Even though this was a voluntary director role there was considerable interest in the two roles.

I was successful and became a director of BoysTown in February 2011. The second director appointed was Peter French.

BoysTown's services included Kids Helpline, youth employment services, two family residential services and various other services. It was a large charity with services and staff spread across Australia.

I don't know why but I remember thinking that I would be able to assist with board meetings and other board matters due to my previous board experience. I was wrong about that. The BoysTown Board was chaired by Brother Ambrose Payne, a De La Salle brother. He was as good as any listed company chairperson I had worked with. I learnt a bit from him about running effective board meetings, rather than the other way around. Further the CEO was Tracy Adams, and she was as good as any listed company CEO I had worked with. Tracy is still the CEO today.

BoysTown was a great organisation to work with and I loved being on the board from the start. I had found the place where I could give back a little for Brad.

Danita and Sasha welcomed their second child, Luka Bradley, on the 24th of September 2010. Luka was my second grandchild. He was a very good baby and a great sleeper. Luka's arrival was special as he was the first baby born after Brad's death. We were still grieving then, and his arrival provided the lift that the family needed. Zoran and Mira continued their active grandparenting role. They wanted to take Luka, with Evie, every Saturday night as soon as they could. They are special family people.

After I had started the BoysTown role I received a call from Kerryn Newton, the owner and Managing Director of Directors

Australia (DA). She knew my background from Carolyn Penklis and wanted to discuss a possible role at Directors Australia. DA specialised in board governance and board recruitment work. Kerryn was looking for a consultant who could assist with board evaluations and other board governance work, preferably with a finance and audit committee background. I had never considered this type of consultancy work. I was very interested as I enjoyed being on boards and working with boards sounded like very interesting work.

I joined DA as a board governance consultant and have been there ever since. It is a flexible role, tailored to DA workflows, which has suited me with my other board and consulting roles. I have particularly enjoyed working with private company boards and facilitating strategic planning workshops. Working with DA has broadened my corporate network and I have made some great friends along the way. Kerryn has been a pleasure to work with and DA has built a very solid reputation in the board governance space.

Our family received an unexpected shock in late 2011. Hans, arguably the fittest, healthiest sibling, was diagnosed with pancreatic cancer. Hans passed away on 6 July 2014 after an almighty battle against this vicious disease. As fate would have it, he passed away on the same day the Gold Coast Marathon was held that year. This was very fitting as he loved this day. Please refer to chapter 18, for more details on Hans's life and death.

Chantal and Pat got engaged on the 7th of January 2012. By then Chantal had graduated from university with a Bachelor of Business (Marketing and HR). She worked at Paradise Gems, a jewellery store in Mermaid Waters. She had become very experienced in jewellery retailing. Pat had a natural flair for selling. He had a variety of jobs selling various products and consistently achieved high sales levels. Chantal became pregnant and they welcomed their first child, Levi Niklas, on the 7th of January 2013. He was born exactly one year after they became engaged.

Levi was a very cute, serious baby. He knew what he liked and didn't like very early. He brought a lot of joy to Pat's family, after the death of Nik in 2007.

Chantal and Pat were married in Vanuatu in August 2014. They chose a destination wedding, and we all combined it with a holiday at the beautiful Warwick Le Lagon Resort, in Port Vila. It was a very memorable wedding for a variety of reasons. The setting was idyllic. The ceremony and reception were both held on the sandy beach on the edge of the lagoon. The ceremony was delayed when there was a malfunction with Evie's, who was a flower girl, hair. A hair curler got caught in her long hair and it took about an hour to extricate it. Evie didn't cry and patiently sat there while it was all happening. Fortunately, it was a relatively small wedding and we kept everyone informed of the delay.

It was my first destination wedding. Whilst it was as idyllic as expected, I noticed something I didn't expect. With all the wedding guests being together for about five days before the wedding there were more pre wedding nerves and jitters evident than at a normal wedding. Fortunately, it all ended like a movie. Chantal was a stunning bride, Pat was a nervous groom, Levi was an integral part of the ceremony, Evie's hair looked great, and it was a fantastic night.

Life continued to be both busy and great for Di and I. Di was the perfect partner for the many corporate functions that I attended, and for the different corporate roles I had. She was equally at home talking to the chair of a listed company or being in a crowded bar at a sporting event.

I recall one big corporate lunch that we attended in Brisbane. I was there hoping to make some new contacts and I was getting a bit fidgety at the pre lunch gathering. I was keen to move around and meet people. Di told me to stay where we were and wait for people to come to us. I did that and within five minutes we were talking to a former premier and former treasurer of Queensland. That little networking session was very successful.

Di and I travelled frequently and managed to fit in a few trips each year to attend family functions and see my family in Wollongong. Di was a huge support to me in my varied corporate roles. She did any administration work, but more importantly she was a very people savvy, intelligent sounding board.

In 2014 I was in one of my regular chiropractic appointments with Lara. She suggested that I have a remedial massage with their massage therapist as that would help with my back issues. I organised the massage with the therapist, Kirralee Campbell. She was a brilliant massage therapist and I have been going to her ever since.

Kirralee was also very spiritual which led to an unexpected extra at some of the sessions. And it wasn't the extra that men immediately think of. I don't profess to have any knowledge as to how these things happen but somehow messages from Brad's spirit were coming through Kirralee. She is what I would call an informal, intuitive medium. She doesn't charge for it and doesn't profess to be able to do it. If it happens, she lets you know so you can interpret the messages.

At my first massage I got quite a shock as I did not know that Kirralee received these messages. Halfway through the massage she said, "There is someone here who wants to talk to you". I said, "I did not even hear the door open", thinking someone had walked in. This was the start of Brad's spirit coming through and it happened consistently from then on. It also happened after Hans passed away.

Several months later I had an appointment with Kirralee after a week of researching and organising to buy a new car. I laid down on the massage table. Kirralee placed her hands on my back and said, "Brad wants to know what you are doing with your car". By then I was used to receiving the messages but this one shocked me as it was so accurate and specific.

On another occasion the message from Brad was around that Di and I should do more travelling. Kirralee suggested that we do up a vision board to include our travel plans. When I got home from the massage that day Di said, "Don't tell me what Kirralee said today as I want to show you something first". She then showed me a vision board that she had started compiling that day and it included travel destinations. Di had never discussed compiling a vision board before.

My whole family has now been to Kirralee, and she has become a close friend of the family.

Lara is also responsible for introducing me to ice baths. She had been going to ice bath therapy at P3 Sports & Recovery at Burleigh and suggested I give it a go. I went and kept going for about three years. I did the hot/cold therapy where you alternate between the ice bath and a very hot bath at 4-minute intervals. Spending 4 minutes in an 8-degree ice bath was very testing, even painful, at the beginning. Like anything you get used to it and I was soon able to do 4 or 5 rounds of the hot and cold baths. If the ice bath was a little warmer, say around 12 degrees, I would sit there for 8 to 12 minutes.

The ice bath therapy was great for my joint pain and general health. The baths all had magnesium in the water which made you very relaxed afterwards. I talked to many people in those baths. They ranged from elite athletes attending for sports recovery, to people attending for physical ailments, to people attending for mental health issues. One man told me once that if he stopped at P3 on the way home from work he then had a good night and did not drink. If he didn't stop at P3 he went home and drank alcohol. I talked to a stripper once who had been referred to P3 to assist with shoulder pain after too much pole dancing. One day I found myself sitting in the ice bath with Sonny Bill Williams, the dual rugby league and rugby union international. He was as friendly as anyone I had ever met there.

I had continued to do consulting work with Villa World from time to time. In mid-2014 I was appointed to the Audit and Risk Committee and then appointed as an independent director early in 2015. I had come full circle with Villa World, from being an employee to an independent, non-executive director. I felt like I had returned to my corporate home.

I now had two listed company directorships, a charity board role, a couple of advisory board roles and ongoing board consulting work with DA. I enjoyed all these roles, and I was achieving my financial targets.

Life has a way of throwing you a curveball when you least expect it. In mid-2015 there were some unexpected developments, which must remain confidential, at CuDeco, after which I decided to resign as a director. There was some fallout from these developments. I then decided not to stand for re-election as a Villa World director in November 2015. I also decided to focus on my advisory board roles and consulting work and not to accept any further listed company directorships.

In 2016 I picked up an advisory board role with City Venue Management (CVM), an aquatic centre and swim school operator, based on the Gold Coast. CVM operate the Rackley Swimming brand. They are a private company that walks the talk in playing a role in the environmental challenges faced by today's world. The CEO, Reece Rackley, and Managing Director, Jay Clarke, have worked together for the past twenty years to drive the company to where it is today. They, and the executive team, are a very refreshing group to work with. They have grown significantly since 2015.The company has a great culture and Reece is a very savvy, high-level CEO. I still have this board advisor role today.

Chantal became pregnant again soon after the wedding. This became a very difficult and dramatic pregnancy. Chantal was hospitalised when she was 21 weeks pregnant. She then had to have an emergency operation to have her gall bladder removed when she was 24 weeks pregnant. She went home for almost 5 weeks when she started haemorrhaging and was admitted to hospital again.

Annalee Angelica Goransson was born 10 weeks premature on the 9th of April 2015. She weighed 1.3 kilograms and spent the next six weeks in the NICU and Special Care Ward at the Gold Coast University Hospital. She was tiny and showed her fighting spirit from the minute she was born. This was an extremely stressful period for Chantal, Pat, and their families. Tina was an enormous help to Chantal through these six weeks. Chantal virtually lived at her and Rob's place so she could leave Levi with them while she went to the hospital all day. Pat's mother, Elke, was also a big help. We all pitched in and rotated hospital visits as much as possible.

Thankfully Annalee was allowed to go home on the 17th of May. She is now a happy, healthy, tall, seven-year-old child with a zest for life.

Little did we know that some of the pre wedding nerves at Chantal and Pat's wedding may have been prophetic. Their marriage broke up towards the end of 2017. Today they are great co-parents, and we are pleased to still have Pat in our lives.

After I stepped down from the Villa World Board, I caught up with Craig Treasure, the CEO, for a coffee. Craig said he thought I could be more useful to Villa World now that I wasn't a director. This was due to my understanding of Villa World's business from my long history with the company. He was a forward-thinking CEO and wanted someone to be able to focus on the company's future strategic planning. I became Villa World's Strategy Consultant, which was a part-time role for the next three years. It is a very small world as Craig and his wife, Debbie, had bought our house at Worongary about twenty years before I worked with him at Villa World.

I had met a lady called Lisa MacCallum through my BoysTown role. Lisa had a long-term executive career with Nike in the USA and had impressed me as someone with a contemporary, fresh approach to corporate strategy. She was an early, strong proponent of the concept that companies must stand for ideas bigger than profit to be competitive in today's world. I was planning a strategy workshop with the Villa World Board and senior management team, and I organised for Lisa to attend the workshop as a guest speaker. The strategy day went very well, particularly Lisa's presentation, and we embarked on a journey to develop a purpose led strategy for Villa World.

The concept of a purpose led strategy is that, in today's world, every business should have a purpose beyond profit. The purpose essentially answers the question as to why that business exists. There is nothing wrong with businesses making a profit, in fact that is essential, but the profit achieved should be the outcome of the business achieving its purpose. I have become a strong advocate of purpose led strategy.

We completed a purpose led strategic plan for Villa World. The purpose statement agreed upon, after consultation from staff and all relevant parties, was "Helping People Reach Home". It was a comprehensive, fulfilling process.

In addition to my strategy role, I assisted in other areas as required. This included working with a new CFO, Lorelei Nieves, who had been promoted from within the finance team. I also worked closely with the Organisational Development Manager, Leanne

Morgan. Leanne had been an accounts payable clerk when I joined Villa World in 2000. 17 years later she was in the senior executive team. A young lady, Kirsty Chapman, was the Digital Marketing Executive. Her father, Warren, was our IT consultant when I was the CFO from 2000 to 2005. I guess that aged me a bit noticing the next generation coming through.

The Villa World Chairman was Mark Jewell, a respected Gold Coast property identity. Mark, Craig, and I had known each other, many years earlier, through our corporate roles when I was the CFO of Villa World. It was a pleasure to work with Mark and Craig again. The Villa World Board were so impressed with Lisa MacCallum that she became a non-executive director.

Unfortunately, we did not see the strategic plan through to its execution. My consulting role ended in June 2019 when the plan had been finalised. A few months later Villa World was taken over, and privatised, by the Avid Property Group. The entire board and most of the executive team, including Craig, left in conjunction with the takeover. That was the end of an era for Villa World and for me.

In 2016, BoysTown moved to a new name and image which better reflected the inclusive nature of its work. The name was changed to yourtown. In April 2016 the Chair of yourtown, Brother Ambrose, announced that he was stepping down due to other commitments. yourtown had always had a De La Salle Brother in the role of Chair. It was decided to appoint a Chair from the existing board members. I was appointed as the first lay, that is not a member of the clergy, Chair of yourtown on the 15th of June 2016.

I was very pleased to be appointed to chair such an incredible organisation. I was quietly proud of myself as I had generally been in 2IC, that is second-in-charge, roles in my corporate career. I considered this appointment to be the pinnacle of my corporate career.

The change of name to yourtown proved to be very successful. The next few years were very busy and rewarding as services were delivered, reviewed, and expanded. We also revised the board structure and at one stage had three young directors, under 35 years of age, on the board. They brought in younger generational thinking and kept me on my toes as the Chair.

I stepped down as Chair in November 2018, and as a director in October 2019. I had served the standard 9-year term. Peter Ffrench, who had joined the board on the same day as me, became the new Chair.

I could not leave entirely, and I am still a member of the Finance and Risk Committee. After being in the corporate world I found it to be refreshing and humbling to work with a charity that does such great work. I had met many more people who selflessly work for their local communities.

I have worked closely with Peter, Tracy, and Julie Kleidon, who has been Tracy's Executive Assistant for the past ten years. It has been an absolute pleasure to work with them and all the other directors, executive team members and staff. They are very special people.

I have been enriched through working with yourtown. I think Brad would be proud of me.

In early 2017 Di and I decided to transition from a life partnership to friendship. We had a fantastic ten years together and our relationship had reached a natural turning point. We decided to hold a "transition to friendship" party on my birthday in May that year. We were still living together at this point. Di was nervous that day as she thought it would be the last time that she saw some of my family members, and the Maksimovic family, all of whom she had grown close to.

Di was wrong about that. At the transition party my ex-wife Tina came up to Di and gave her a present. She told Di that she wasn't going anywhere, and she still expected to see her at our family gatherings. And that is how it has been since then. Di and I have maintained our close friendship. She and her new partner, Les Howson, come to our family gatherings. I know that all sounds a bit weird, but it works for us.

In January 2020 I took on what I think will be my final board role. I was asked to become a founding director of Byron Bay Wildlife Hospital. This was a newly formed charity founded by a veterinarian named Steve Van Mil. The purpose of the charity was to build a mobile wildlife hospital. This hospital could then be transported to areas of need, such as bushfires, as required. Steve had recruited three other veterinarians as co-directors and they needed a director with governance and finance experience.

I accepted the role. The charity had no funds at the start of 2020 but by the end of 2020 it had funded and taken delivery of the mobile wildlife hospital, and I stepped down as intended. My role was to assist getting it set up and that had been done.

I enjoyed this role and am pleased that the mobile wildlife hospital is now the subject of a television series called "Wildlife Rescue Australia."

Steve was a very good fundraiser and I discovered that the Australian public are generous in their support of our wildlife preservation.

Looking back on my board and various board advisory roles I thoroughly enjoyed them and learned something from each of them. Occasionally I was involved in board decisions which were very difficult to make. These decisions were made easier by the board having a sound decision making process, the directors remaining calm and logical and the board being cohesive. These boards ensured that the board room was a place where individual input by directors was encouraged while also ensuring that the final decision was a collective one accepted by all directors. I found that boards often became stronger if they weathered a crisis, or made a very difficult decision, as the directors respect and appreciation for their fellow directors was generally enhanced.

I received some nice, useful feedback early in my board career when I was sitting on a body corporate committee. After I had been on the committee for about six months I was in a meeting when one of the committee members commented that they, the committee members, don't argue with each other anymore. Another committee member remarked "That's because Gerry is here now". I had subconsciously brought cohesion to that committee. It was useful for my board career as it made me more aware of my boardroom style and confirmed the importance of a cohesive environment whereby robust discussion is encouraged but respect and willingness to listen to other viewpoints is always maintained.

Several years ago, I attended an annual governance summit in Melbourne. There were a few thousand directors at this summit. One of the speakers was very thought provoking and somewhat "tongue in cheek" commented that the majority of corporate directors in Australia were "pale, male and stale". He was referring to the historical corporate board structures that generally comprised Anglo-Saxon males over sixty years of age.

I realised that he was talking about me although I would like to think that I hadn't reached the "stale" stage yet. Board composition in Australia has improved significantly over the past decade with greater gender, skills, age and cultural diversity on boards, and board performance has been enhanced accordingly. It would be rare to find a board now that comprises only "pale, male and stale" directors. Nevertheless, the phrase "pale, male and stale" is a great reminder to all directors to continually undertake professional development and stay up to date in their area of expertise. This is particularly relevant in today's digital world where directors should be digitally literate.

I loved working with growing private companies, either in a board advisory or a board consulting capacity, who were willing to improve their corporate governance processes. They understood the vital importance of having a great culture and that good governance is good for business.

Whilst I enjoyed all my board roles and Villa World was like a second family to me, there was something extra special about being on the yourtown board. On one occasion I attended a morning tea presentation at the Kingston office which provides training and employment services for young people. After the presentations I was sitting with a few of the staff when a young Aboriginal person, aged around 16, asked to join us. She wanted to thank me for the services yourtown were providing for her. She told us that she was determined to break the generational cycle of unemployment in her family. It was a very meaningful discussion; it really grounded me and stayed with me. I thanked her as she was inspiring us and demonstrating how worthwhile the work done by charities like yourtown is.

And lastly re corporate matters I will pass on my number one leadership tip, for what it is worth. It is to be a good, active listener. For many people, there is a natural temptation in a conversation to think about the next thing you are going to say while the other person is still talking. I know because I have done this. This can quickly lead to a person not fully hearing what the other person has to say. A good technique to use to become a better listener is to restate back, succinctly and respectfully, to the person what you think they have said to demonstrate to them that you heard them properly and to clarify what they really meant. You only have to do this a few times and your listening skills will naturally improve. Becoming a good, effective listener demonstrates empathy, a willingness to learn from the other person's input, and promotes respect from the other person.

With a family as large as the Lamberts there will always be some family members with challenges or tribulations at any point in time. There have been several serious medical issues over the years. I would like to acknowledge one family member, Lily-Rose Burnell, who is currently facing very serious health challenges. Lily-

Rose is the daughter of Pauline Wilson and her former husband, Lee Burnell. She is Dianne's granddaughter.

Lily-Rose is 16 years old. She has had a major health battle for more than two years. Her life went from being a normal active teenager, who dedicated her life to dance, to a life when getting out of bed can be a major achievement. She has been diagnosed with several major illnesses and syndromes including Postural Orthostatic Tachycardia Syndrome (POTS), Functional Neurological Disorder (FND) and Gastroparesis. She has spent many months in hospitals and long periods in a wheelchair.

Lily-Rose's medical conditions are very complex, and she still has a hard road ahead. She has been beyond courageous in the battle to date. She wants to live the life of any normal teenager. This is Pauline's, and the entire families', biggest hope and wish for her.

In August 2019 Chantal met a guy called Dave Turnbull. They met through Danita as Luka and Dave's son, Jordan, had started playing soccer in the same team. Love blossomed and they have been together ever since.

Dave has three children, Paige, Damien, and Jordan. He moved to Australia from South Africa in 2018 to set up a business in Australia. Chantal and Dave have now created their own "Brady Bunch" and it is going very well. Having a meal at her place, when all the kids are there, reminds me of my childhood. I was there recently for "Taco Tuesday". The kids had at least five tacos each. I had three.

Dave's kids are 15, 13 and 11 years old so they are older than Chantal's children, Levi and Annalee. It is amazing how well they all get on. It is very good for Levi and Annalee to have older kids around growing up. Levi and Jordan play sports together non-stop. Paige, Damien, and Jordan are polite, friendly, and practical children. I am quietly thrilled that they call me Opa. Dave and the kids have enriched our family unit.

Dave is a very interesting person, so I have two of them with Sasha always being interesting. I thought the Lamberts were sports mad and then I met Dave! He is very hands on with his kids' sporting activities and is interested in all sports. Chantal and Dave both run their own businesses. Their lives are extremely busy.

Danita and Sasha are also very busy, but perhaps not as hectic as Chantal and Dave. They both work in their business, SDM Consultants, which provides accounting, taxation, and business consulting services. Sasha has built this into a very good business and his clientele increases each year. He is also an astute investor. Their kids, Evie, and Luka are also active with sports and school activities. Danita and Sasha are hands on, great parents.

Danita and Sasha have joined the Gold Coast boating community, purchasing a Riviera M370 Sports Cruiser in July 2021. They are very generous in hosting family and friends on boat trips. These boat trips are very popular. As we know boating can be an expensive hobby. Sasha keeps asking me to "bring my credit card" and I keep telling him "I have lost it".

CHAPTER 17

BRADLEY LAMBERT
— 29TH NOVEMBER 1981 TO 3RD OCTOBER 2009 —

As noted in Chapter 15 Brad sadly and unexpectedly passed away on the 3rd of October 2009.

His funeral was held on a beautiful, sunny, spring day on the 9th of October. It was quite a big funeral with about three hundred people in attendance. I delivered Brad's eulogy. The composition of it was a combined family effort and I was told after the day it provided the perfect summary of Brad. I am including the eulogy in full as follows even though there is some duplication with stories mentioned earlier in the book:

My speech is going to be a bit different with hopefully as much joy as tears. In fact Brad would like some clapping so can we start with a round of applause to welcome Brad.
I am going to touch on a few things in around 10 minutes.
- *Brad's disorder*
- *The last couple of weeks*
- *Some highlights about Brad the person*
- *Some thank you's*

Brad was diagnosed with Obsessive Compulsive Disorder when he was around 16. It was quite severe and it manifested itself with thoughts in his head that would never go away. Brad very bravely and openly battled with his disorder until his death. His disorder contributed significantly to his genetic addictive disposition and Brad was one of those people who became easily addicted to alcohol, drugs, and medication. He had many good periods and tried to rehabilitate several times, but OCD was always looming and ready to pounce. Brad explained to me that people without OCD could not understand what people like him go through.

A significant turning point for Brad happened in August 2008 when he achieved a good outcome from a Court case. It also provided a serious and timely warning and it became the catalyst for what would be arguably the best year of his life:

- He quickly got a great job with Technigro which he held until the time of his death. This job provided Brad with a good income and over that year he was very generous at birthdays and celebrations, and I knew he was very proud of that. He paid out a loan that I had taken out for him and became financially independent.
- Around the same time, he and Jacqui (or Jackson to Brad) found each other, and she became his first serious relationship. Brad was settled for the first time.
- He also moved in to rent at Matty's place and this provided him with a secure home that he really liked.

Things started to unravel for Brad a couple of months ago and he broke up with Jacqui, got injured at work (which left him with too much time on his hands) and started to drink quite heavily again.

This led to a major incident on the 22nd of September this year. Brad was hospitalised for a day and was facing various charges. I picked him up from hospital the next day and asked that he be admitted as I considered him to be at high risk. However, he was released as his problems were considered to be long term rather than things the hospital could sort out in the short term. I took Brad home for a night and then he went back to Matty's place. However, he quickly found another place to live as Brad was aware of the effect of the impact of his recent actions. I think this incident really affected Brad as he considerably overstepped the level of his previous misdemeanours, and he was facing the real possibility of going to jail.

Brad's psychiatrist has explained to me what is likely to have happened on the night that Brad passed away. He could have been quite normal during the day, and this appears to be the case. Rafer spoke to Brad around 4pm and "everything was sweet". This is the last conversation we are aware of Brad having. With people like Brad everything depends "on that moment at that time".

It is likely that Brad drank excessively through the night, the bad thoughts kicked in and they would have been exacerbated by the recent events. He wrote a note and took an overdose of prescription medication. We are awaiting autopsy results, but we are very confident that Brad died in his sleep without pain which is very comforting. It is important that I emphasise that before Brad's "moment in time" hit him that night he would have had no intention of doing what he did and there is plenty of evidence that it was not premeditated.

His note has not been released to us due to police protocols, but they have read me the parts they could decipher. I am going to share the key parts with everyone as I know a lot of people are looking for answers.

- He was sorry and loved his family and wanted to thank them. He loved everyone in his life
- It is no-one's fault.

- Special, positive references to anyone he thought may have felt guilt.
- "Don't cry for me – I had fun".
- There was no anger in the note at all and the underlying tone was that he had had enough.

Brad wanted peace, he had battled for long enough and I think he has shown tremendous courage to both battle with his demons and then do what he wanted or needed to do in the end.

Brad wanted to make his family proud and because I know he is listening now I want him to know that we have all never been prouder of him than right now. For a person who had an ongoing battle with disorders and addictions he had an amazing impact on everyone he met. His "life of the party" persona, genuine friendship and generosity are his greatest legacies.

This brings me to Brad the person. The following speakers will recall some experiences so I will limit mine to a few that typify Brad:

When Brad was 13, I sat him down for the father/son chat. I said to him I would like to have a talk about sex, and he immediately responded with "What do you want to know Dad?"

Secondly, for Brad's 22nd birthday I asked him what he wanted to do. His response was "I just want to buy my mates a drink" so we went off to McGinty's at Broadbeach with five of his mates and family. I had told Brad I would spend $500. The night was going along very exuberantly when Danita suggested I check the tab. It was over the limit, and it was not 9pm yet. They had all gotten smashed and I had not even noticed. Brad loved it!

About two years ago one of the Dutch cousins, Wayne Berkelmans, came to stay for a while and work with Villa World. He arrived on my birthday and initially he appeared quite conservative and informed us he did not drink. He ended up sitting next to Brad at the restaurant and surprise surprise, he had a beer in his hand very quickly. Brad persuaded him that you must have a drink on your first night in Australia. Wayne got smashed and he and Brad were inseparable for the rest of his trip.

Brad was the king of nicknames. If you didn't have a nickname, he would call you by your last name and then that stuck as your nickname. Who else would give their dog a first and last name, Ernie Dingo. I will be happy to be called Gedro forever now. He was also the master of his own language and sayings. He is probably looking down on me now saying, "neck up you parrot!"

I did not know that Brad was a champion at something until this week when Undies came over one night. He recalled the night that Brad got knocked out three times in one night. I was duly informed that this is an all-time record and further I should be proud of that. So yes, I am now proud of that!

I would like now to touch on Brad's intelligence. Brad used to love asking me Sale of the Century style questions in front of his mates as he thought I knew everything. As the years went on, he taught himself an enormous amount from the internet and it was interesting to observe that he gradually began to know more answers than me. He liked to dumb himself down a bit, but he was extremely intelligent and could retain a lot of information. His knowledge of English soccer and boxing were great examples of this.

Brad's generosity knew no bounds. He was there if anyone had to move house or fix something. He would spend his last dollar on a shout at the bar and he always managed to get some money out of me if he needed it for his mother's or sister's birthdays. More importantly he was very generous with his time. He would sit down and talk to older people, play with kids, spend time talking to his mates' girlfriends. He loved people and being with them.

I would like to thank and acknowledge a few people:

- Brad's doctors, particularly Arthur and Mark Whittington. Great job!
- Brad's workmates. I understand he was highly regarded at Technigro, and I look forward to meeting some of you later.
- Brad's mates and their families. For Brad, life was all about his family and his mates and he invariably became part of their families. I don't know how many meals he had at the Harts' but he loved your cooking Di! The six pallbearers have been friends of Brads for many years, and I know he has many more close friends from recent years who I am keen to meet. A special thank you to Matty for providing Brad with a home for the last year of his life. Also, thanks to the 50 mates who gathered last Sunday and took up a collection for the funeral. What a gesture! You paid for that rather large notice in the Bulletin, and we all know that Brad would have loved that.
- Jacqui, she helped Brad mature and make his last year a very good one.
- Everyone else here today, particularly the travellers. We appreciate your love and support. Also, the many people who have supported us this week. Our house has been full of people, flowers, cards, and food. A special mention to Bill, Karen and the Cunninghams (who are like a second family for Brad).
- Tina's family. There are too many to name, but David, Ryan, Luke, Natalie, Patsy and Cheryl have all played a major role in Brad's life. A special acknowledgement to Joan, Brad's only surviving grandparent. It is great to have her here today. Also, Scott Baxter who shared a bond with Brad and supported him

unconditionally.
- My family. As most of you know I have eight brothers and sisters and they have all flown in for the funeral, together with most of the cousins. My six brothers will do a reading later in the service.
- Brad's family. He loved and adored his two sisters and Sasha and Patty, and he was also fiercely protective of them as Patty found out the first night that he met Brad. They had some great special times together. It is wonderful that Brad got to know Evie, his niece, but very sad that she won't have Brad in her life.
- Brad's mum Tina. The mother/son bond was very strong, and Brad loved Tina, or Old Cheese as he called her, with all his heart. Tina, together with her husband Rob, gave Brad tremendous support over the last few years. It is fitting that Brad sent his final text message to Tina. What an honour!
- My beautiful partner, Dianne, who has been very supportive and enlightening for me in my journey with Brad. She understood Brad better than me, and they formed a strong bond. Speaking of Di reminds me to thank everyone who has supported me in my journey with Brad.

Brad, we love you and are very proud of you, look over us.
We will never forget you.
Rest in the peace that you have craved.

At Brad's funeral wake a man came up and asked to talk to me. He told me that he owned a few strip clubs in Surfers Paradise and knew Brad well, as a regular patron at the clubs. I wasn't surprised. He thanked me for explaining Brad's illness. He had no idea that Brad had mental health issues. He said he always would have wondered why Brad did it. Quite a few people asked me about OCD that day.

A few weeks after Brad's death a letter arrived from his probation officer following up on a missed appointment (he had been on probation from a previous Court matter). I opened the letter and immediately called the probation office to advise them of Brad's death. I expected to leave a message with the receptionist, but she said that Brad's probation officer would want to talk to me. I don't know why but I was expecting to be put through to a stern, male probation officer (like in the movies) but instead I found myself talking to a quietly spoken female voice.

She started crying as soon as I told her what happened and then we were both crying. After we composed ourselves and I had told her what we thought had happened she said something like "we don't get many good people through here, but your son was one of the good ones!". She explained how Brad was always polite and cooperative and they were determined to keep him out of jail. She knew that Brad had mental health issues and said that jail was not the place for people like Brad. This was a very emotional phone call and I felt very proud of Brad after it.

Brad was always open about his mental health issues. He always told me that he was happy for me to talk about it if it helped anyone else. Hopefully one of Brad's legacies is greater awareness.

I can't finish Brad's story without talking about the ducks. I had organised for Brad's funeral notice to appear in the Gold Coast Bulletin. On the morning of publication, I got the paper and went outside to read the funeral notice. I was the only one awake, so I had some quiet time to myself. As I was reading the notice two ducks flew into our swimming pool and started swimming around. I got up and walked over to the pool. One of the ducks then got out of the pool and stood ramrod straight looking at me. I fed the ducks, and they flew off. I had never seen ducks in our swimming pool before.

When everyone got up, I told them about the ducks. The consensus was that the duck who looked at me was sending a message from Brad's spirit. Once again, I was in it, but didn't understand it. I don't feel these messages like some people do.

About six months later Di and I caught up with a group of people. They included a few of Tina's cousins and one of their husbands, Greg Dillon. Greg had attended Brad's funeral, and this was the first time we had caught up since then. Greg asked me if we could talk about Brad, which I was always happy to do. We had a long chat and I told Greg about the ducks. He said something like, "One of those ducks was Brad, Ged". He really liked hearing about the ducks and was energised by the story.

Tragically Greg died suddenly the following Sunday, following a heart attack. I did the same thing with his funeral notice the following week. His family had told me what day the notice would be in the paper. I went outside again to read the funeral notice. Once again, as I was reading the notice two ducks flew into the swimming pool and started swimming around. I named them Brad and Greg. They were the only two times I saw ducks in our swimming pool.

Tina and I have both had the "Duck" ringtone on our mobile phone since then.

I have been asked the question "If I could say one thing to a suicidal person what would it be?" Please note that I can only answer this question based on my experiences with Brad. I cannot offer any medical advice in relation to mental health and my answer should not be interpreted professionally or medically.

My answer and message to that suicidal person would be for them not to think that their family is going to be better off without them. In Brad's case I believe that one of the reasons he committed suicide was to relieve the pressure and stress that he believed he caused for his family. My belief is based on our interactions and also his suicide note which stated, inter alia, that he regretted not making his family proud and was "sick of being a f..k up".

I must acknowledge that I did experience some relief after Brad passed. This was both for me and my family, in relation to the stress that often came with Brad's life, and for Brad, as his pain was finally over. However, any stress relief was quickly replaced by grief, loss, and the knowledge that this lively, caring, loving person would never become a father or be an uncle to my grandkids. I really believe that Brad would have flourished in his role as an uncle and that life would have been different, and better, for him if he could have hung on until then.

The fact that we still talk about Brad in our everyday conversations, and the extent to which I have written about him in this book, highlight that the pain of the loss is far greater than any relief gained.

I would also try to incorporate into the conversation (with the suicidal person) how important it is to have a few people you can rely on to talk to in times of crisis. It is hard enough having mental health issues to deal with; it is much, much harder trying to deal with them alone. We were very fortunate with Brad that he was very open about his mental health issues, and I would like to think that this made his journey a bit more bearable.

Brad had a core group of friends from school. These included Rafer Hart, Arley Obarzanski, Cameron Snow and Justin Underwood. After school it expanded to include Nick Baxter, Corey Willis, Nick Heathcote, Matty Snow and many more. Brad lived for his mates or "the boys" as he called them. Brad was also very good with any of his mates' girlfriends. He was very inclusive and would spend time with the girls as well as the boys. Carley Snow, Cameron's wife, recalls how attentive Brad was to their daughter, Harper, when she was born.

Brad was also very close to his Widdicombe cousins, David, Ryan, Luke, and Natalie. Brad and Luke were more like brothers than cousins. I'm not sure that Brad was always the greatest influence on him. Luke loved every minute of his time with Brad.

Brad did not see his cousins from my side of the family as much because they all lived in Wollongong or Sydney. However, as it was with Brad whenever they did catch up, they had a ball. He was very popular with the Lambert cousins. I'm pretty sure he encouraged his cousin, Byron, to have his first alcoholic drink at one of the family weddings.

Brad had a nickname for everyone. This included Danita and Chantal, who were "pig" and "piglet." Evie became "Stevie Wonder". In return Brad was called "Bert", "Bertie" or "Bertdog".

By now you can see that we have many great memories of Brad, and I am going to finish off with three more of my favourite ones.

When he was about eight years old a funny thing happened. I used to give the kids one dollar every Saturday morning and then take them to the local shop so they could spend it. I was backing the car out of the driveway when Brad started crying hysterically. I turned around out to see what had happened. He told me he had swallowed his one dollar coin. He had been mucking around with it. I thought he must be choking and jumped out of the car to attend to him. When I opened his car door, he said he was fine. He was crying because he now didn't have any money for his lollies.

We did not get to the shop that day. We went straight to our local doctor's surgery. The x-ray revealed this shiny one dollar coin sitting comfortably in Brad's stomach. The doctor advised us that Brad should pass the coin naturally. If he didn't pass it in fourteen days, they would have to consider surgery to remove it. Brad then had to stay home and do his "number two's" on a pot. We had to check every time to see if the coin was in there. We were very relieved when it arrived about a week later.

I did replace the one dollar for Brad, and we eventually made it to the shop.

Another amusing incident occurred when Brad was about 13 years old. We decided it was time to open a bank account for each of the kids. I organised the accounts with the Mudgeeraba Suncorp Metway branch. At that time, it was normal practice for the manager of the branch to meet the three kids, explain their bank account to them and give them their debit card. I took the kids to meet the bank manager and get their cards. He told them he was going to give them a PIN number each and they should change it to their own number as soon as possible. Before he got the card Brad confidently said that he was going to get a good number. The manager handed them each their envelope and said they could have a look at their number but not tell it to anyone else. He emphasised the importance of confidentiality.

Brad opened his envelope and started laughing uncontrollably. He showed me his number, which he should not have, and then I joined him in the laughter. It got to be too much for the bank manager. He asked Brad to show him the number so he could see what was so funny. He said he would just give him another PIN number. Brad's PIN number was 6969. Brad kept the number. I don't think he ever changed it while he had that account. I never found out how Brad knew that was such a funny number.

The final one is a story from my Villa World days, and it is a typical and great Brad memory. In 2002 John Potter and I were granted employee options. These were options to purchase shares in Villa World at the market price at that time. They were incentives in that if Villa World performed well and the share price increased then we would benefit by the amount of the share price increase if we converted the options and sold the shares.

I was granted 1 million options. The allocation of the options to John and I was reported in an article in the Gold Coast Bulletin. Brad found out that I had been allocated the options by reading it in the Bulletin. Well, he thought that was the greatest thing ever. However, Brad either failed to, or did not want to, understand the difference between options and shares. He would just announce something like, "Gedro's loaded, he just got 1 million Villa World shares".

He was very proud of me and proceeded to tell all his mates and anyone else he thought should know. I did explain to him that I would only make money if the share price went up. I'm sure he did understand that, but nothing was going to stand in the way of a good story for Brad. It brought him a lot of joy to brag about me a bit and it led to many humorous moments. Sasha never missed an opportunity to ask Brad, " How are Ged's shares going, Brad?" That would lead to another discussion with Brad confidently predicting how much money I would make.

We talk about Brad often. He is still in our lives. His nieces and nephews know all about their "Uncle Bertie".

I now live in a building called Freshwater Point. It is situated on the vacant lot where Brad used to search for the dead body. Due to this connection, I feel like this is my spiritual home.

CHAPTER 18

HANS LAMBERT

— 7TH AUGUST 1950 TO 6TH JULY 2014 —

In December 2011 Hans started to feel unwell and looked a bit jaundiced. He was quickly diagnosed with pancreatic cancer. He underwent a whipple procedure, which is major surgery, on Christmas Eve that year. His surgeon told him that he enjoyed operating on Hans as he was the skinniest person that he had performed it on. It made his job to access the tumour much easier.

The operation provided Hans with some valuable time. He underwent several rounds of chemotherapy. He tried alternate medicine through a naturopath in Sydney who specialised in liver related cancers. He visited this naturopath every fortnight. Hans's wife, Diane, John, Fuji, and Ossie rotated driving Hans to the naturopath. Fuji drove Hans most of the time. He recalls that they had deep, meaningful conversations on these trips. A couple of our friends also offered to drive Hans if ever required. I don't think that ever happened as the family rallied around Hans and there was always a family member available to drive him.

I turned 60 in May 2013 and had a party on the Gold Coast. Even though I had seen the entire family at a wedding in Sydney the previous weekend Hans was determined to come to the Gold Coast for my party. He was quite ill with the cancer and did not want to miss any significant family events. He could not fly so our mutual friend, Haze, drove Hans up for the party. Haze said that they talked for the entire trip. He treasures that memory, and I was very grateful to Haze for driving Hans up.

Hans had a great weekend at mine and Di's place. He could not do much so he would sit out the back, with a cup of tea, and talk to whoever was around. He and Di talked for hours. She recalls that he was warm, gentle, insightful, and wise during these chats. He made a great speech at my party, again making sure it was about me and not about him.

The last time I did something with Hans was a visit to Lakeside Cemetery at Kanahooka. Hans could still drive, and he met me there. We had organised this visit so he could show me where Jack Van Krevel's ashes were. When I arrived Hans was waiting for me with a thermos of tea, which was typical Hans and very welcome. After finding Jack we strolled through the cemetery and paid our respects to several people who we knew were buried there, including Ross Greenfield and Joe Pearson. It was a very special time with Hans.

Hans passed away on the 6th of July 2014 after an almighty two-and-a-half-year battle. He timed his passing very well. He made his wedding anniversary two days before, Ossie's birthday the day before and then he passed on the Gold Coast Marathon Day for 2014. He never complained about getting cancer and never became self-indulgent with it. This was despite him leading an extremely healthy, active life. He was one person who would have been entitled to say, "Why me?"

Hans's funeral was a beautiful, fitting service held on a glorious winter's day. It was a massive funeral, which reflected Hans's ability to make friends and influence people. At the funeral his children shared what their dad meant to them. Here are some excerpts:

Josh, "A great son, brother, husband, father, uncle, and friend. Dad was truly a great man"

Ali, "Dad was one of my dearest friends...it didn't matter what you did or said. Dad always loved and supported"

Bek, "He was my sounding board, someone I could turn to for advice, a walking buddy, my gardening teacher, a vet to our pets, a role model showing me how to live life, a friend, but most importantly, the best father I could have ever asked for"

Fuji's speech included, "Hans was not perfect, but he was our imperfect, determined, humble, generous, forgiving and stubborn Dutchman who was the new and improved version of his own mother and we will forever have pride in our voice when we say the words, Hans Lambert".

It was a very emotional service. The Unanderra parish priest, Father Mark, was shattered by Hans' death and told Hans' family they could do whatever they wanted to in relation to the funeral service. It was unusual for a priest to say this.

The final paragraph from the eulogy aptly described Hans:

"Hans was a peacemaker and always put everyone else before himself. He enjoyed encouraging others and felt privileged to share in their joy as well as be there in times of need. He was very loved by his immediate family, eight siblings and all his extended family and friends. He will be greatly missed and remembered fondly for his acts of service, friendship, and love."

A few years ago, Hans's son, Josh, came to stay with me while he was competing in the national judo championships, which were being held on the Gold Coast. Josh performed well in these championships. On his last night we had dinner together. We were discussing the sports similarities between Hans and Josh in that they were both very good and determined at any sports that they tackled. During this discussion I said to Josh, "Imagine how good your dad would have been if he didn't get shot". Josh went quiet and I suddenly realised that he did not know about Hans getting shot in the knee with a blank rubber bullet at a school cadet camp.

We discussed this and neither of us were surprised that Hans had never told them. He would not bring that attention to himself. I also think that he thought that getting shot did not affect him at all later in life. I checked with Hans's wife, Diane, after this and she also didn't know about the cadet camp incident.

Hans did not get the same opportunity that I have had to tell his story. That conversation with Josh that night was one of the reasons that I decided to do this book. Even though it is primarily my story I am taking the opportunity to write this chapter about Hans, so his descendants have some appreciation of the wonderful person that he was. Hopefully you have already got the impression that Hans was a special person, and a big brother that I very much looked up to.

Hans was a solid student through his school years. He was well behaved, did his homework and studied conscientiously. He left school when he passed his School Certificate at the end of 1966.

Hans loved animals from an early age. His interest extended beyond the usual dogs and cats. He loved rabbits, pigeons, and chooks. His interest in chooks started when we moved to Albion Park Rail in 1961. He was eleven years old. Dad built a cage so Mum could get chooks, both for eggs and for the family roast chicken lunches. Hans helped Mum with the chooks right from the start. He once noticed wheat seeping through the cracked floorboards at the Albion Park Produce Store, which was near the railway station. He gathered up the wheat and took it home to feed the chooks. After about six months of doing this his guilty conscience got the better of him. He went to the owner to ask permission to take the wheat. I'm pretty sure that permission was granted.

Hans showed Fuji and I the way through the wheat episode. Later in life, we gathered sawdust from the Albion Park Building Supplies for the guinea pigs' cages. We did seek permission right from the start.

One day Hans, Fuji and I were out exploring, and we caught a duck. We brought it home and Mum and Dad let us keep it in the backyard. We made an enclosure, which included a bath. The duck grew quickly and was soon fully grown. Hans loved that duck, as we all did, and he looked after it. One Sunday, a few months later, we returned home from church to find that Dad had killed the duck and was getting it ready for Sunday lunch. We were all very upset, particularly Hans and Fuji. I don't think any of us ate much of the duck. After seeing how upset we were Dad realised that this was different to killing a chook. However, the practicality of getting a meal on the table outweighed the sentimentality for Dad.

Hans's love of chooks also illustrated that he was a conservationist way ahead of his time. He was interested in the vegetable garden from a young age. He helped Mum quite willingly whilst the rest of us considered it to be a chore. He always gathered up the chook droppings for the garden. He also gathered up horse and cow droppings from around the neighbourhood. He was an early user of lawn clippings, and other waste, for the garden. He did not like to see anything go to waste.

Like all of us Hans found whatever jobs he could. His first jobs were moving school toilet cans and selling newspapers at the Oaks hotel.

Hans loved his sports right through school. He was outstanding in athletics at primary school, and very good, but not outstanding, in athletics at high school. He always loved running. He started playing tennis when he was at school. Hans tackled every sport he played with discipline and hard work. He was always happy to practise, and he listened to the coaches. He wanted to improve in whatever he was playing.

After leaving school Hans commenced work at Australian Iron & Steel (AIS) as a commercial trainee. He went to Wollongong Technical College and completed three courses. He enjoyed his job and made plenty of new friends through work. He later joined a department where another guy from Albion Park Rail, John Marley, worked. Hans knew John from school, and from around town. He got a lift to and from work with John and a great friendship developed between them. It was an unlikely friendship as John was the star footballer and a real extrovert. It appears Hans had that innate ability to attract friends from an early age.

Hans got his first car, an old model Morris Minor, around 1969. He loved it and was very generous in driving us kids around if we had to get somewhere. Through the 1970's we had many great times through our common sporting interests and being in the same big circle of mates. Hans got drunk at times, like everyone else. Generally, however he was content to have a few beers and leave it at that. Like most of the Lamberts he decreased his alcohol consumption through his 20's and 30's. He was virtually a teetotaller later in life.

Hans told his daughter, Ali, about his 20th birthday. He said that everyone forgot that it was his birthday. He then decided to tell everyone that it was his 21st birthday, to make up for the forgetfulness. Everyone then bought him drinks all night and he got very, very drunk.

I don't know how it started but Hans loved a song called the Music Man, that starts with, "I am the music man, I come from down your way, and I can play". He learnt all the lyrics. He started singing this song at parties. It was surprising as he wasn't the type of person to get up and perform. When he got up to do the Music Man he transformed into an extroverted entertainer. He didn't have to be drunk to do it, but he was more entertaining if he had had a few beers. Hans couldn't sing but he could sing the Music Man.

We pestered Hans to do the Music Man more often than he wanted to. He almost always obliged. It became legendary. I can recall renditions when around 100 people gathered to watch. Everyone joined in with, "What can you play?" and "How does it go?" It always brought the house down and made many parties more memorable.

I have many distinct memories from Hans's rugby league days with Albion Park. I never saw him run down if he had clear space in front of him. He had one season of prolific try scoring where the team would always try to get the ball to Hans with an overlap, as they knew he would score. He was probably the fastest winger in Group 7 that season. One of his team-mates from those days recently told me that he thought Hans was probably the fastest player to ever play for Albion Park.

Fuji recalls that Hans decided to enter a 100-metre sprint competition that was being held at Nowra. The competitors included amateur runners and footballers. Fuji accompanied Hans on the day. Hans won his heat and then his semi-final. He asked Fuji to stand on the finish line so he could see if Hans won. Fuji said that Hans was the winner, but they awarded the win to the second-place getter. Fuji said that Hans's finish was blistering. Hans was not interested in disputing the result. He told Fuji. "If you think I won that's good enough for me." Hans also told Fuji that he was happy that he now knew he was a competitive runner. However, he decided not to pursue a running career beyond that race.

Every Sunday night we would gather around a radio at home to hear the Group 7 football scores. They read out the try scorers for first grade. Hans's name would often be read out, and we were just as thrilled each time. There was one occasion when the radio announcer called him Harry Lambert. I think this is where his lifelong nickname, Harry, came from.

Hans was the treasurer of the Albion Park Oak Flats rugby league club for several years. If they played at Albion Park, he brought all the gate takings home. He would count the cash out on the dining room table home before he went back to join the rest of the team at the hotel or RSL club.

Ali has reminded me that his favourite sport to play was cricket. I played cricket with Hans at Albion Park cricket club for 12 seasons from 1971/72 to 1983/4. He was always a grade or two higher than me. He became a regular first grader. He opened the batting and became a specialist in the short leg fielding position. He was a very good fielder and took many great catches. He got the nickname "Claw" for a while because of his catching prowess. He was a solid batsman, without being a prolific run scorer. His job in first grade was to open the batting and stay there for as long as possible. He became a very good technically defensive batsman and learnt how to read the ball out of the bowler's hand, something I was never able to achieve.

As with all sports he tackled, Hans was "all in" with cricket. He attended training sessions, helped prepare the grounds for play and was a very active club man. We often worked together preparing the club's newsletter, which was the club's main source of revenue.

Later in life Hans loved going to watch his three nephews, Jacob, Nicholas, and Isaac, play cricket. The second last time I did something with Hans was to join him watching Jacob playing cricket for Albion Park first grade at Kiama. Hans was the same as always, sitting quietly by himself enjoying the game and just being there.

Hans worked at AIS until 1977. He then worked at Kembla Coal and Coke from 1977 to 1995. After he started this job, he enrolled at the University of Wollongong to do his Bachelor of Commerce degree, majoring in accounting. He completed his degree part time and became an accountant. In later years he worked in business management roles at St Mary Star of the Sea College, 1995 – 2005, and Chevalier College, 2006 – 2013.

Hans always encouraged me in my university and work career. He was very proud of me when I became the first sibling to go to university. That pride was reversed when Hans obtained his degree. He had done it a much harder way, compared to me. He spent many years studying part-time whilst he had a full-time job. It was a testament to his hard work and determination.

Hans was first and foremost a family man. He lived for his wife, Diane, and children, Joshua (Josh), Alison (Ali) and Rebekah (Bek), and later in life for his grandchildren. Ali told me that Hans subtly adapted himself for each of his children. Josh loved various sports, particularly hockey. Hans supported Josh through all his sporting activities. He became interested in whatever sport Josh was playing. He became involved but was not pushy. Ali liked to walk and talk. Ali found that he was always available for a walk. He would mainly listen and talk about anything that Ali wanted to discuss. Bek was an animal lover. Hans became an animal lover with Bek. If Bek saw an injured bird Hans would pick it up and take it to the vet. They shared a love of breeding tadpoles. Ali recalled that when one of their cats had to be put down Hans was shaking so much that she had to hold the cat for the vet.

Hans was very happy at his home of many years in Figtree. He continued his love affair with chooks and gardening at this home. He and Bek added tadpoles along the way. Any visit to Hans and Diane's home included a compulsory garden tour and chook update with Hans.

Both his and Diane's extended families were very important to Hans. He visited Mum and Dad very regularly, particularly in their later years. He loved catching up with his siblings, collectively or individually. These catch ups often included six handed, competitive, games of euchre with the Lambert brothers. Ali recalls that the Lambert family Boxing Day gathering was his favourite day of the year. He became an integral member of Diane's family. He and Diane's father, Maurie, enjoyed many quiet chats together.

Hans always jogged for fitness. He loved running and had a "runner's" body. He weighed around 70 kilograms all his life. As noted in Chapter 14 Hans organised several of our brothers, and a brother-in-law, to run in the 1991 Gold Coast Half Marathon. Hans then ran in ten half marathons and one full marathon over the next 11 consecutive years. He finished in 2005, at the age of 54, completing twelve half marathons and one full marathon. Ossie finished in 2011 after completing thirteen half marathons. I think Ossie wanted to equal Hans's total number of races, but not pass it.

Hans loved both the running and the social side of the marathon weekend. He was always well prepared for the race. His times were always the best of the Lambert brothers, although our brother-in-law, Vince, was always competitive with Hans. His best time for the half marathon was 1:27:48 in 1997, when he was 46 years old. Any time under 1:30:00 is considered fast for a half marathon.

Hans thoroughly enjoyed the weekend of bonding with his brothers, Vince, and various friends who raced over the years. It was always at my place. It got crowded when I had the three-bedroom unit but none of us minded. We played cards, watched the footy on TV, had a carbohydrate loading meal on the night before the race and a big barbecue after the race. Hans was always up for a chat on those weekends.

After running a few gold coast half marathons Hans decided to organise a run in the Wollongong area. He had a vision for a run around Lake Illawarra and he organised the first one in 1998, in conjunction with his running club, the Kembla Joggers. It was called the Gong Run. He developed, promoted, and almost single-handedly organised every aspect of what still stands as the longest ever Kembla Joggers race. His wife, children and brothers were his main helpers. Hans told his kids that he organised the run to show his kids that you can do things to help the community.

Hans was a long-term member of the Kembla Joggers running club. He became heavily involved and was appointed to several committees over the years.

Hans loved attending working bees. These included school, family and friends' working bees. Hans always picked the hardest jobs to do. He was quite handy and could have a go at most things. In the early 1980's a group of the Lambert siblings decided to paint the exterior of Mum and Dad's house over a few weekends. This was the first repaint in twenty years. It was a fibro house, and it was not easy to paint. Hans was in the thick of this job. He was one of the organisers and never missed a session. He tackled the job enthusiastically while some of us, including me, couldn't wait to finish. We did finish it and it looked great.

Hans greatly assisted Mum and Dad in their later years. He was on the work roster for their domestic duties. When they went into the aged care home Hans was appointed as Dad's guardian. Dad was not as amenable in aged care as Mum was. There would have been many stressful times for Hans with Dad during this period. He took it in his stride and was an invaluable support for Dad in his final years.

Hans and Mum had some very similar personality traits. They were both quiet, unassuming people who were happy not to take the limelight. They were both very good listeners who made the person they were talking to feel like it was all about them. They could influence a person without the person knowing they were being influenced. They both lived for their families.

I suspect that each of the siblings would feel like they had their own special relationship with Hans, because Hans made you feel like that. He loved all his siblings and relished any time he had with them. He was a great big brother role model for me. I followed him into sports activities all our lives. He was a very stable, older influence and a great sounding board for me growing up.

Hans had a way of saying very meaningful things in cards. When I turned 50 some of the wording in my card included, "Our family is much stronger, more understanding, loving in our own way and a large part of it all is due to you." I'm sure I'm not the only sibling who received messages like this from Hans which were very personal and thoughtful. Ironically, I feel like Hans's words apply more to him than me. He made our family much stronger, more understanding and loving in our own way, without us, or at least me, fully realising that he was doing that.

Hans was always honest and ethical in his work roles. He always expected people to do the right thing. Ali and I have discussed our perception that Hans could not accept it when people did not do the right thing. He was black and white about this.

This caused Hans considerable stress in a couple of his jobs. There were people he worked with who had a lower threshold than him of what "doing the right thing" meant. He had trouble letting go if he saw questionable actions or behaviour tolerated. Fortunately, his last job at Chevalier College was very enjoyable and stress free for Hans. They valued him and he valued them.

I commented earlier that Hans was an early adopter of not wasting anything. This led to Hans adopting some behaviours which may be described as frugal. It would be remiss of me not to mention a couple of these. On one occasion he was on the Gold Coast for a family holiday. I was due to meet him at dinner time. He asked me to meet him at his resort hotel room as he had decided to have dinner there. I got there to find his family had all gone out for dinner. However, there were a couple of bananas still to be eaten so Hans had decided he would have them for dinner on a few slices of bread. They were returning home the next day, so the food had to be eaten. Hans could not waste it. I'm told that Hans often had banana sandwiches.

Hans was also renowned for his multiple uses of one tea bag. He loved a cup of tea and could easily get three cups from one tea bag. My reflection on this is that Hans retained some of our childhood ways of living all his life. I think that the financial struggles we experienced as kids ingrained into him never to waste anything. He also retained his catholic faith all his life, which stemmed from our strong catholic upbringing.

Danita's 21st birthday celebration in March 2001, with her Nan and the Widdicombe cousins. (L-R) David, Natalie, Ryan, Luke, Chantal, Joan, Danita, Front - Brad

Dad's 80th birthday celebration in November 2001. Back row (L-R) Ossie, Steve, Dianne, Me, Fuji, Hans, Terry. Front row - John, Dad, Mum, Toni

Mum's 80th birthday celebration in March 2003, with Br Bell who taught all 7 Lambert brothers. Back row (L-R) Fuji, Me, Toni, Br Bell, Mum, Dianne, Terry, Ossie. Front row - Hans, Steve, John

A photo from our emotional visit back to Parkes in January 2002. Hans, John, and Me standing in the middle of Pearce Steet, Parkes - the street which was the dirt road that we grew up on.

The house that Dad built at 26 Pearce Street, Parkes

Nine siblings inside the Kaylaur Crescent house on the day in December 2003 we met to clean out the house. Standing (L-R) John, Fuji, Toni, Hans, Terry
Sitting (L-R) Dianne, Me, Ossie, Steve

Me standing beside the garage that we all lived in while Dad built the main house

Me, Danita, Brad, and Chantal at Brad's 22nd birthday celebration in November 2003. Brad was working outdoors at that time and had a deep tan.

The newspaper article featuring our visit to Parkes in January 2002.

Danita and Sasha's wedding in March 2006. Brad was resplendent in his bright green suit which was tailored for the occasion. (L-R) Chantal, Sasha, Danita, Tina, Me

Melissa's, Toni's daughter, wedding in May 2007. This was the last family wedding attended by Mum. Mum is very happy, in her wheelchair, in the middle of this Lambert family photo.

Brad and I at Danita's wedding in March 2006.

Brad with his beloved dog, Ernie Dingo, in early 2006. Note the position of Ernie's paw.

The Lambert siblings with their partners at Fuji's 60th birthday celebration in April 2012 (L-R) Me, Ossie, Jodie, Vince, Terry, Fuji, Dianne, John, Hans, Toni, Steve, Rita. Seated – Di, Julie, Rae, Diane

Me and Di (Dianne Harland) at a wedding in 2013

Hans with his beloved chooks in December 2013

The last photo of the 9 Lambert siblings in January 2014 when Hans was very sick with cancer

Hans with his family in January 2014. Back (L-R) Rebekah, Diane, Alison. Front (L-R) Josh, Hans

Chantal and Pat's wedding in August 2014, with parents and partners. (L-R) Narelle Reed, Tom (Pat's father), Alan Spencer, Elke (Pat's mother), Pat, Chantal, Tina, Rob, Di, Me

Steve with Nejmere at his PhD graduation ceremony in December 2015

Me with my 4 grandkids in August 2017 (L-R) Annalee, Me, Levi, Luka, Evie

Group photo, including the Maksimovic family, from Danita's 40th birthday celebration in Fiji in March 2020. Back (L-R) Sasha, Mira, Davor, Jelena. Front (L-R) Me, Alex, Ollie, Luka, Levi, Chantal, Danita, Annalee, Evie, Romy, Zoran

I guess I am good at breaking up! Here I am with my former wife, Tina, and former partner, Di, and Tina's husband, Rob, in June 2022. That is Marnus, Chantal and Dave's dog, in the foreground

Danita, Tina, Chantal, Me at Xmas lunch in December 2021

Evie's stunning self-portrait drawing in August 2022. This was done for a class assignment at school

Group family photo in September 2022. This is my family and a great photo to finish with. Standing (L-R) Levi, Jordan, Damien, Paige, Evie, Luka, Annalee. Seated (L-R) Sasha, Danita, Me, Chantal, Dave

A few newspaper clippings from my corporate career

EPILOGUE

THE LAMBERT SIBLINGS, MUM AND DAD, MY FAMILY

Hopefully you have obtained a reasonable sense through the book about the Lambert siblings.

Toni's succinct word for us is that we are 'stable'. We have led stable lives. Some might say boring, but I agree with Toni that stable is the right description. Our kids can rely on us, and they don't have to worry about us. We are good at managing our money and have generally achieved a reasonable level of financial independence.

We are not adventurous or extravagant and maintain reasonably modest lifestyles. We do not try to "keep up with the Joneses". We are resilient and have generally accepted the realities of life. While writing this book Terry commented to me that, "we were bred to be accepting". We are happier sitting around a dining room table playing cards than going to a fancy restaurant for dinner.

Most, but not all of us, are people of routine. I have many routines including regular meals, same shopping time each week, getting up at the same time every day, never being late and an exercise routine. I have had the same accountant, solicitor, doctor, and dentist for the last thirty years. Toni assures me that she has more routines than I do.

We have had good, even outstanding, work ethics all our lives. Fuji has said to me, "We just get things done". This has applied to our work and personal lives. In our work lives we could be relied upon to get our jobs done and go the extra mile if required. We were generally that staff member who would step up if there was a problem or a stressful situation that required resolving. We took pride in our work. A Lambert would have to be sick to take a sickie.

We were honest and ethical in our work lives. We had a high threshold expectation of what "doing the right thing" means. I mention in Hans's chapter that this caused him some stress during a couple of his jobs. He was not the only sibling to suffer this type of stress. I encountered it but generally managed to work through it.

We have generally led happy, healthy, reasonably active, lives. Four of the Lambert brothers, Hans, Fuji, Terry, and Ossie have weighed around 70 kilograms all their lives. We have generally been plain eaters. We have been largely resistant against the winter flu and colds, and other minor illnesses. Perhaps both the physical and mental aspects of our childhood helped us develop great immunity systems.

That does not mean we have always been idyllic. We have had our fair share of tragedies, hardships, divorces, accidents, medical and mental health issues and the usual stresses of day-to-day life. The resilience we developed during our upbringing has stood us in good stead to face these challenges and get on with our lives.

There is a history of mental health issues in the family. Brad had severe OCD. There have been other cases of OCD in the family as well as cases of ADD and ADHD. It is above my pay grade to offer any medical opinions regarding these issues. However, it does appear that they have arisen partly through genetic inheritance from Dad's side of the family.

We are independent, which seems somewhat ironic after a childhood with so many people around all the time. By independent I mean that we can get by on our own and are happy in our own company. Dianne and John have happily lived on their own for many years. I have happily lived on my own for the last five years. Fortunately, there have also been many long-term happy marriages and partnerships, Toni and Vince, Fuji and Rita, Terry and Rae, Ossie and Jodie, Steve and Justin and Hans and Diane, until Hans's passing.

We are friends as well as siblings. We enjoy each other's company, both collectively and individually. We like to make each other laugh. Hopefully that applies to all the partners as well, although it must be different marrying into a family with so many in-laws. I have never had a serious argument or fall out with a sibling. I'm not aware of any rifts that have become serious.

However, we do enjoy "putting shit on each other" which never stops. There are also plenty of robust discussions and differences of opinion about the usual things, including sport and politics. We are competitive in games, tipping competitions and sports.

Whilst there are many similarities between us there are also many differences. These are exemplified by John still running his business full-time at the age of 73, while Ossie happily retired at the age of 58.

I mentioned earlier in the book that Toni was a typical eldest child. She was babysitting before she was ten years old and virtually raised the little kids. This background, together with her becoming a young mother, led Toni to generally maintain a responsible, serious approach to life. She did not go through the typical adolescent drinking stage. Toni has been a teetotaller almost all her life.

Toni loves catching up with the family. She enjoys a good conversation. She can be quite forthright with her point of view. She loves a good laugh. She is still very good with little kids. They respond to her even though she is strict with them. Toni is possibly the best money manager out of the siblings. She has had to be at times.

Toni started entering competitions many years ago, both for something to do and to see if she could win. She has become a prolific competition winner. She has won several trips that she and Vince have enjoyed, and many minor prizes. At the annual Lambert boxing day gathering Toni lays that year's unused prizes out on a table for anyone to take. She even won a competition once that was only between competition winners from various countries. She still walks the shops obsessively looking for competitions.

Toni and Vince have raised a "Brady Bunch" having three kids each when they married. There were some trying times in the first few years but it all came together. They now have a large, diverse, happy extended family, including Savannah, who is the first great grandchild for a Lambert sibling.

Toni has suffered from OCD and anxiety all her life. Her OCD has made her pretty quirky. Vince must cook the meat for every meal on the outside barbecue as Toni can't tolerate cooking in the kitchen. We all know to take our shoes off when we visit Toni. Toni is very knowledgeable about her mental health and mental health illnesses more broadly. She is very generous in sharing that knowledge.

John is possibly the most unique of the siblings. He has operated his business, Lambert Kitchens, since 1978. Even though it has stressed him at times he has always loved it. Many years ago, I had a conversation with him about how hard he was working. I was trying to influence him to slow down a bit. He looked at me and said, "You know how you love Fridays, well I love Mondays". He could not wait for the weekend to finish so he could get to work. He should feel proud of the legacy of Lambert Kitchens. There are thousands of happy customers using their Lambert kitchen every day in the Wollongong area.

John and his former wife, Barbara, both worked very hard to build the business. Barbara worked in the business and ran the household. John recalls that she did everything with the kids' activities as he was always at work. She was a great hostess and fantastic cook, and they hosted many Lambert family gatherings over the years. Their hard work provided a great upbringing for their children, Kristy, Daniel, and Jessica.

John's main point of difference is his hobbies. He loves online auctions, and breeds finches. If he decides to do something he is "all in". He has always liked finches and, after many years without them, he decided to get some again about a year ago. He built his own cages, and they are 6-star luxury. I don't think the finches would fly away even if he left the doors open.

He is very funny, very generous, and very tidy. Many of the family members have benefited from a low-cost kitchen over the years. He has a quick wit. I was talking to him recently and I asked him, "Did you see Four Corners this week, it was about dementia?" He responded immediately with, "I can't remember." We both laughed so much we had to finish the call.

John had a major scare recently. During a night of heavy rain, he went into his ceiling to check a water leak. Being John, he had lights in the ceiling in case he ever had to go up there. He got to the leak and was positioning a board so he could stand on it and check the leak. He knew that the plaster was too wet to take any weight. Somehow the board slipped, and he and the board fell straight through the plaster ceiling to the kitchen floor.

He was injured but still conscious. He managed to call Ossie, who came straight over with his son Nicholas. They got him to the hospital. He was severely battered and bruised. His only significant injury was a torn bicep muscle. The outcome could have been much, much worse. John thinks that he rode the board down and it partly cushioned his fall.

John has reminded me that this was not the first time the "cavalry has arrived". A few years earlier Fuji and Ossie had to get him from his bathroom floor to a hospital when he had severe back pain.

Hans has his own chapter. In relation to the siblings the best way I can summarise Hans is to say that he could make every sibling feel like you were his favourite. In return it would be hard for any of the siblings not to pick Hans as their favourite. Not that we have favourites, but it helps to explain Hans.

Fuji is a shining example of a person who has adapted his life to get the most out of it, through its various stages. He was quiet and serious through his school years and his first few years of work. He then bloomed from his late teens into possibly the most well-known young person in the Wollongong area. He thrived in the drinking, partying environment. He was generally the centre of attention and he loved it. Everyone wanted Fuji at their party or night out.

He played his part by regularly getting drunk and doing the cheeky, naughty things that everyone wanted him to do. It is fair to say that he got away with doing things in clubs that would have got other people thrown out. In hindsight I saw that Fuji was playing a game. He was entertaining enough for he and everyone with him to have a great night, but not too much to get into any real trouble. He never got into or caused fights. He could also stop drinking at any time and often went weeks drinking orange juice.

When he met Rita and it was time to settle down and get married, he changed again. He recalls that he had already decided that he would reduce his drinking when the time came. He did not want to be one of those regulars at the pub or club every night. He reduced his drinking to the point where he quickly became a very light, occasional drinker. Fuji and Rita settled into a happy, long marriage. He blended in to become an integral member of Rita's extended Italian family.

Fuji has been a highly respected real estate agent in the Wollongong area since 1988. He has a reputation for doing the right thing for his clients. I'm pleased to report that he still carries his trademark cheekiness from his adolescent years. He can still be quite risqué.

Fuji is an avid walker and book reader. He reads so many books that he had to join the library to keep up the supply.

The letter R is important in Fuji, Renee, and Rita's family. They named their kids Ryan and Rachel. Ryan married Rhiannon. Their first child is named Rochelle. Thankfully Rachel married Simon and didn't wait for an R to come along.

In relation to my role with my fellow Lambert siblings, it would be logical to think of me as a "glue" type of middle child. I had been called the "glue" at Villa World and I have been told that I bring cohesion to a board room. However, within the siblings I am no more a glue than anyone else. Most of the siblings are good, natural organisers and "glues" in their own lives.

My other point in relation to the siblings is that I probably "bite" more than anyone else. I have been known to be a quick, over reactor. This sometimes led to me responding too quickly and taking the bait, that is "biting", when someone was trying to stir me up. This can become a self-fulfilling prophecy as the more you bite the more people will try to stir you up.

A humorous side to this occurred one night at John and Barbara's place many years ago. Daniel, their son, decided to imitate me. He raised his right eyebrow the same way I did when I had "bitten". I did not realise how easy I was to read, and I was learning from a teenager.

I would like to think that with the benefit of executive coaching and some self-discipline I have become much better at not "biting".

Dianne has worked very hard all her life. It started after her first two children, Pauline, and Graeme, were born. She decided to go to night school to obtain her Higher School Certificate. She became a single parent in 1986 when her youngest child, Christine turned one. She rented an old duplex in Botany and they lived in this duplex for the next twenty years. She had the kids virtually full time as her ex-husband Joe was in the army.

After her marriage ended Dianne knew that she would require a secure job in a few years. She decided to enhance her nursing qualifications and completed a three-year Diploma in Nursing at Sydney University. After she completed the diploma she commenced work, as a nurse, at St Vincent's Hospital. She went on to obtain a Degree in Nursing. This required an additional two years of part-time study while she was working full-time. At this point she had a huge workload with four children at school, work, and university.

Dianne's children became independent from a young age. They knew how to look after themselves. Dianne recalls that Belinda, her third child, obtained her first job at the local grocery store when she was 13 years old.

Dianne went on to have a stellar nursing career. She has worked at St George Private Hospital for the past 27 years. She became a Speciality Team Leader of Cardiac, Livers and Vascular Surgery. She now works part-time as she transitions to retirement. Her retirement will be very well earned.

Dianne went out with a few men after her marriage ended, but she has not re-partnered. She has been very happy with a life focused on her children, grandchildren, extended family, and work. She has eleven grandchildren, the most of any Lambert sibling.

Dianne has practised meditation since 1997. She is a great believer in the benefits of meditation. She has been fortunate enough to travel to India and the USA to practise meditation.

The interesting thing about Terry is that he was always Mum and Dad's favourite. This wasn't a favouritism that was blatant or caused any issues. It was just a nice thing that Mum and Dad always had a soft spot for Terry. He doesn't know why he was, but he told me that it started as soon as he left school, when Dad bought him a brand-new set of tools to start his carpentry and joinery apprenticeship. It was the first time Dad had done something like this.

There is something about Terry as Brad was drawn to him as well. They didn't catch up very often but when they did Brad loved a chat with Terry.

Terry completed his carpentry and joinery trade course in 1979. Since then, he has worked as a carpenter and joiner, and he is good at it. This included a nine-year stint working with John at Lambert Kitchens. The building game can be tough, and Terry has shown great resilience to work in it for so long. At times he has had to travel for work and live away from home.

Terry also played rugby league with Albion Park for around seven years. He was a handy player and won a third-grade premiership in 1981.

Terry is a very laid-back, easy-going person. He and his wife, Rae, decided many years ago to choose the country lifestyle.

They both prefer life away from the hustle and bustle of the cities. They have lived in a variety of country towns in New South Wales, recently settling in the seaside town, Harrington.

With Terry it doesn't matter at all if you see him less frequently; we are all still just as close. He is always the same, so easy and conversation just flows as if you saw him yesterday. Terry enjoys gardening and camping and likes the quiet life. He has kept himself physically fit and looks like he could still play a full game of touch footy.

Terry has a great, individualistic family. He and Rae have chosen their own lifestyle. Their children, Tanaya, and Byron are taking after their parents and living life their way. It is refreshing to observe their independent thinking. They are a tight family unit. Terry is very family oriented and always places his family first.

Ossie had a similar professional journey to Hans. After leaving school in 1978 he studied part-time, while working full time. He completed his Bachelor of Commerce (Accounting) in 1988 and the CPA Programme in 1994. He had long careers at Wingecarribee Shire Council and Illawarra Retirement Trust.

He has always been a very active sportsman, both on and off the field. He played cricket for Albion Park for many years and won the Clubman of the Year award in 1981/82. In his later years he probably eclipsed Hans as the best sporting sibling. He has played touch football since 1979 and became a representative player. His team won the National Touch Championship in 2008 and 2012, making him the only sibling to become a national champion. He is a Life Member of the Albion Park Touch Association.

Ossie and Jodie are very well matched. Together with their three sons, Jacob, Nicholas, and Isaac, they are a very tight family unit. They still do plenty of things like holidays and sport as a family even though their boys are adults.

Ossie is proactive with his siblings and the broader Lambert family. He organises a tipping competition for every rugby league State of Origin game. He has recently commenced a monthly Family News Update, distributed by text message. The content grows each month and family members love receiving these updates.

Ossie is there when he is needed. As noted earlier he is a member of John's "cavalry". After two of my major life events, Brad's death, and my marriage breakdown, he flew straight to the Gold Coast to support me, both times with John.

He likes telling jokes and he likes laughing at his own jokes. This is understandable as most of his jokes are quite funny. He is very infectious when he laughs. He loves board games and is an avid book reader. Ossie's sons have inherited his sense of humour. Nicholas has chosen the nickname Ivon Avin, meaning "I want to win", for our footy tipping competition. I wish I had thought of that one.

Ossie had a successful corporate career. His last role was in the aged care industry. He decided to retire at the age of 58. As the second youngest sibling he has perhaps shown the older siblings that there is more to life than work. He is a very happy retiree and doesn't know how he ever had time to work.

Steve has led a very interesting life. After leaving school he left home, at the age of 17, and joined the Christian Brothers. He trained to become a teacher, and a Christian Brother, for the next four years. After these four years Steve decided not to continue as a professed Christian Brother. He became a teacher and worked in Wellington in New South Wales, and Innisfail in Queensland for the next eight years.

Steve then decided to focus his education and teaching skills in an area that had become an emergency in Australia amongst the gay community, education about HIV and AIDS. This resulted in a change in career for Steve and was one of the reasons he had decided this was the time to come out as gay. He worked in HIV education and public health for the next eighteen years. He completed his Masters Degree in Public Health in 1997 and obtained a PhD in Public Health in 2015. He became the first sibling to be called Dr Lambert. Steve switched to broader medical education training, using the cross disciplines in health and education, in 2011.

During the early part of his academic career Steve became a renowned leader and speaker in HIV education in Australia. This was a very important area as HIV/AIDS was still a major health threat in Australia and around the world. This has included participation in national and international events where world leaders were involved, including the World AIDS Conference in Barcelona in 2002.

Steve recalls that he was surprised on one morning of this conference when he arrived to see security personnel everywhere. He thought it was another normal conference day. He took a seat near the stage, noticed some commotion, and looked up to see Nelson Mandela and Bill Clinton walking onto the stage. They were the keynote speakers that day.

Steve has been with his life partner, Justin Cooper, for over twenty years. They became engaged on the 9th of December 2017, which was the date that same sex marriage was legalised in Australia. While Justin prefers to stay in the background, he is an integral part of the family. He understood Brad very well and was an invaluable support to me in the period following Brad's death.

Steve and Justin are book collectors. They had a small book shop in Toowoomba several years ago and they have stored the books from that shop and have been adding to their stockpile ever since. They have around eighty thousand books in storage. They are planning to open a boutique book shop down the track.

Steve is another proactive sibling. He has always lived away from all the other siblings. He makes sure he sees everyone regularly. He always stays in touch. Steve is a great person to go on holidays with. He organises everything.

Mum and Dad were a solid married couple. They stuck together through thick and thin. When we were kids, they never argued in front of us. Dad was the boss and Mum was happy for him to be the boss. That was the way marriages were in that era. They undoubtedly had differences of opinion. There would have been times that they would have been frustrated with each other, more so Dad frustrating Mum. They kept any of that to themselves. Looking back Mum was the real boss as she led and influenced us in her quiet, amiable way.

Dad was a complex man. He was adventurous, intelligent, hard-working (until his accident), extroverted and charming when he wanted to be. On the other hand, he was argumentative, he could be arrogant, and he liked to feel important. In some ways the expression, "Arrogant Dutchman" applied to Dad.

Toni recalls that Dad always wanted the nine siblings to be well educated. He took us all to the library every Friday night for years and encouraged us all to read. On the other hand, it would be difficult to get Dad to go out of his way to do some of the things that other parents did.

Looking back on Dad's complexities and contradictions, Toni and I believe that Dad suffered from an undiagnosed mental health illness, probably depression. At that time only extreme cases of mental health illness, such as manic depression, were diagnosed and treated by doctors. From my conversation with Brad's pediatrician and Toni's research it is highly likely that some family members genetically inherited mental health illness from Dad's side of the family. Dad also displayed symptoms of depression. From the time that he injured his knee he slept for three to four hours every afternoon. He also constantly talked about illnesses that he might have. It was almost as if he wanted to be sick to justify how he was feeling.

I'm not saying the above to have a go at Dad. In fact, writing this book has made me appreciate him much more than I had. I have a much better understanding of the hardships he and Mum endured, as well as the sacrifices they made, to give their children the best life they could. I think that I also have a better understanding of why Dad sometimes acted the way that he did. As an example, he always wanted to be financially successful. When that didn't happen, he adopted certain coping behaviours just to get through life.

The reality is that Dad was successful in areas much more important than money. He and Mum raised nine wonderful children who have become good, solid citizens in their local communities. Mum and Dad are at the head of a Lambert family tree that now comprises 105 people in a happy, diverse, connected family group. The end outcome for Dad was success in life and he can rest easy.

Mum was also complex however worked hard to show the opposite. She was amiable, selfless, accepting, resilient and much more astute than she appeared to be. She influenced and guided us by modelling behaviours, rather than by telling or teaching us. She did this in her quiet, unassuming way.

She was happy to play the role of a stay-at-home mother. She supported Dad the whole way, from agreeing to migrate to Australia to going to work when Dad injured his knee. It is very difficult to grasp the hardships Mum endured along the way, particularly leaving her family behind in the Netherlands. I hope this book has given some sense of that.

Mum loved the simple things in life. She liked knitting, playing cards, jigsaw puzzles and board games. She liked having a good conversation.

Mum never complained. She just got on with life. As I noted above all nine of us can "just get things done". That is a legacy from Mum. As John said at Mum's 80th birthday party, Mum was a saint. She can also rest easy. She would be beyond proud of the 105 people in the Lambert family tree.

In terms of my own children, Danita and Chantal are very tight as sisters. They always were and Brad's death tightened the bond even further. They are both very family oriented, both for their own families and their broader family groups. They are both very good cooks, great at hosting people in their homes and at running a household. They learnt these skills from Tina, not me.

They have both got that Lambert attribute of being able to "just get things done". They are very health conscious, and each provide healthy diets for their families. Chantal starts everyone's day in her household with celery juice. They are great daughters and I think they worry a little about me living on my own. They don't need to, but I do like the frequent dinner invitations.

They are also excellent parents. A few years ago, I had the revelation that they are now the main adults in our family. Tina and I had subconsciously passed the baton. Our family is in safe hands, and I can comfortably fade into seniority. I prefer that terminology to old age.

Danita is probably now the "glue" of the family. She is the proactive organiser for family celebrations and holidays. She has become an integral member of the Maksimovic family, and often organises them as well. Danita is confident but can also get anxious at times. She has a wicked sense of humour. She is the only one of my children who has left home and not returned. She works with Sasha in the family business.

She is an emotional person. This has resulted in her probably being the worst public speaker in the family. At my 50th birthday she got up to make her prepared speech. She burst into tears and could not get one word out. This happens every time.

Chantal has had a tough journey over the past seven years since the premature birth of Annalee and her marriage breakdown. She has shown how resilient and tough she is. There have been many times that she has reminded me of Mum and my sister, Dianne, through this period. She has come through it extremely well. Her and Dave have a busy, happy merged family unit.

Chantal is very sociable and extroverted. She is also emotional, but she will pick up the remnants of Danita's speeches and deliver them. She will let you know what she is thinking. She is competitive and does not like to lose a game of spoons. She has a core group of friends, who have remained close, from primary school. She now runs a children's clothing business, Coco Kidz, with Tina. She is a hard worker.

I should point out that it is hard for me to keep calling her Chantal, as she has had the nickname Bub, in the family, all her life. Maybe it is time for a new nickname.

Evie is a very special child with some unique talents. She is reserved and has always done things her way. She is a natural artist. Some of her paintings and drawings are breathtaking. She is also very handy and practical. One day Sasha was trying to put a trampoline together. He was getting frustrated. Evie had a quick look, suggested what to do, and the rest went smoothly. Evie is a nature and animal lover. She is already handy in the kitchen. She likes organising games at family gatherings.

Luka is a confident, outgoing, friendly child. He is very good with people. He can just walk up to someone and start having a conversation. He has a quick wit. He can be very caring when you least expect it. He is the "king" of his male cousins. They all want to play with Luka. He is sporty. After many years playing soccer, he recently switched to basketball.

Levi is an old soul. He has always demonstrated a level of understanding or seriousness that is typical of someone much older. He was a seriously cute baby and provided us with many hours of entertainment with his unusual antics. He is a fussy eater, something he has inherited from his father. He is soccer mad, both playing it and following it. He is quite intelligent and a good student at school. He also has a quick wit. He can be very affectionate.

Annalee is precious. She was clearly meant to be here. She loves everyone and everyone loves her. She is very caring and very family oriented. She is bright and very helpful at seven years of age. She offers to help Chantal with any household chores and is happy doing them. She is also very good with people and likes the company of adults. She loves playing games.

I love and appreciate my family.

AUTHOR'S NOTE

Tracey Whelan compiles an annual Lambert Family calendar. Tracey is Toni's daughter and Mum and Dad's eldest grandchild. Tracey decided to do it after Mum died in 2008. The first calendar was produced for the 2009 year. The quality of the calendar improves each year. It now contains details of each family as well as a calendar of all birthdays. On behalf of the Lambert family thank you Tracey for your ongoing hard work in producing this calendar. It is invaluable.

The details of the relevant past family members are:

Mum's full name was Martha Maria Van Ammers. She was born on the 5th of March 1923 at Westwoud, the Netherlands. She died on the 4th of January 2008 at Albion Park Rail, NSW, Australia.

Dad's full name was Adrianus Engelbertus Reinier Lambertus Lambert. He was born on the 28th of November 1921 at Oude Tonge, the Netherlands. He died on the 15th of December 2005 at Albion Park Rail, NSW, Australia.

Mum's parents:

Johannes (Jan) Van Ammers – 22nd of March 1887, the Netherlands to 17th of October 1946, Hoorn, the Netherlands.

Joanna (Jansje) Ruiter – 14th of February 1888, Zwaagdijk, the Netherlands to 21st of July 1939, Westwoud, the Netherlands.

Dad's parents:

Johannes Engelbertus Willem Lambert – 29th of November 1894, Oude Tonge, the Netherlands to 6th of June 1977, Bemmel, the Netherlands.

Antonia Maria Scheepers – 23rd of May 1895, Oude Tonge, the Netherlands to 6th of September 1982, Bemmel, the Netherlands.

Sheer numbers and space prevented me from talking about all the births and lives of the many further Lambert grandchildren. Tracey's and Melissa's births were brought into the story as they were born much earlier than the other grandchildren and they were an integral part of the family story to that time. In their early years they were virtually the 10th and 11th Lambert siblings. Byron's birth was included as it was so significant in relation to the extent of the prematurity.

I had some very interesting coincidences and memorable experiences during the writing. At one point I was trying to contact some old school friends from primary school when one of them contacted me "out of the blue" through Facebook. It turned out that school friend, who I had not spoken to for at least fifty years, had all the information that I was looking for.

I always listened to a radio station, that played older music, when I was writing. A very eerie thing happened to me while recalling the Outset dances and in particular the bands who had performed. As I was writing the paragraph about Jeff St John & the Copperwine (in Chapter 8), their biggest hit, "Teach Me How to Fly" came on the radio. I had not heard that song on the radio for at least thirty years and I took that as a good sign for my book.

It was a common occurrence to hear songs that related to Brad, like "True Blue" by John Williamson, or Hans, like "Piano Man" by Billy Joel, at just the right times.

It was very enjoyable contacting old work colleagues, school friends and other friends, many of whom I had not been in touch with for many years. Without exception they were happy to have a chat and contribute what they could to the book.

As this is a Lambert book, I will share the Ken Tate player assessments for the three Lamberts who played in the 1972 Outset rugby league team:

"John Lambert (Lock). Good cover defending lock who on his day is the equal of any of our forwards. A player who if he put his mind to it could be one of the top locks in the competition. A great team man who will give everyone else a run before himself. It's blokes like Sticks that have made Outset the great team it is.

Renee Lambert (Wing). Fast running winger who is a very good finisher. Has very safe hands. He was unlucky to have broken his collar bone through the year, but I am sure he will come back better than ever. He is a tough winger who at times gets a little hot under the collar when niggled.

Gerry Lambert (Wing) Very capable winger who on his day is the equal of any in the competition. Very safe hands. He is an elusive, big-striding runner who has a fine sense of positional play. Has the ability to score a try when it is most needed."

I have had a journey filled with family, friends, love, and loss. Writing this book has made me more aware of the importance of family and friends in my life. My journey has been rewarding.

ACKNOWLEDGEMENTS

I'm grateful to my siblings, Toni, John, Fuji, Diana, Terry, Ossie, Steve, and Hans's wife, Diane, for sharing your memories, taking my many calls, answering my emails, searching your photos, and allowing me to include you in my story. This book has been enriched by the lives of my siblings. An extra thanks to Steve for his invaluable, informal edit of the book and to John for significantly contributing to the resources required to produce and publish the book.

I'm grateful to my daughters, Danita and Chantal, for their love, support and assistance through the whole process. An extra thanks to Chantal for organising the photos. I'm sure I talked about the book a bit too much at times and I appreciate their indulgence.

A special thank you to my gifted granddaughter, Evie, for her drawing of the Lambert family home.

I'm grateful to my former partner, Di, who filled a much-needed sounding board role, assisted with the administrative work and kept me going with support and encouragement.

I'm grateful to the many people who have allowed me to include them in my story. There are too many to name, but I must acknowledge Tina, my former wife, Paul Newman, Les Ward, John Potter, and Shannon Hill who allowed me free rein to write about them.

I have been amazed by the genuine interest in the book by many relatives, friends, and former work colleagues. Their encouragement, support and assistance have been wonderful.

Jelena Maksimovic suggested that I consider a book coach and referred me to Vanessa Barrington, the Book Doula. I thank Jelena for both her interest in the book and for the referral.

A special thank you to Vanessa Barrington who was both my book coach and editor. I completed her Book Doula program prior to writing the book. It taught me "what I didn't know" about writing a book and gave me the confidence to go ahead. Vanessa's input was concise, insightful, and necessary.

I'm grateful to Maja Wolnik, Maja Creative, who was the book designer. She is great to work with, knows her stuff and I was extremely pleased with the end result.

AUTHOR'S BIOGRAPHY

GERRY LAMBERT

Gerry is the middle of nine siblings from a family that migrated to Australia from the Netherlands after World War II.

Gerry has a very wide circle of family and friends and thrives on continuing to build and nurture these relationships. He is an active contributor to the Gold Coast community where he resides, and has volunteered with several charitable organisations.

Gerry is an experienced company director and senior corporate executive and has previously held a variety of senior finance, chartered accounting, business consulting and academic roles in a career spanning over forty years.

Gerry loves sport and games, and isn't afraid to say he's a little competitive at the club trivia he attends each week.

Our Journey Is My Reward is Gerry's first book.

My family loves a funny photo, taken in September 2022

CPSIA information can be obtained
at www.ICGtesting.com
Printed in the USA
LVHW041541030123
736349LV00010B/728